Dave Pelz's Putting Bible

ALSO BY DAVE PELZ

Dave Pelz's Short Game Bible:
Master the Finesse Swing and Lower Your Score

Putt Like the Pros

Dave Pelz's
Putting
Bible

The Complete Guide to
Mastering the Green

DAVE PELZ

with James A. Frank

DOUBLEDAY

NEW YORK LONDON
TORONTO SYDNEY AUCKLAND

PUBLISHED BY DOUBLEDAY
a division of Random House, Inc.,
1540 Broadway, New York, New York 10036

DOUBLEDAY and the portrayal of an anchor with a dolphin are
trademarks of Doubleday, a division of Random House, Inc.

Photo Credits are on page 395.

The Library of Congress has established a record for this title.

ISBN 0-385-50024-6

Book design by Tina Thompson

Printed in the United States of America
July 2000
First Edition

10 9 8 7 6 5 4 3 2 1

Dedication

To my dearest JoAnn

My incredible, wonderful, beautiful wife,
You have truly become the light of my life.

You run the company, and our schedules, too,
Let there never be doubt, I'd be lost without you.

You fill our days so full with such pleasure,
With you at my side, each one is pure treasure.

I feel so lucky on you to depend,
As my companion, partner, soulmate, and friend.

So I dedicate this book, to your beauty and glow,
To your caring and talents, the most wondrous I know.

In every way, my most beautiful sight,
My unwavering, beautiful beacon of light.

I'm so grateful to the force in the somewhere above,
For letting me live (and work) with the woman I love.

All my love.

Contents

Acknowledgments

It is slightly overwhelming to think of how many people actually contributed to this work and deserve my thanks.

From the technical point of view, my thanks go to all the PGA and LPGA Tour players who have contributed to our understanding of what can and cannot be accomplished with hard work. I appreciate your trust in coming to us with your putting-game problems and sharing your results, frustrations, and rewards over the years.

In addition, I want to give a special thanks to Jim Simons, Tom Jenkins, Allen Miller, Joe Inman, Tom Kite, Andy North, Eddie Pearce, D. A. Weibring, Tom Sieckmann, Peter Jacobsen, Vijay Singh, Jesper Parnevik, Beth Daniel, Paul Azinger, Lee Janzen, and Steve Elkington. These players have a special place in my heart for the way they have helped me learn, and I thank them for being my friends, as well.

Another player I want to thank, posthumously, is my friend Payne Stewart. Payne, I know you are there, and I was so looking forward to doing some special things in this book with you. I will never forget your focus and determination in working on your routine, which you maintained perfectly as you made the best three putts in the history of golf to close out your second U.S. Open win. And we all know those were your least important accomplishments over the last few years. We are proud just to have known and worked with you.

I also want to thank my technical staff, especially Pete Piotrowski, Eddie Pelz, and J. D. Pelly, for their contributions to the Pelz Golf Institute testing results.

Putting this book together, I thank Joel Mendelman, Bryan Allison, and Dave Watford for their graphical talents, Eddie Pelz for project management, Leonard Kamsler for his unparalleled photographic talents, and Tina Thompson for her talent in laying out the book as well as her patience with my "occasional" changes.

I also thank my good friends at the best magazine in golf, GOLF MAGAZINE, for their contributions, and especially my editor, Jim Frank, who helped me cut the size of this book from ridiculous down to just "really more than you want to know about putting." Jim, really, I appreciate your talents after this one more than ever.

And finally, I want to thank my instructional staff at our Scoring Game Schools. To you twenty full-time teaching professionals, you are the best in the business, and I couldn't have done this book without you. And Bob Scott, your editorial contributions were awesome . . . thanks.

Introduction

My Putting Bible

I want to start this book with a short explanation. Look closely at the title. Notice that I don't claim this to be "THE" putting bible. I call it *Dave Pelz's Putting Bible* because it truly is "my" bible on putting. It is a compendium of my research, my studies, my test results, my teaching philosophy, and my beliefs about the art and science of putting. It is my bible—or, if you prefer, my notebook or data log book—into which I have transcribed my thoughts, interpretations of test results, observations, and theoretical work that have been instrumental in forming my understanding of putting. It is also from this work that I draw my philosophy for teaching the putting game in the Dave Pelz Scoring Game Schools.

My putting bible is a work in progress, because as I continue to study putting, which I do almost every day, I'm sure I will learn more. The information you'll read here is what I've learned so far. It started with my playing, thinking about, and studying my own game.

I started playing golf when I was six. I played throughout my childhood, was the number-one player on my high-school teams, played in numerous local tournaments, and had some minor success. I attended Indiana University on a four-year golf scholarship; more important, as it turned out, I also majored in physics. After college, I tried—unsuccessfully—to become a good enough player to make it on the PGA Tour back in the early 1960s. So I began a 15-year career at NASA, conducting research in space, launching satellites into earth orbit and beyond, and studying how the sun controls our atmosphere.

Since then, having changed my focus from the stars to the little white ball, I have studied the performance techniques and results of many tour professionals and amateurs, golfers of all sizes and skill levels, whenever and wherever I find them. I also have studied thousands of putting greens, balls, the behavior of balls on those greens, myriad putting implements, and many of the varied techniques of putting. I have filled most of my last 25 years measuring and trying to improve the teaching and learning techniques for putting and the short game. I have had some success improving the putting of my students, from beginners to Tour pros, all over the world. As I write this today, I am deeply involved in several continuing (and very exciting) research projects relating to how players can learn to putt and play better.

Again, this is "my" research and "my Putting Bible." But I've put it in a form to help you become a better putter.

I'm a Researcher

Several years ago, I founded the Pelz Golf Institute, which has as its mission "research for the good of the game." We chose that charter because it is a noble purpose and fits very nicely with what I'm trying to do—help golfers of all handicap and skill levels play the game better and enjoy it more. This has become my life's work—and better work you could not find! But we also have taken this mission one step further: That is, we want to make the game simple enough to understand that everyone can "get it," and, therefore, shoot lower scores and have more fun. To make teaching and learning the game this simple, we have to study it in depth. Luckily for me, that is something I dearly love to do.

It's obvious to me now that all my previous experience—my years playing junior, high school, and collegiate golf; my first career conducting space research at NASA's Goddard Space Flight Center (where my Indiana University book learning changed into real knowledge of how to conduct valid, scientific research); the in-depth studies I made of my own game; and my most recent work conducting research with the Pelz Golf Institute—were merely preparation for what I'm doing now. It's taken me 54 years (since I first picked up a club at age six) to be ready to tell you, and show you, how you can improve your ability to sink putts while understanding the game better and enjoying it more.

As you'll soon learn, one of the keys to lower scores is better putting. And the better you learn to putt, the more you will enjoy the rest of the game.

Why This Book?

That's easy: I had to write this book because putting is so important. Furthermore, besides being a researcher, I'm also a teacher.

But let me explain that I did not write my Putting Bible to change the concepts I wrote about in my previous book on putting, *Putt Like the Pros*. In fact, not much in *PLTP* has changed. But since writing that book more than 10 years ago, much has been learned. True, we're still using flat-faced sticks to strike a round ball and try to roll it into a 4¼-inch hole. But I've learned a great deal in those 10 years about stroke techniques, greens, wind effects, green-reading, and practice technology. I've also seen, learned, and tried teaching techniques that can significantly help your putting skills. The purpose of this book is to try to bring putting knowledge, understanding, and instruction to the next level.

So why this book for you? Because too many golfers pick up a putter based on its looks and off they go. Is that you? If it is, and you already putt well, then it's okay. It's also perfectly fine if all you want to do is have fun watching the ball roll any which way.

If, however, your idea of fun in golf is scoring well, putting well, and holing putts—and you don't putt well using your "natural" stroke—then you're in the right place. My Putting Bible is meant to help you understand putting well enough to make it simple (acquainting you with the realities of putting), to explain both what and how to improve your putting, and then help you actually learn to putt better.

This is not your normal "how-to" instruction book. My Putting Bible is much more of a "what, why, and how-to" book. This means not only learning how to improve your stroke, but also understanding the mechanics of your putting stroke and what happens on the greens. That's why I've followed a format of first explaining what has to be learned and why you need to learn it (Chapters 1–9) before getting into how you learn to improve your putting (Chapters 10–15).

I hope you won't cheat and skip over the understanding and jump right to the instruction part of the book, because you'll only hurt yourself. I've learned from many years of teaching that understanding what and how you need to learn makes learning much easier. And it helps to understand both the theoretical and practical sides of golf's problems when you are struggling with your solutions. One of the goals of this book is to make you knowledgeable enough to become your own best teacher. To do this I must erase your belief in "old wives' tales" (a process I hope I've already begun), and clear up any misunderstandings about how you should practice.

One more very important goal is to prove to you that putting can be simple, and that the better you putt, the simpler it gets. My friend Willie says it best: "Just start the ball on the right line and give it the right speed. You can understand that, can't you?" So if you want to putt better consistently, to hole putts more frequently, and permanently improve your ability to score, please read on.

Dave Pelz's Putting Bible

PUTTING OVERVIEW

CHAPTER 1

What Is Putting?

1.1 Putting Is a Different Game

Putting is simple. It's rolling a small ball into a large, round hole. It always ends in success. A holed putt is the successful finish of every golf hole you play (although this success takes a little longer on some holes than on others).

However, some golfers don't think putting is so simple. As the late, great Ben Hogan once said, "Putting is a different game." And he meant it! Ben thought putting was so different that it shouldn't count in one's score. He believed the person who hit the ball best with a full swing, the one who hit the most greens in regulation, or the golfer who consistently hit his shots closest to the pins should win.

Hogan was not alone in this belief. My friend Peter Jacobsen, one of the best ball-strikers I've ever had the privilege of working with (and taking data on), once told me his father believed the same thing. So when Peter, his two brothers, and his father played, they picked up their balls as soon as they reached the green. In their foursome, there was no putting. Because if they didn't slow down to putt, they could get in more holes, strike more shots, and hit more greens when they played. And anyway, as they all knew, anyone can putt.

Erling Jacobsen was a good man, and he raised three fine sons who could all hit the golf ball incredibly well. But he was very wrong about putting. Because while putting is different from striking drives and irons, it *does* count. In fact, it counts almost a disproportionate amount. There is no recovery opportunity from bad putting. When you miss a short putt, you add a stroke to your score and you have to putt again (unless you *really* putted badly, in which case you might have to putt twice more, or chip). A two-foot putt counts the same as a 300-yard drive—one stroke. The putt is only one of several types of swings golfers make, but it accounts for nearly half of all the swings made—43 percent (plus or minus about

2 percent)—and perhaps as much as 80 percent of the anguish derived from the game.

So putting does count, and is a vital part of golf. The question is, Where does putting fit into an overview of the game? If you examine golf under a microscope, as I have tried to do (Figure 1.1.1), you find that putting is much more than the most frequent shot golfers make. Based on my studies, putting is an entire game in itself, one of six different and distinct games that make up golf (as shown in Figure 1.1.2). In golf, the ball always reacts to the decisions and motions we make in the putting game, the short game, the power game, the management game, the mental game, and the physical fitness game, and our skills in these six games determine our abilities as golfers.

Putting is part of what I call the "scoring game"; the other element of the scoring game is the short game, those shots from 100 yards away to the edge of the green. While most golfers think that the drive from the tee and the next shot to the green comprise the game of golf, what they don't understand is that they will probably make two, three, or four more scoring shots before finishing the hole. If you look back through golf history, the best ball-strikers have never been the best putters. And the best putters (who have been relatively poor ball-strikers) have never been the best short-game players. Look at the table in Figure 1.1.3, which shows my list of the world's best power- and putting-game players, and you'll see that none of them cross over between lists. If you think about it, this is a perfect illustration of my point that the games are all really very different from one another.

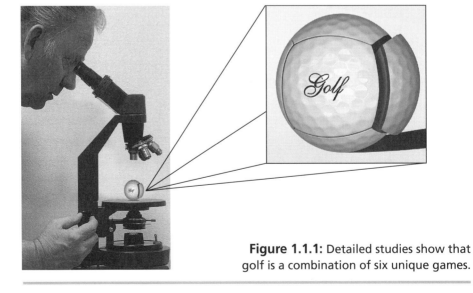

Figure 1.1.1: Detailed studies show that golf is a combination of six unique games.

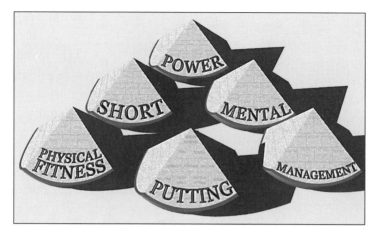

Figure 1.1.2: The six games of golf.

The World's All-Time Best	
World's Best Ball-Strikers	*World's Best Putters*
Moe Norman	George Archer
Ben Hogan	Ben Crenshaw
Lee Trevino	Dave Stockton
Tom Weiskopf	Loren Roberts
Tom Purtzer	Bob Charles
Johnny Miller	Brad Faxon
Tiger Woods	Greg Norman

Figure 1.1.3: The best-ever power-game players and putters.

The mechanics that make a golfer a good putter will not stand up well if employed in the full swing. Similarly, if you try to use a throttled-down power swing for your putting stroke, you will struggle on the greens. The motions don't cross over because their purposes are so different. The requirements of good putting are twofold: the accuracy of the initial line and the precision of rolling the ball at a specific speed, which, taken together, allow it to roll and curve gently into the hole. When putting, there is never the problem of achieving enough distance to carry a lake or creating enough power to get the ball to the hole. The requirements of a good drive or 2-iron swing are to hit the ball as far as possible within the constraints of reasonable accuracy. This means propelling the ball about as far as your golf swing will allow, with whatever club you choose, while keeping it out of trouble. There is very little trouble on a green, and missing the target by half an inch is rarely reason for despair on a full swing.

So I agree completely with Ben Hogan and Erling Jacobsen that putting is a game unto itself. But despite what Ben and Erling desired, it counts. And it should! Putting is an integral part of golf, and one of the most challenging.

1.2 All Golfers Can Putt

The mechanics, physical motion, and mental strength required for putting are vastly different from what's required for every other swing in golf. And putting is different in another way: It is one of the few skills in all of sport in which any player, regardless of size, strength, speed, gender, or education, can compete equally with—and have a realistic chance to beat—the best professionals in the world.

In the first two World Putting Championships (WPC), it was proven to the world that any golfer can compete with the world's best putters. Just ask professional golfers Len Mattiace and Raphael Alercon, who won the first two WPCs. In the finals, after more than 127,000 competitors had participated worldwide, these two touring pros had to beat (Figure 1.2.1):

- 95-year-old former Olympic discus thrower Ed Alofs
- 12-year-old Kentucky state putting champion Derek Penman
- four U.S. Open winners—Andy North, Tom Kite, Payne Stewart, and Lee Janzen
- the 10 best putters (statistics) from the PGA, LPGA, and Senior PGA Tours
- and 27-year-old Bill Rockwell, who putted in bare feet, standing on one foot, holding his putter between his toes. And let me tell you, this man can putt!

1.3 Putting Combines Science and Art

The science of putting is relatively unknown, rarely practiced, and almost completely misunderstood by amateurs and professionals, teachers and novices. The art of putting, on the other hand, is well-known and appreciated. It is widely practiced, but with very poor results. One of the goals of publishing my Putting Bible is to help all golfers see putting for what it really is.

Putting science: A simple series of physical motions using a flat-faced stick to roll an almost-round, fairly well-balanced ball into a hole on a relatively smooth

Figure 1.2.1: Among the best 300 putters
(finalists in the World Putting Championships).

surface, under the essentially unknown scientific influences of gravity, slope, green speed, and footprints. Always remember—nothing rolls like a ball!

Putting art: Painting pictures in one's mind of smoothly undulating green contours, gently arcing ball tracks, the rhythm and pace of a swing and a roll, of wonderful things yet to happen (and all this before you make the stroke).

Putting is a unique combination of these two disciplines, science and art. To master putting (or to even come close), you have to master, and understand, both. One is not more important than the other, and you cannot master one without the other and still putt well. While some combination of art and science exists in all of golf, including the striking of balls with the power swing, the art of imagining ball flight through the air is much more obvious to golfers than the curving ball tracks of putts rolling at unknown speeds on unknown surfaces.

But please don't, as so many golfers do, believe for one minute that putting is a "black art," that it involves some sort of voodoo or is something that can't be understood. Yes, putting is seldom taught, and yes, it may be the least understood part of the game, and seeing how putts will roll may not be intuitive to many golfers. It is even true that some of the world's greatest players have driven themselves away from the game because they lost their ability to putt. But most all of this is because golfers fear what they don't understand. That doesn't mean golfers can't learn to putt once they understand *how to learn to putt.* I'm here to tell you that all golfers can learn, and that includes you.

While it is sometimes tempting to be lazy and not deal with improving your putting, I assure you it's really not that difficult. Of course, if you are a bad putter and have tried to improve your putting without success, it is easy to conclude, "I just can't putt. Never could. Never will. I just was not meant to be a good putter." But that, my friend, is just not true.

1.4 Putting Results Are Uncertain

Golfers are always looking for a cause-and-effect relationship. It's human nature to want an explanation or reasons for why things happen, especially when you are trying to enjoy yourself but you keep seeing putts miss the hole. In golf, as in other areas of life, the phrase "the easy way out" comes into play. Many golfers choose to hope or spend money in an attempt to buy improvement, rather than have to read, practice, or learn how to improve. But putting does not succumb to such desires or offers of cash. Rather, just to make things interesting, the game throws in a number of unknown and unknowable factors that make success a statistical uncertainty.

The statistical nature of putting is one of its charms. As shown in Figure 1.4.1, the world's best putters (the golfers on the PGA Tour) make only about half of all their putts from six feet away; however, if they were on perfect and known surfaces, their strokes are so good that they would hole approximately 90 percent of these same putts. As you will see later in this book, there are good reasons for putting results to be uncertain and hard to understand. And those reasons don't change much over time. Once you understand them, they are easy to accept as part of the game. But putting is, was, and likely always will be difficult to comprehend for those who don't understand the true rules of the game.

Much of the inconsistency in putting is the result of the complexity of the way golfers swing their putters. I sometimes rate putting strokes on a scale from one to ten (Figure 1.4.2). Don't take the player names or the rankings too seriously, as they are simply my opinions on the complexity (that is, the difficulty of repeating) of the motions made by these players. But don't totally ignore my evaluations either; I haven't taught thousands of students without learning a few things about putting stroke mechanics. One thing I have learned for certain is that the more complex the stroke, the less repeatable it is. And the simpler the stroke, the more repeatable it is.

My point is that putting strokes are complex enough to always provide something to blame when misses occur. But my research shows that in many cases, the golfer had nothing at all to do with the reason for the miss. The reality of the game

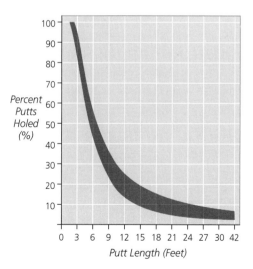

Figure 1.4.1: The percentage of first putts holed in PGA tournaments vs. putt length.

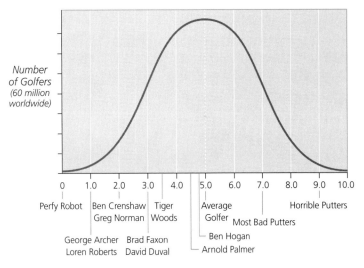

Stroke Complexity (10=maximum complexity)

Figure 1.4.2: As putting stroke complexity increases, putting proficiency decreases.

of putting is that not all well-struck putts go in, and that sometimes poorly struck ones do. Statistically speaking, your chances of making any given putt improve with the quality of your putting skills. But your odds of success will never be anywhere near 100 percent, even if you are perfect in every stroke you make.

1.5 Putting Looks Simple

Putting looks, and can be, simple. A short putt looks so easy that most golfers are embarrassed when they miss one. But miss them they do (Figure 1.5.1). And since there are many seniors and youngsters who putt very well, "regular" golfers get extremely frustrated when they can't hole a simple-looking putt.

This frustration is based on expectations. If golfers have unrealistic expectations for holing putts, they are building frustration and disappointment into their games. If they never expected to make a putt, they would be thrilled when they made one. But the opposite is also true. If they expected to make all of their six-footers, they would be devastated when they made only half of them (even though a 50 percent conversion rate would rank them with the best putters in the world). Add enough disappointment and frustration and it's easy to understand why simple ol' putting sometimes drives even good golfers from the game.

Perhaps a reason putting abilities are sometimes attributed to mystical skills is

Figure 1.5.1: Short putts look easy.

the embarrassment caused by missing those so-called simple putts. One of the easiest solutions when a golfer doesn't understand his or her failure is to consider putting a "God-given talent," albeit one that God did not impart to them.

So we know that putting is but one of the six games that make up golf, and we know how confusing it can be. But we also know that this is only one view of putting, the reality (science and art) of which escapes most golfers, the success of which is statistically controlled by factors unknown to most golfers, the apparent simplicity of which makes it embarrassing if you are not excellent at it, and the mystery of which creates unrealistic expectations in golfers about how well they should perform. And, oh yes, the importance of putting is so great because it comprises almost half of the game.

From this view, it's amazing that we enjoy golf as much as we do.

1.6 Great Putters Are Made, Not Born

What I want to show you with this book is the other side of putting, the Pelz side, the positive view of putting. As I have studied putting in great detail (Figure 1.6.1), I have found it to be a game based on 15 well-defined building blocks, each of which you already have and own (Figure 1.6.2). I say you already own these 15 skills, in one form or another, because every time you putt you use them all. Every

Figure 1.6.1: Upon close examination, putting combines many skills.

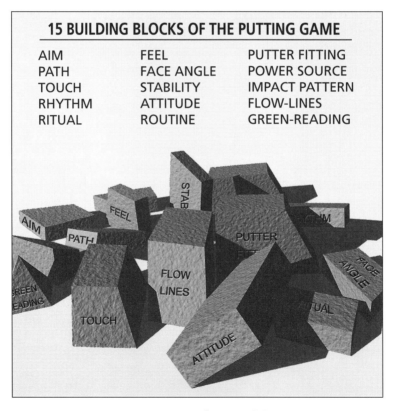

15 BUILDING BLOCKS OF THE PUTTING GAME

AIM	FEEL	PUTTER FITTING
PATH	FACE ANGLE	POWER SOURCE
TOUCH	STABILITY	IMPACT PATTERN
RHYTHM	ATTITUDE	FLOW-LINES
RITUAL	ROUTINE	GREEN-READING

Figure 1.6.2: The 15 building blocks of putting.

time you swing your putter you aim it, you swing it in a stroke path, and your touch is always either a little strong, a little weak, or perfect.

The only question, then, is how well have you developed each of your 15 skill blocks, and how well have you fit them to work together? Are all your blocks formed properly, with edges straight and smooth, fitting together as they should with the rest of your game (Figure 1.6.3 top)? Or do you have a few blocks slightly out of shape or with rough edges that won't fit, causing your putting to be a rough spot in your performance (Figure 1.6.3 bottom)?

The good news is that most golfers (you included) are usually pretty good at most of these putting-skill blocks. The bad news is that few golfers have all 15 of them formed and polished well enough to make putting a strength of their game. Those who have them polished are the golfers we watch winning tournaments on Sunday afternoons (Figure 1.6.4).

Where does this leave you? In a perfect position to find the blocks that cause problems in your putting game, and fix them. Whether this means polishing a few edges or changing the shapes of the blocks is yet to be determined. And how many of your blocks need improvement is yet to be measured. But measure, determine,

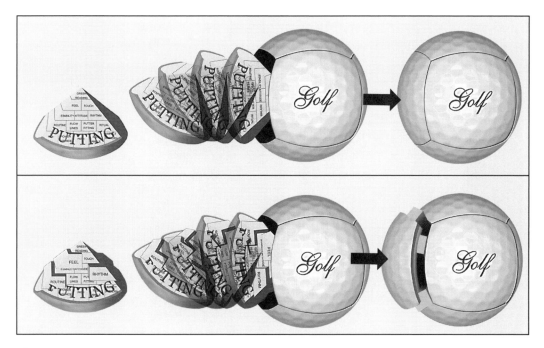

Figure 1.6.3: Does your putting fit perfectly, or does it have a few rough edges that won't let it fit . . . or perform, in your game?

Figure 1.6.4: A great putter, Payne Stewart, winning the 1999 U.S. Open.

and improve is something we can do. We've been doing it for years in our schools, and we can do it with you through this book—if you can bring your understanding of the game to where it needs to be.

I don't want to mislead you, so please read these next statements carefully. Putting good is easy, but *learning* to putt good is not! It's learning which part (block) of your putting to work on, and learning how to work on it, that's difficult. The putting motion is simple; it's the simplest motion in golf. If you can hit the ball at all, you can learn to putt very well (the world's best putters are using simpler motions than you use).

All you have to learn is *what to learn and how to learn it* to improve your putting game. The actual improving is easy. Find the right blocks, fix them, and you've got it. Your building blocks can be arranged and assembled in many different ways. Not everyone has to look the same to putt well, because as long as certain ball–putter interactions occur, good results can be achieved (Figure 1.6.5). However, leave one or more aspects of your putting skill weak and you will be stuck like most golfers, putting poorly for most of their golf lives with only hopes and glimmers of good putting on rare occasions (Figure 1.6.6).

Just because there's a lot of both science (physics) and art (imagination) in putting doesn't mean it's hard to do. Putting isn't made difficult by the conditions of gravity, impact energy transfer, or imperfect balls rolling on imperfect sloped surfaces. These conditions just make it impossible to make *all* your putts. And I say thanks to them, because if every golfer was holing every putt, what fun would it be?

Putting *is* both science and art. It *is* a different game. It *is* sometimes confusing (because of statistical effects you can't see). It *does* look easy (yet isn't). However, it

Figure 1.6.5: All great putters do not look the same.

Figure 1.6.6: Many golfers "hope" to putt well, and don't understand why they don't when they don't.

is not a skill one is born with or without, and I will prove that in this book. As you read my Putting Bible, understanding will replace wonderment; confidence will replace anxiety. And I promise, you will learn—and learn how to learn—to improve your putting.

So press on. You will see just how simple and fun putting can become for you.

CHAPTER 2

Problems on the Greens

2.1 No Net Luck in Putting

If you think you did something wrong every time you missed a makable putt, you need to read this book.

Part of the charm of putting, indeed of the game of golf itself, is the occasional unfairness of the results versus the quality of the swings. Put another way, some of the best-stroked putts in history have not gone into the hole, while some of the worst have. And you know what? I think that's charming. Unfair, but charming. Because I think golf is, and should always be, a test of more than your athletic ability and your swing plane. The challenge of putting includes an examination of your ability to accept adversity and move on. That means it is a character check, as well as an evaluation of your judgment, preparation, eyesight, nerves, concentration, organizational prowess, work ethic, and feel, touch, putting stroke, and ability to read greens.

In the previous chapter, I said that putting is not a black art. That's true. However, it is also true that almost every putt can involve an element of luck. When you read a putt incorrectly, then roll it just the way you want to, it should miss the hole. But sometimes it hits something and goes in. That's good luck. When you read a putt perfectly and make a good stroke, sometimes the ball is knocked off-line and misses. That's bad luck. Both of these happen all the time. As I mentioned in section 1.4, putting results are statistical in nature. By this I mean that if you stroke a good putt on the proper line at the proper speed, your chances of making it on a "good" green are maybe 5 to 3. If, however, you don't stroke it well, your odds drop to 3 to 5. And these are for good greens; on poorer greens, your odds of success may drop by 20 or 30 percent or more.

No putting result is ever for sure until the ball stops rolling. And the factors that cause this uncertainty are many and varied, some of which you can see and some you can't. That does not mean that all putting is the result of luck, or that good putting is just lucky putting. There is no such thing as overall or long-term luck in putting. The good and bad breaks that occur to an individual always balance out over a golf season, so in the end the players who make the most good strokes always hole the most putts. There is no net luck, good or bad, in putting.

2.2 Easily Seeable Hazards

So forget about luck, both good and bad (which you can't control anyway), and look for the factors that you can control (or at least influence) to determine results. Also become aware of the influences outside your control that can affect your results. Many of them are visible and, therefore, easily recognized. Some, however, are invisible to the human eye, and are much more difficult to deal with (see section 2.3).

I don't mention these outside-influence factors to make the game seem more difficult, but to help you recognize and understand them, so that when you witness unexpected behavior on the greens, you won't panic. And I mention them now, before getting into any mechanics of good putting, so you keep things in perspective, keeping what you can and can't control separate. If you can always keep the "big picture" in mind, and ignore the short-term statistical uncertainties, you can better accomplish your tasks of playing the game and focusing your attention on those things you can control.

We can see—and, therefore, know about—the obvious imperfections on the surface of a putting green caused by disease, spike marks, and pitch marks. These often cause balls to go somewhere other than where we wanted them to go:

- When grass is diseased, it dies or withers, leaving a depression between the healthy and unhealthy areas.
- Spike marks—bits of grass roots pulled up by the cleats on the bottoms of golf shoes—can create ball deflectors (Figure 2.2.1).
- Pitch marks, caused by the impact of incoming shots to a green (Figure 2.2.2), regularly go unrepaired, which is bad etiquette as well as bad strategy, since that same pitch mark—or one someone else didn't repair—could come back to hurt you.
- The ragged edge of a cup can cause a putt to lip out (Figure 2.2.3).

All of these green imperfections can have a negative effect on putting, especially when the ball is moving slowly (as it does near the end of its roll). And you know what? There is nothing you can do about it. But all of these are seeable, so golfers understand them and know they are part of the game. If you miss a putt

Figure 2.2.1: Spike marks from one step of a U.S. Open champion.

Figure 2.2.2: The unrepaired pitch mark.

Figure 2.2.3: A worn or ragged cup edge can cause unfair lip-ins or lip-outs.

because of one of them, you mark it down to a bit of bad luck, assume that your good luck will come, and don't worry. But most important, you don't change your stroke because of them.

2.3 Measurable (Although Difficult to See), and Therefore Knowable, Factors

What about some factors that golfers don't see? There are many. The length of the grass on a green (determined by the mower that cut it that morning) has a tremendous effect on how fast balls roll and how much putts break that day. The moisture in the surface of the green influences green speed: A light covering of dew, water from a recent rain or the irrigation system, even the sand content near the surface of the green (which affects water retention), all can change a putt's roll, speed, and break. Each of these factors can be measured and known by golfers (in fact, I'll discuss them in Chapter 7), but they rarely are.

What about grain, the direction the grass grows (Figure 2.3.1)? The stronger the grass blades and the stronger the forces of nature (such as nearby water, sun angle, and wind, all of which cause grass to grow in certain directions), the greater the likelihood that the grain will influence your putting. Again, grain can be accurately measured and known, but not in the time a golfer has while sizing up his next putt. (For a more detailed look at grain, see section 7.10.)

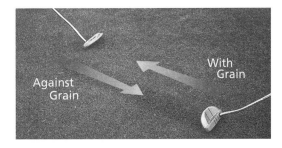

Figure 2.3.1: Grass usually grows in a direction (grain) other than straight up.

Here's one few golfers consider: the ball's balance. Most golfers assume that all golf balls are perfectly balanced, but I assure you, they are not. In many balls, the center of gravity (CG) or mass (the center of weight distribution) is not exactly at its geometric center. To understand this, imagine a golf ball as shown in Figure 2.3.2, which is perfectly balanced except for a small mass of lead positioned horizontally from its center. Such an imbalance could be caused by a bad operation in the construction of (or mud on) a ball. Imagine if such a ball was rolled perfectly side by side with a perfectly balanced ball on a perfect green. Due to the imbalance

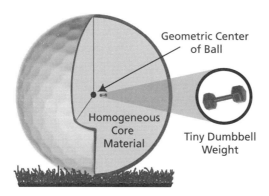

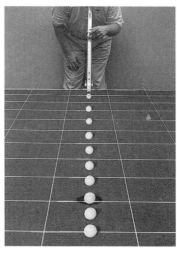

Figure 2.3.2: An otherwise perfect ball would be thrown off-balance by the addition of a small lead dumbbell off-center.

of weight, rather than rolling in the desired direction (Figure 2.3.3 right), the ball would roll off to the side (Figure 2.3.3 left) and miss the hole. Worse than the lost stroke, the golfer probably would think he had just blown a short putt that he should have made, leading him to change his stroke to fix a problem that didn't exist. The problem, which the golfer never knew of or even suspected, was the ball (see sections 9.8 and 9.9).

Getting a little scared? Don't be. True, putting can appear to be very complex. And things, at times, will get still worse, believe me. But believe this, too: It's no problem. Because in the end, once you learn to not be bothered by all these "nit-noy" problems, the more good strokes you make and the better you read the greens, the more of your putts that will find the hole.

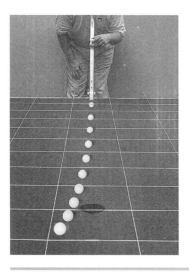

Figure 2.3.3: The perfect roll of an out-of-balance ball (left) and a perfectly balanced ball (right).

2.4 Unseeable and Unknowable Factors

Years ago, as I began pondering the inconsistencies and uncertainties in putting performance, I became fascinated by the possibility of learning enough about putting to help golfers learn to do it better. I had a breakthrough—a moment when I knew I'd truly be able to help people—when I started studying the footprints golfers left on greens. As I watched a ball I'd filmed in slow motion roll innumerable directions on a single putt, it seemed as though an army had marched across the green on the line of the putt. I examined that area of the green at sunset. I sat in amazement, watching the shadows lengthen, wondering how anyone could hole any putt over such an uneven surface. There seemed to be thousands of footprint lines, humps, bumps, and heel-print edges in the grass, any one of which was capable of turning a slowly rolling ball in a different direction. I realized that even a perfectly stroked putt, rolling over that green, would have a very good chance of being diverted from the hole. I also realized that an imperfectly stroked putt rolling over that same green would have a chance of being knocked into the hole.

The Lumpy Donut
That was one of what I consider the critical "learning moments" I've had in golf. Looking closely at that green from ground level, I decided to measure the severity of this effect on the entire course. I got up early the next morning and followed the first group while the greens were still covered with dew. This allowed me to actually see and count the individual footprints. I learned that a foursome often makes more than 500 footprints on each green it plays. Even worse, these footprints were not evenly distributed: Most were within six feet of the hole, because half of all putts were from less than six feet away. They created a trampled-down area between 6 feet and 6 inches away from the hole (no one was so inconsiderate as to step within 6 inches of the cup) and 360 degrees around it. I began referring to this area as the "lumpy donut" (see Figure 2.4.1).

There's no way a golfer can know how many footprints are between his ball and the hole before a putt. That's true even if you are in the first group to tee off, when the greens are in the best possible condition to allow putts to roll straight and true. Because even then, one of the men who cut the grass on the green or cut the cup into the green earlier that morning may have left one footprint dead in the path of your putt as it slows near the hole. And if this one footprint turns your putt away from the hole, you're going to get disgusted and assume it just isn't your day (or worse, think you made a bad stroke). If, however, this footprint turns your ball into the hole, you do a little dance (making more footprints!) and assume you

Figure 2.4.1: Four players, nine putts, more than 500 footprints: a lumpy donut surrounds every hole.

hit a great putt. Again, this is one more example of the unpredictable and statistical nature of putting. You can't do much about it, but you should be aware of it because you'll never detect or be absolutely sure about these invisible land mines that lie in wait on the greens.

The Ramp

There was something else I noticed while collecting my lumpy-donut data. On greens where the traffic was particularly intense, there was a ramp—a raised area—all around and leading up to the hole. The golfers had trampled near the cup, but they were very careful not to step inside the six inches immediately around it, so that area was elevated inside the center of the lumpy donut (Figure 2.4.2). These ramps, I learned, cause many putts that are slowing down and dying as they near the hole to be stopped short or turned away. I measured and found that if those same slow-rolling putts were hit at the same speed on a perfect surface, they should have, and would have, fallen into the hole. So because numerous golfers before you were respectful of the hole, your putt missed.

Wind

Here's a factor that you can't see but you can feel. Of course, if the wind is blowing 50 miles an hour, you might see it blow your ball off-line as it rolls to the hole. But what about a light breeze? Does it affect your putts? In Chapter 9, I've quantified what wind can do to a putt. It's just one more unknowable factor that you might want to be aware of so you can play your best golf.

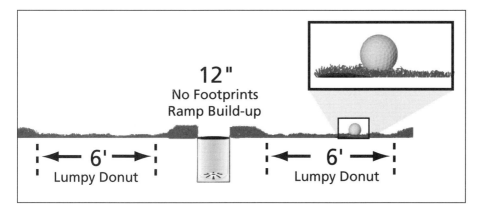

Figure 2.4.2: After multiple players putt out, a small ramp (exaggerated for clarity) forms around every hole.

2.5 A Multiplicity of Options

Let's get off the greens and look at another common factor, another bump on the road to consistently effective putting. That would be the thousands of ways in which you can swing a putter. It is precisely because there are all these options that so many golfers believe putting to be "personal." I know you've heard or read of golf professionals teaching that putting is individualistic, idiosyncratic, or a matter of personal taste, and that you should do "whatever feels right to you."

Wrong! Nothing could be further from the truth. For many golfers, there is absolutely nothing natural about a good putting stroke. When I've measured them, most golfers putt pretty badly when they try to do "what feels right."

There are as many body types as there are golfers. And while there are only a few proper ways to stroke a golf ball perfectly, in trying to accomplish those few fundamentals, each golfer can look unique. However, this does not mean putting is individualistic; what it does mean is that when taking a perfect stance and perfect posture for the perfect address position, different golfers will look different.

How about grip? There is a single best putting grip for every golfer. But there is not one perfect putting grip for *all* golfers. Different golfers have hands of different sizes, and for some, one hand is larger than the other. Each golfer's forearms, wrists, hand strength, instincts, and even metabolism are different. So while there may be many ways to putt, there is only one best way for each golfer to putt.

There is a best stance for you, a best address position for you, a best grip and a best stroke for you. Just as when you're sick, there are thousands of pills you could take. But you don't take the one that just looks or tastes good. You take the one that makes you better. In putting, the key is to find which options help you putt better, then practice and groove them until you own them. Once grooved and working well, they will begin to feel comfortable and become natural. Only then will they "feel right."

2.6 Misunderstanding

There are occasions when golfers cause themselves problem on the greens as a result of not understanding some of nature's "rules of the game."

Here is a fact: Straight downhill putts are usually easier to make than straight uphill putts. This may be the opposite of what you think and have heard on television when announcers mention that "Joe Pro is happy to be below the hole facing an uphill putt." But what they don't say—perhaps because they've never studied it—is that on downhillers, the force of gravity tends to hold putts on-line, minimizing the error caused by a slightly open or closed clubface at impact. On the same length uphill putt, however, gravity maximizes the result of the same error, actually increasing the possibility of missing the hole (Figure 2.6.1).

All that said, it's easier to three-putt a downhiller than an uphill putt of the same length. The reason is speed: Downhill putts require a more delicate touch to control rolling speed. If you stop and think about that (which, I'll bet, you never

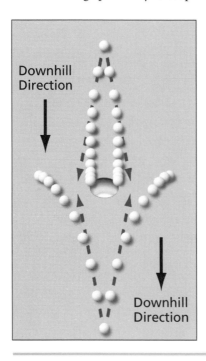

Figure 2.6.1: Gravity tends to focus the line of downhill putts, while helping uphill putts to diverge.

have), it's pretty obvious. But obvious isn't factual, and obvious doesn't give you a sense of the severity of the problem. So look at Figure 2.6.2, which shows how far five balls on a flat green will roll when putted with perfect-length backswings, made with a pendulum stroke, to produce putts of 3, 6, 9, 12, and 15 feet. Of course, they roll 3, 6, 9, 12, and 15 feet. Using my True Roller, I can produce the same release energies for putts of 3, 6, 9, 12, and 15 feet. In both series of putts, the spread of distances between the shortest and longest ball is 12 feet (15 feet − 3 feet).

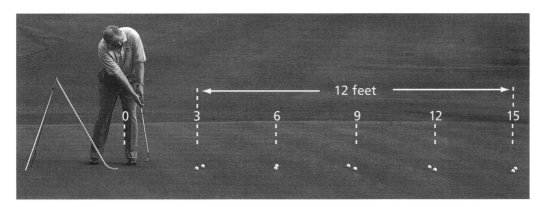

Figure 2.6.2: The True Roller has exact release heights to roll putts known distances repeatedly.

The True Roller

Years ago, I created the True Roller, a simple ramp device to control the direction and speed of simulated putts (a 1978 photo is shown below). It turns out to be one of the most useful devices I've come up with for rolling balls and testing on the greens.

Figure 2.6.3: The original True Roller in use at Congressional Country Club (1978).

The first True Roller was eight feet long and very cumbersome, but later versions have included laser-aiming attachments, refined ball-release mechanisms, and a level to ensure that the release ramp is always perfectly vertical and releasing balls in a straight line (Figure 2.6.4). The original intent of the True Roller was to simulate putts near the end of their rolls, because the initial release of a ball differed from the initial roll of the putted balls (putts start out slightly lofted and sliding along the grass, whereas the ball is already rolling as it leaves the True Roller). However, after we tested and calibrated the True Roller to simulate putts, we found no essential differences in putting results between balls putted versus those released from the True Roller.

You will see many balls and test results from balls rolled from the True Roller in this book. Remember that the True Roller is simply starting each ball in a given direction at the given speed. And that is what putting is all about.

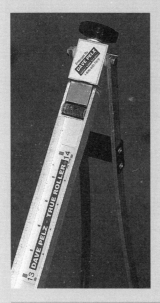

Figure 2.6.4: A leveling mechanism assures that the True Roller is vertical before rolling every putt.

Look next at the top of Figure 2.6.5, which shows how far the same five balls will roll on an uphill putt (released from the True Roller, each with the same energy as before). The uphill putts stop closer together (the distance between the longest and shortest balls is 7.5 feet), indicating that on uphill putts, balls tend to roll closer to the same distance. This means the roll of an uphill putt is less sensitive to the length of the stroke than putts on a level surface. The lesson is that even if you don't hit all of your uphill putts the right speed, be sure to get them past the hole.

Figure 2.6.5: Five putts rolled at the same energies as in Figure 2.6.2, roll closer together uphill and farther apart downhill.

That gives them a chance to go in, and the longest ones will probably stop near enough to the hole to leave no-brainers coming back.

Now look at the bottom of Figure 2.6.5 to see how far these same putts roll, given the same amount of starting energy, on a straight downhill putt. There's a big difference from the level and uphill putts. Of course, each downhill putt rolls farther, but more important, the spread of distances between balls has increased, meaning the roll distance is more sensitive to energy input. Now the distance between the longest and shortest balls is 18 feet. So your downhill stroke has to be about three times more precise than your uphill stroke to stop a putt at the right distance. When putting downhill, make a stroke of the wrong speed and you'll have trouble making your next putt.

I'm not saying that understanding putting like this will make you a great putter. But I am saying that understanding nature's rules and where the dangers lie in putting can help you be a better putter. And not understanding what putting is all about will make it even more difficult for you to learn to putt well.

So if you don't know that downhill putts break more than uphill putts on the same slope (covered in Chapter 7), then you won't be making many downhill-breaking putts. Or, if you believe that Bobby Locke and Ben Crenshaw struck their putts with overspin to make them dive into the hole, then it's unlikely that you'll work on those aspects of your putting that actually can help you putt better (see section 4.9).

2.7 Poor Learning Environment

It might seem about now that I'm being very negative about putting, that I'm pointing out how hard it is, how much you don't know, and how much you have to learn to be a good putter. I'm not trying to be negative, but I am trying to point out how much you have to learn. Learning is what good putting is all about: It's not hard to putt well; it is hard to *learn* how to putt well. And the difference is crucial. I place much of the blame for the difficulty in learning squarely on the putting green. The green provides a very poor environment in which to learn.

Standing on the putting green, golfers have no idea why they miss putts or why they make them. After missing a putt (even on the practice green), most golfers assume their stroke mechanics were to blame. However, they may have stroked a perfect putt but it hit a hard-to-see footprint, which caused the putt to miss the hole. Or they might make a putt and assume they stroked it perfectly when they actually hit a terrible putt but misread it just the right amount to compensate, and—only luck can explain it—roll it into the hole.

I learned a long time ago that if you learn from your mistakes, things usually get better. But if you continue to repeat the same mistakes over and over again, things get pretty bad. Then I read a book on learning theory and learned that immediate, accurate, reliable feedback is the key to efficient learning (Figure 2.7.1). This, in fact, has become the basis of all my teaching (I wrote about it at great length in my *Short Game Bible*). The basic notion is that if you don't know right from wrong in

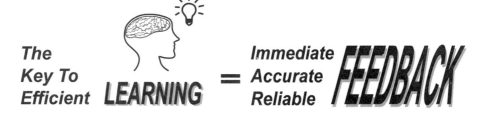

Figure 2.7.1: The key to efficient learning.

practice, there is no way you can improve. If you don't know a good stroke from a bad stroke in practice, you are just as likely to groove the bad one as the better one. If you make a perfect putting stroke from a bad setup position and then blame your miss on stroke path, you'll never learn to set up perfectly. Or if you blame your heart, your courage, or your self-worth when you miss putts, then you'll never fix your aim, your path, or the impact problems that truly are at fault.

Don't Be a Pigeon

A student in one of our Scoring Game Schools told me a story. In a laboratory devoted to the methodology of learning, scientists were studying how pigeons learn to feed themselves from pellet dispensers. In one cage of pigeons they placed a number of dispensers, all of which released one pellet every time a pigeon bumped or stepped on the release lever. Every time the lever was hit, a pellet fell out. It took just two days for every pigeon in that cage to learn how to feed itself: hit the lever, get a pellet.

There was another cage of pigeons, which had the same number of identical-looking pellet dispensers. But these dispensers worked differently. They released pellets randomly. Sometimes pellets were released without the levers being touched. Sometimes they were released when the lever was touched once. And sometimes when the lever was touched nothing would happen. In time, some of the pigeons thought that when they lifted their right wing, a pellet was released. Some of the pigeons thought that if they chirped they would get a pellet. And some of the pigeons believed that if they turned in circles in front of the dispenser, they would get a pellet. In two months, none of the pigeons learned to feed themselves. In fact, it was humorous watching the second cage: every pigeon practicing a different move, hoping to release a pellet.

It reminds me of a practice putting green filled with golfers. One golfer is practicing a new grip. Another has widened his stance and is bending over more than he used to, while his friend is trying the split-hand grip he saw on television. Another golfer is trying to learn a short backswing and "pop" stroke. All these golfers practicing something that they actually did just before they happened to make a putt, hoping it will help them make another one.

And that is what you see if you look at many putting greens today. Golfers practicing, practicing, and practicing—who knows what they are practicing?—all hoping their putting will improve. Some of them practice a different thing every day and use a different stroke in every round. Some golfers even use several different strokes during one round. Yes sir-ee, they remind me of a bunch of pigeons!

2.8 How Well Can You Putt?

Something else you need to think about before actually beginning to work on your stroke are the answers to a few questions. They are important questions, but only if you want to know just how good your putting can get: (1) How good are the world's best putters? (2) How well do you putt now? (3) How good can one get at putting? (4) How good will your putting be in the future?

Let me answer these as best I can:

I believe the best putters in the world are playing on the PGA Tour. My proof is the results of the first two World Putting Championships, where the Tour pros were seriously challenged by some Senior Tour players, several LPGA Tour players, and a number of amateurs, both young and old. However, the PGA Tour players placed higher as a group than any other.

Also, my data on the percentage of putts holed from different distances shows that the PGA Tour players lead all other groups. Don't think that you can look at the statistics quoted in the newspapers and find this information, because the number that the papers publish (provided by the Tour) simply show how many putts the players average on greens hit in regulation, which is affected by the quality of their iron shots (the better the iron play, the shorter their putts). And these are the new putting stats. Years ago, the Tour's statistics measured putts taken per green, which was influenced by how many greens players missed and how consistently they chipped close to the hole (again, leaving them shorter putts). Neither of these statistics measures the quality of a player's putting, because both are strongly influenced by the quality of different shots (approaches and chips).

The true measure of the Tour pros' putting is indicated by the percentage of putts they make ("convert") based solely on the length of the putts (shown in Figure 1.4.1, page 7). The shaded curve is data on PGA Tour players taken between the years 1977 and 1992, and shows the spread between the best and worst conversion percentages. It has now been almost 10 years since we measured how well the pros putt, and the Pelz Golf Institute is in the process of repeating this test. We hope we'll find that the percentages have changed in recent years (they remained fairly consistent in the period from '87 to '92) as the conditions of greens improve and as players improve their skills (and perhaps as some of our teaching is taking effect).

If you want an answer to question 2—"How well do you putt?"—you must measure your percentage of putts holed from each distance. You can do this, but it will take some effort. You have to record the distance of each putt on your scorecard as you move around the course, and indicate those you hole. After 10 to 15 rounds (and at least 5 to 10 putts from each distance), you'll begin to be able to plot your own conversion chart and compare it to those of the pros.

As for question 3—"How good can one get at putting?"—the answer depends on a number of things: the quality of the greens, how well a player reads those greens, and the quality of the player's stroke and touch. Although none of these questions can be answered definitively in this book, I assure you that all of the above are getting better all the time. As greens improve, putting strokes improve, and golfers learn to read greens better, a higher percentage of putts from every distance will be made in the future.

Finally, "How good will your putting be in the future?" That depends on your ability to learn the mechanics of a better putting stroke, your ability to learn better putting feel and touch, your ability to learn to read greens better, and your ability to produce the right stroke at the right time. Depending on your lifestyle, your determination and intensity, your focus, your self-discipline and practice habits, and your ability to learn, only you can provide this answer.

2.9 Stop Three-Putting

For most golfers to improve their scores, it is often easier to reduce their number of three-putts than it is to increase their number of one-putts. This is generally true for golfers with handicaps greater than 20, although it is even true for some very fine, lower-handicap players. As you can see in Figure 2.9.1, the length of the most frequent first putt on greens hit from outside 60 yards is 38 feet. (This distance

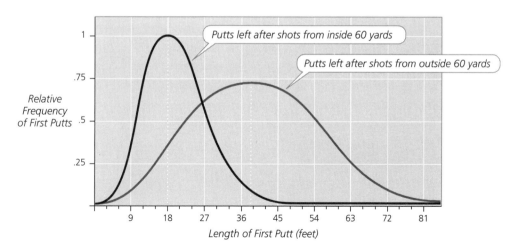

Figure 2.9.1: The length of first putts for 20 (±5) handicappers.

varies a little with the handicap of the players measured, but, obviously, there are many more long first putts than short ones.) This figure also shows that the most frequent first putt to follow shots hit from inside 60 yards is an 18-footer. If you combine these two curves and add in all the second and third putts that become necessary after the first putt is missed, you can see a typical value for the number of putts of each length golfers face per round over a season of golf (Figure 2.9.2).

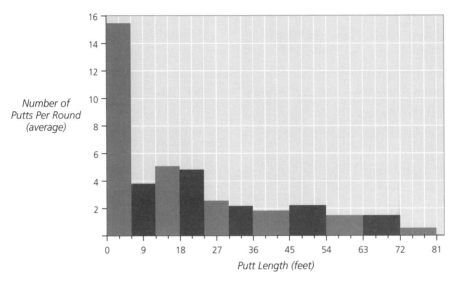

Figure 2.9.2: Average number of putts per round.

Now look at the conversion curve for this group of 15- to 25-handicap golfers (Figure 2.9.3) and the frequency with which they three-putt versus the putt distance (Figure 2.9.4). By comparing these data, you can see the importance of making short putts, as well as learning that you can save several strokes per round by eliminating three-putts from outside 30 feet. This means that you shouldn't practice only short putts; the long ones are also important. And you must stop three-putting those long ones if you want to be a good putter.

2.10 Learn to Lag Putt

For those not familiar with "lag putting," some explanations:

- To lag a putt is to minimize thoughts of holing it, instead concentrating on stopping the ball as close to the proper distance and as close to the hole as possible, thus minimizing the possibility of three-putting (which is first priority).

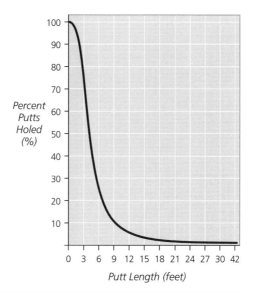

Figure 2.9.3: Putt conversion efficiency of my Scoring Game School students (20±5 handicaps).

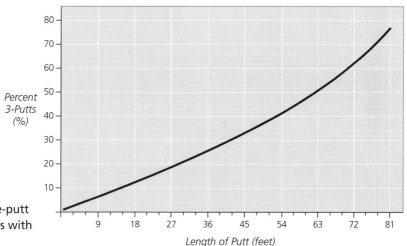

Figure 2.9.4: Three-putt probability increases with length of putt.

- To putt aggressively is to concentrate on rolling putts at the optimum putting speed to maximize the chance of holing out.
- To jam putts is to roll them at a higher than optimum speed to minimize the amount of break required to be played.

Lag putters (golfers who always seem to be lagging their putts) usually leave more than half of their putts short, which is not good when you are trying to hole the maximum percentage of makable putts (those inside 30 feet). But to be a good

Practice Tips

After learning the benefits of lag putting, some advice:

- When you warm up before play, or go to the practice green for a true practice session, practice lag putting first, concentrating on stopping all putts from more than 35 feet close enough to make the second putt a virtual tap-in. You don't need to sink long putts, but you must get them close enough so you almost never three-putt.
- Practice putts of intermediate length—6 to 30 feet—second, and concentrate on rolling them at a speed that stops any that miss about 17 inches past the hole.
- Finish your practice with putts of less than six feet, focusing only on rolling them into the cup at a firm, brisk pace.

lag putter from outside 35 feet is one of putting's more important skills.

Figure 2.10.1 shows typical lag patterns (for putts between 50 and 60 feet) of some Tour pros we work with, compared to our Scoring Game School students. You can see that if the amateurs improved their lag patterns so they were closer to the hole by a factor of two, they would not only reduce their number of three-putts significantly, but they also would increase their number of putts holed by a factor of four. (The percentage area of the hole, relative to the lag pattern area, changes by the square of the lag-area radius.) So better lag putting not only reduces the number of three-putts, but also leads to more long putts holed (but still a relatively small number).

Don't Be Discouraged

In mentioning some of the problems inherent in putting (all of which will be explained in more understandable detail in later chapters), I've thrown a fair amount of information at you, and we have yet to even begin examining the putting stroke. However, please don't be discouraged about the complexity of putting or the confusion you might be feeling right now. You need to understand the realities of putting so you'll be more tolerant when unexplained things happen to you on the greens. You need to believe—no, you need to *know*—that there is no net luck in putting no matter how your putts seem to be rolling, bouncing, or deflecting that day.

Once you understand the reality of the problems of the game, and the often cruel statistical nature of its results, you will be better prepared to proceed with your learning program, which will lead to your improved putting. Always remain alert to the importance of immediate, accurate, reliable feedback *and* what it can do for your practice and on-course putting. So take heart, and realize your better scores will come from more areas than simply improving your stroke mechanics. There's much more to good putting than that physical stroke motion of yours.

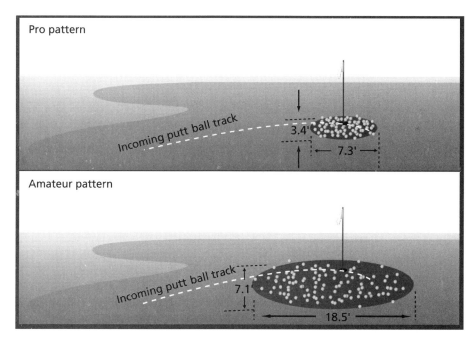

Figure 2.10.1: Typical lag-putt patterns from 50- to 60-foot putts.

CHAPTER 3

Methods of Putting

3.1 Simpler Is Better

There are many different ways for golfers to putt. Having said that, it does not mean that I'm advocating all, or any, of these methods. But it's important that you are aware of the choices a golfer has, and even a few he doesn't, unless he doesn't care about the Rules of Golf (which I think you must if you're going to be serious about this game).

The old adage "different strokes for different folks" is very meaningful, because some putting strokes work better than others for certain players, while no one stroke works perfectly for everyone. While no strokes, even perfect ones, make all their putts, some really awful strokes do make some putts. And sometimes the differences between good and bad strokes are very difficult to measure or see. But believe me, the differences are there.

Before I discuss some of the many methods you could employ, let me pass on to you the one thought, the one axiom that governs all my theories on putting. It is this: Simpler is better. You'll find research test results in many different disciplines that validate this conclusion. It is certainly true in almost all of sports. Why? Because regardless of your level of talent, the less you give yourself to do (and still get the job done), the more consistently you can learn to do it. Whereas the more compensations that must be made in your putting stroke, the more difficult it will be to repeat in such a way that it actually makes your putts. The more complex a putting stroke (that is, the more compensations that must be made to make it effective), the more uncertain (or inconsistent) its results by any golfer regardless of skill level.

All this may sound routine, and you may have heard it many times before, but that doesn't mean it isn't true. And more important, that doesn't mean it shouldn't be taken seriously. So there's no question about it: In putting, simpler is better.

The simpler and easier the stroke is to execute, the more precisely and repetitively you'll be able to learn to execute it, especially under pressure. And that's why all my teaching begins with that principle.

3.2 The Easiest Way to Putt

Let's examine some specifics about the many ways you can putt. First, we'll look at two of the easiest ways, which are both illegal according to the USGA. Why? Well, for one thing, they really aren't putting at all, although they are very effective ways of rolling the ball on the green and into the hole. But they don't utilize a stroke. Therefore, according to the USGA, they aren't putting. And I must agree with them: They aren't really putting.

The True Roller

After about 24 years of research, I've determined that the easiest way to putt (notice I say "easiest," not "easy") is to roll putts from the True Roller. As shown in Figure 3.2.1, you can see that there's no stroke at all: Simply aim the True Roller and then release the ball from the height required to provide it with the necessary speed. Looks easy, right? The True Roller never pulls or pushes putts, its backstroke never moves inside or outside the line, so you might think it would be unbelievably easy to make putts using it. But it's not that easy because you still have to know where to aim it and how fast and how far to roll the ball.

The True Roller is the easiest way to putt because it is as simple as starting the

Figure 3.2.1: The True Roller is the easiest (but not an easy) way to putt.

ball on the right line (in the right direction) and at the right speed. But that doesn't mean it is easy. I know, because I use it all the time in my research to determine the right speed and the right line, and it can take me many tries to find the perfect release point and direction. But once I've got them, I can roll the same putt, exactly the same way, over and over and over again. And ultimately, that's what you want your putting stroke to do. So the True Roller is as close to the ideal as I've found.

Shooting Pool

Not quite as easy as the True Roller, but fairly close, is rolling the ball as if you are shooting pool. In Figure 3.2.2, I'm demonstrating this technique on a practice putting green. I've actually putted like this a number of times, on a number of different greens and grass types, because it proved to me just how important speed is to good putting. When "pool putting," starting the ball on the chosen line is simple, but it doesn't help you choose the line, and giving the ball the proper speed is just as difficult as it is when standing up and using your putter. Again, this is not a method I think the USGA should allow. I'm merely explaining that it's not nearly as easy as you might expect it to be. (If you don't believe me, get a pool cue and try using it on some breaking putts on your practice green.) Just as with the True Roller, you have to find the right speed if you hope to make anything.

Both of these methods are easier than other types of putting, because they

Figure 3.2.2: Shooting pool is the second easiest way to putt.

remove, or at least reduce, the difficulty of starting the ball on the desired line. But the pool method for sure (and to a certain extent the True Roller) is just as difficult as most other methods in transferring the correct speed to the ball.

This is a point worth repeating, because most golfers don't think enough about the speed of their putts. Rather, they focus on line. If you are a "line" putter, try putting with a pool cue or a True Roller and I promise you'll learn to appreciate the importance of speed in making putts.

3.3 It Gets More Difficult

So we've disposed of two methods that no one can or should be allowed to use. What about some techniques that have been tried and, in some cases, are still in use?

Croquet-Style

Next on the "easiness" scale (which means it's a little more difficult than the techniques above) is standing so you face the putting line and putt croquet-style between your legs. Yes, this really has been used. Bob Duden and Bob Shave Jr., two PGA Tour pros who had been struggling with their putting, used this technique back in the 1960s. I've never been sure whether the USGA banned this method because it was too easy, too nontraditional, or it just looked bad when viewed from behind. It certainly made putting easier, because it gave the golfer the best view of the line before the putt and a clear view of what the ball was doing immediately after it started to roll.

Both of these views provide critically important feedback that golfers generally miss when putting in the conventional style (that is, standing to the side of the line). Croquet-style putting has other benefits: It removes all rotational motion of the forearms (which opens and closes the putterface during conventional putting), it forces the wrists to remain solid (no breakdown), and it creates the perfect in-line stroke path, straight down the intended putting line.

Croquet putting is so easy that it was used by no less a legend than Sam Snead in the mid-1960s (when he was in his mid-fifties) to counter a case of the yips. Snead actually putted this way (Figure 3.3.1)—with one foot on either side of the target line—during the 1966 PGA Championship, where he finished tied for sixth. Perhaps it was seeing the great Samuel Jackson Snead putt from the wrong direction, or perhaps it was deemed to reduce the skill required to play the game—in any case, croquet-style putting was quickly outlawed by golf's powers that be.

So Sam modified the method slightly, changing to "sidesaddle" (Figure 3.3.2),

Figure 3.3.1: Sam Snead putting croquet-style.

Figure 3.3.2: Sam putting sidesaddle.

doing everything as much as he could the same, except bringing both feet to the same side of the target line. Snead continued to putt this way until the end of his competitive career, and his creation is, I believe, the next-easiest way to putt.

Just as with croquet-style, Sam found that putting sidesaddle allowed him to bend over slightly and look down the line of his putt. But more important, it still did away with the breakdown of his wrists. I'm sure golf's grand pooh-bahs didn't like what they saw, but either they couldn't figure out a way to outlaw the sidesaddle technique without getting sued, or maybe they didn't have the heart to drive Sam out of the game. Thank heavens they didn't, because it was wonderful watching him play the game, even putting from the side, for all those years.

Another Variation on a Theme

Someone else started with Snead's sidesaddle style and made a modification of his own, which produced the best putting I've seen to this day. Rather than using a standard-length (roughly 35-inch) putter, a fellow came to me putting sidesaddle, but with a longer-than-normal (about 42-inch) putter (Figure 3.3.3). He stood beside the putting line facing the hole and swung the putter along a perfect vertical pendulum, with his top hand and the top of the putter tucked under his armpit. He leaned over to set his eyes directly over the putting line, then balanced his weight by extending one foot away from the line.

Figure 3.3.3: Sidesaddle putting with a longer putter.

I can't remember the name of the man who figured this out, but I give him credit: He found something that really does work. He started every putt by standing directly behind the ball and pointed from his ball to a spot out in front of it on his intended starting line. Then he addressed the ball and again pointed down the line to make sure he was aligned correctly. Finally, he stroked the ball and held his finish pointing at the same spot again exactly down the putt starting line.

This technique produced the consistently best putting I've ever seen, and it is legal. But I'm certain that if someone switches to this style and starts winning with it, the USGA probably will ban it.

3.4 The USGA Way

One of the tenets of the USGA, the ruling body of golf, is to protect and maintain the integrity of the game, in part by preserving its challenge and difficulty. I support this noble purpose, and think most golfers feel the same way. If we lost the challenge in the game, it wouldn't be nearly so much fun. Having said that, we all want to make our own putting strokes simpler so we can hole more putts, score better, and enjoy the game to its fullest.

In keeping with their tradition of maintaining the game's challenge, the USGA would prefer that golfers putt in what they describe as the "traditional style." While this technique is not as simple or easy as the methods described above, it's not necessarily all that difficult, either. Lots of putts have been and will be made the USGA way.

Up to this point, I have been going from the easiest to more difficult ways to putt. Now I have to reverse that. In discussing the following ways to putt, all of which conform to the Rules, I will begin with the most difficult and work down to what I perceive to be the easiest way to putt.

The USGA would be happiest if every golfer would putt like Bobby Jones (Figure 3.4.1) used to putt, and would use a putter similar to Jones's old "Calamity Jane." Jones putted standing perpendicular to the intended putting line and made what appeared to be a miniature golf swing. While this sounds like it might make putting easy, being like all the other swings in golf, in reality it makes putting quite a bit more difficult.

If the putting stroke is a miniature chip shot, which is a miniature 5-iron swing, which is a miniature driver swing, it makes down-the-line vision difficult, involves a slight rotation of the body, and encourages rotation of the forearms. This also encourages rotation of the putterface, provides far more power than is needed, and brings to bear critical timing requirements, all of which make putting so difficult and traumatic to so many golfers.

Figure 3.4.1: Bobby Jones putting with his "Calamity Jane" putter.

3.5 More Methods That Work

As I continue to detail the various options you have for putting, you should know that some of the legal ways are easier than others (yet not one is truly easy). And here's the kicker: Only one will work best for you.

As I mentioned above, I'm moving from the more to the less complex, in terms of having to perform manipulations and actions to make these strokes happen. That means I'm going to finish with the method I think is the easiest. You can skip ahead if you like, but I'd suggest reading through the less desirable methods so you don't someday find yourself doing something that you think is good but is actually hurting your chances of success.

Body Putting
One putting method you rarely hear about is "body putting." As shown in Figure 3.5.1, the arms, wrists, and hands are locked onto the body, so the putter is swung by the rotation of the body around the spine. One reason it's rarely mentioned is that you've never seen a Tour professional putt this way for any length of time and with any measure of success. I have tried it, and yes, putts can be made with this stroke. But that doesn't mean you should do it.

Body putting does help eliminate the wrist collapse and forearm rotation problems so many golfers suffer from. However, the body turn is so powerful, it doesn't allow golfers to develop the delicate touch for dealing with fast greens. Body putting also relies on the very thing that most golfers want to avoid on the

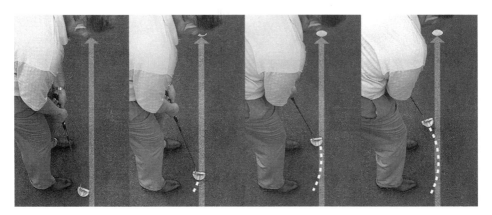

Figure 3.5.1: In body putting, the large torso muscles rotate the body and putter around the spine.

green, and that is unwanted body motion. Watch golfers, particularly amateurs, and you'll see them unknowingly make all manner of body movements when they putt, particularly swaying back and forth, which puts them out of sync with their stroke. Because it destroys timing, body motion is one of the leading causes of inconsistency and havoc in traditional putting.

The Power Stroke

A number of very fine players putt with what I call the "power stroke," by which I mean a stroke in which the power comes from the muscles of the hands, wrists, or forearms. Some power-strokers use their wrist muscles, hinging their wrists the way Arnold Palmer did very successfully in the early part of his career (Figure 3.5.2). Another power-stroker, Tiger Woods, doesn't break his wrists, but supplies power with his arm muscles (Figure 3.5.3).

Both Arnold and Tiger like to force things to happen, to control their putts and make them do what they want them to do. And we all know that they both have so much talent they perform this way very well. I think, however, they would both putt better if they used less hit and more stroke in their putting motions. (What do I mean? Have you ever seen Arnold or Tiger blow a short putt four feet past the hole? That's what I mean.)

No matter what provides the power, there are two big drawbacks to a power stroke. First is the likelihood of a "power surge," which can be caused by adrenaline resulting from anxiety or excitement; this significantly degrades the touch of most players under pressure. Second is the uncertainty of controlling the wrist hinge, if there is one, when the muscles are tight under pressure. Either way, consistency usually suffers.

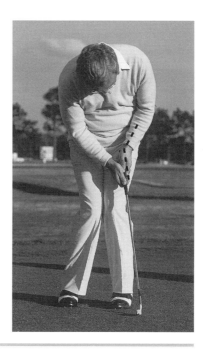

Figure 3.5.2: Arnold Palmer uses wrist-muscle power to roll his putts.

Figure 3.5.3: Tiger Woods uses arm power to control the roll of his putts.

The Pop Stroke

Next down the easiness scale comes the "pop stroke," which was used quite successfully by both Gary Player and Johnny Miller early in their careers. The backstroke is shorter than normal and there's virtually no follow-through after impact, so the ball is "popped," or jabbed, forward (Figure 3.5.4). Neither Miller nor Player stuck with the pop stroke through his career, because they said it lacked consistency; when I've asked them about this method, neither would recommend it. However, both won many tournaments popping their putts, so it may not be as bad as they recall.

The pop stroke does have one advantage, and that is it keeps the putterface angle essentially square at all times, which is a good thing. However, it uses the muscles of the hands and arms for power, and is, therefore, a difficult method to use if you want to develop really good touch.

Figure 3.5.4: Johnny Miller and Gary Player "popped" their putts.

The Hook Stroke

One of the more interesting putting techniques in golf history is the so-called "hook stroke" of the great South African Bobby Locke, who won more than 80 tournaments worldwide between the 1930s and '50s, including four British Opens. Many golfers have told me that Locke put hook spin on his putts, which made them dive into the hole. That may have been what both they and Locke thought, but I'm sure it was not the case.

I've seen photographs of Locke, from which I can imagine that his stroke traveled on an in-to-out path with the putterface slightly closed through impact (Figure 3.5.5). Such a stroke motion would make one think he was trying to hook putts, and he may have actually put a very small amount of initial hook spin on his longer putts (his stroke proved both very consistent and very successful— Locke's putting prowess was legendary). But I'm sure his putts were not spinning to the left or downward when they found the hole. They rolled in just like other golfers' putts, except they may have done so more consistently than any other player of his time. (In section 4.9, you'll learn that the surface of the green takes all the spin off a putt within the first 20 percent of its roll.)

Bobby Locke was a great putter, but his putts did not hook into the hole.

Figure 3.5.5: Bobby Locke preparing to roll a putt.

The Cut Stroke

While there's no such thing as hooking putts, it is possible to cut across the path of one's putts, which is precisely what Chi Chi Rodriguez did while winning more than 30 tournaments in his career. Chi Chi actually putted fairly well in the early years of his career, consistently cutting across the ball by swinging the putterhead outside-to-inside across the line (Figure 3.5.6). But his putting failed him later on, because a cut stroke makes putting more complex than it needs to be.

It takes a talented athlete like Chi Chi to swing his putter to the left while holding the face open to the right, and successfully make his ball go straight. But even he couldn't do it all the time, which is why I think he would have won quite a few

Figure 3.5.6: Cutting across the intended line requires a slightly open putterface to make ball roll straight. Chi Chi Rodriguez was as good as I've seen with a "cut" stroke.

more tournaments had he grooved and owned a simpler stroke. (Don't think the cut stroke spins putts enough to make them slice across the green. The friction of the grass takes all spin off of putts, the same as with hook-stroke putts.)

The Wrist Stroke

Another unusual—I wouldn't go so far as to call it unique—putting style was put to good use for many years by Billy Casper. He locked his arms against his stomach and powered his putts purely by hinging his wrists (Figure 3.5.7). Once again, Casper no longer uses this method and steers others away from it, saying that it took far more time, patience, and practice to keep sharp than the pendulum stroke that is now popular among Tour pros.

However, in his behalf, I have to say that Billy won a lot of tournaments putting with his wrists, so you know it can be done. I caution you, though, that you will have to devote yourself to hours and hours of practice for years and years, and also play under enough pressure to learn how to handle the effects of adrenaline the way he did.

The Block Stroke

Here's a method that sounds almost ridiculous: Aim the putterface a foot to the left of your target on a straight putt, then block the ball toward the hole. That's what Lee Trevino has done throughout his career (Figure 3.5.8).

Figure 3.5.7: Billy Casper's wrist stroke.

Figure 3.5.8: Nobody "block-strokes" better than Lee Trevino.

Every part of Lee's game is built on aiming to the left, then blocking his swing through impact, so it's little surprise he does this when putting, too. In my opinion, Trevino is another great player who achieved greatness in spite of his putting, not because of it. And he agrees: Lee told me that if he had putted as well as Jack Nicklaus, you might never have heard of the Golden Bear.

I believe him. He has always been a great ball-striker (the best I ever measured), and he putted reasonably well, but never great. He is a very talented player who did well with a somewhat complex putting stroke. But he would have putted better and won more with a better (which to me means simpler) putting stroke.

The Blend Stroke

Next on my list of strokes (still moving toward simplicity) is the "blend" stroke, a combination of the power stroke and a pure pendulum stroke, usually employing a slight wrist hinge. A number of fine players putt this way, including Brad Faxon, Lee Janzen, D. A. Weibring, and Ben Crenshaw (Figure 3.5.9). Every one of these players is a wonderful putter, and every one uses a predominantly pendulum motion with just a little bit of power provided by the hand muscles.

The small amount of wrist hinge each employs is done down the line, so it doesn't cause directional difficulty. When I've asked them about this motion, they all say that their best putting days come when the stroke is more pendulum and less wrist. More proof that simplicity is the key ingredient in good putting.

Figure 3.5.9: Faxon, Janzen, Weibring, and Crenshaw use the "blend stroke."

The Push Stroke

The "right-hand push," or "push stroke," used by Jack Nicklaus has been a repeatable, reliable performer for a long time. A friend once told me that Jack really wasn't that good a player: He was just on a 30-year hot streak! Indeed, Jack has putted consistently well throughout most of his career. Even today, Jack's putting remains unshakable, perhaps the strongest part of his game.

Look at Figure 3.5.10 and you can see his right arm and hand are behind the left, pushing the putter through impact like a piston firing straight down the line. There is no putter rotation, no forearm rotation, and no wrist breakdown through the impact zone. The push stroke at its best, and Jack at his best, are and were almost unbeatable.

Figure 3.5.10: Jack Nicklaus
"pushed" his putter down the line.

The Long Putter

We are nearly at the simple end of the USGA-approved putting techniques. And it's here that you encounter the long-putter method, which is probably one option the ruling body would like to outlaw. But as long as it remains legal, I suggest you give it a try (if for no other reason than to experience the feel and vision of a true pendulum motion). Because, when done properly, the long putter creates a wonderfully simple stroke (as demonstrated by Sam Torrance of the European Tour on the left side of Figure 3.5.11).

The solid shaft of the long putter eliminates any chance of wrist hinge or breakdown, and minimizes the tendency to rotate the putterface with your forearms. I've tested thousands of students in my Scoring Game Schools and found that the majority of them make more putts of six feet or less with a long putter than when putting any other way, including the conventional way. It is a very simple way to putt, especially on short putts.

My tests also show that the long putter hanging vertically (from under the chin) is marginally more effective than the long putter anchored against the chest (right side of Figure 3.5.11), and better than the midlength putter anchored below the chest. But all three of these options, because they employ a longer-than-normal-length shaft, eliminate the problem of wrist breakdown that hampers many golfers.

The negatives of putting with a long putter are learning to roll putts the right distance (it requires learning new feel and touch for distance), and occasional instability in windy conditions. However, both problems can be handled with a little practice, leading me to believe they aren't inherent problems but caused by a lack of experience.

Figure 3.5.11: Sam Torrance (left) suspends his long putter from his chin, while I demonstrate a long putter stroke from my chest (right).

The Pure Pendulum Stroke

And that brings us to the simplest, easiest, most repeatable, most reliable, and therefore best way to putt—the pure, no-hit, pendulum stroke. By this I mean a putter swinging in rhythm with the arms and hands, with no power input from the hands and wrists whatsoever. If the pendulum is pure and swings down the line with no face rotation, it is as simple a motion as can be made under the Rules of Golf. And that's why it is the method I recommend most often to my students. And I recommend it to you.

To see it in use, watch George Archer on the Senior PGA Tour, who has produced the purest and best pendulum stroke for the longest period of time of anyone I've ever seen (Figure 3.5.12). Over a 20-year period, playing against Nicklaus, Palmer, Player, Watson, Crenshaw, Ballesteros, Faldo, and Norman, Archer holed a higher percentage of his putts than all the rest.

The list of others who make pure-pendulum strokes reads like a who's who of great putters, including Bob Charles, Greg Norman, Dave Stockton, Andy North, Loren Roberts, and Phil Mickelson (Figure 3.5.13). Having now looked at these great putters, and seeing how simple their strokes are, doesn't it make you want to start putting that way? If it does, you are reading the right book, because my Putting Bible is mostly about why, what, and how to do it!

Figure 3.5.12: George Archer swings the purest pendulum.

Figure 3.5.13: Great putters using pendulum strokes: Bob Charles, Greg Norman, Dave Stockton, Andy North, Loren Roberts, Phil Mickelson.

3.6 The Simplest Okay Way

Back to what I said at the beginning of this chapter: Simpler is better. Because the mechanics of a pendulum motion get the job done, and because they are the simplest, then they must be the best. And they are the best because they are easier to learn and master than any of the more complex motions.

But be careful, because there is not just one single pendulum motion. A pendulum stroke can be swung down the line, around the body, or across the line. It can be swung with the face rotating or with the face kept square. It can be pushed or pulled, or allowed to swing in a consistent, natural rhythm.

The best of all these is the simplest of the simple, the pure-in-line, vertically swinging, face-always-square, natural-rhythm pendulum. It is the way to go if you want to putt your most consistently and most successfully.

I know it took a little time to get through all the possible strokes, from the hardest to the easiest. But it is important that you understand the big picture of putting. It will help if you want to putt your best, because at some point in your putting practice you're going to doubt that what you're doing is right, that what you're doing is working. And that's when you're going to fall back on the knowledge imparted here, that to putt your best you must commit to the simplest stroke that will work for you, and then believe in it. Come hell or high water—or missing 20 putts in a row—you must believe in the stroke you have committed to, and stay with it until you groove it and own it. Only then can you ever hope to move toward achieving your personal optimum putting performances.

So let's get into the putting methods, techniques, and systems most golfers use, find out which is best for you, and learn how to incorporate them, mold them, refine them, and fit them into a system that will allow you to improve and then optimize your ability to putt.

THE FIFTEEN BUILDING
BLOCKS OF PUTTING

CHAPTER 4

The Seven Building Blocks
of Stroke Mechanics

4.1 First, Some Definitions

In this and the next three chapters, I will discuss the 15 building blocks of putting, what they are, how they work, and what they mean to your ability to roll your putts into the hole. First I'll list them all here (Figure 4.1.1), then define a few terms to enable us to keep our communications straight. Then I'll jump in by detailing the seven blocks that deal with putting stroke mechanics.

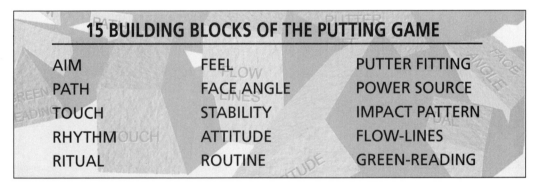

15 BUILDING BLOCKS OF THE PUTTING GAME

AIM	FEEL	PUTTER FITTING
PATH	FACE ANGLE	POWER SOURCE
TOUCH	STABILITY	IMPACT PATTERN
RHYTHM	ATTITUDE	FLOW-LINES
RITUAL	ROUTINE	GREEN-READING

Figure 4.1.1: The putting game requires skills in 15 areas.

Defining How the Ball Rolls

Before getting into the mechanics of the putting stroke, I'll define some vocabulary, which will help keep things simple and easy to understand throughout the book. In our Scoring Game Schools, we routinely use words or phrases that you may not be familiar with. We do this because we've found that many golfers refer to the same things using different terms, and sometimes use the same terms to describe different things.

Obviously, this can lead to unnecessary confusion and disagreement. It helps to be more explicit in how you describe and define some of these concepts. For example, my staff and I never talk about "putting to there," or putting "that way." Rather, we talk about the "Aimline" you intend to start the ball rolling on, the "initial line" you actually start the ball on, and where the "ball track" goes after that.

Ball-Hole Line and Target Line

When we talk about the "ball-hole" line for any putt, we mean the straight line between where the ball sits (before you putt it) and the hole (Figure 4.1.2). However, because the hole is always your ultimate target, some golfers call this their "target line." But many golfers use "target line" to describe the line between their ball and the point at which they are aiming, the line on which they hope to start the putt rolling. But you seldom try both to aim and start your ball rolling along a straight line at the hole and expect it to keep rolling on that line, because most putts break at least a little bit.

Therefore, it is clearer to refer to this direction as your ball-hole line. Also realize that the ball-hole line extends forever in both directions (as shown), and that it is the ball-hole line that most golfers walk to and stand on, behind their ball, as they first try to read the break of their putts.

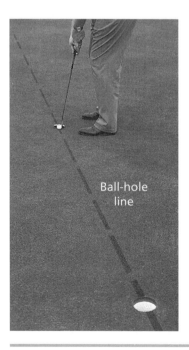

Figure 4.1.2: The "ball-hole" line is the straight line between your ball (before you putt) and the hole.

Aimline

Standing behind the ball trying to read the green, most golfers decide how much they think the putt is going to break and then where they are going to aim. They select a point or a direction where they intend to start their putt, and we refer to the line from the ball to that point or direction as the "Aimline," or desired initial starting line of the putt (Figure 4.1.3). It's best called the Aimline because it is the line along which you align your body, feet, and (it's hoped) your stroke, because you want to start the ball rolling along that line. It's where you're aiming. If everything was figured properly, the ball starts on your Aimline and will roll the proper speed and break (because of the slope of the green) gently into the cup.

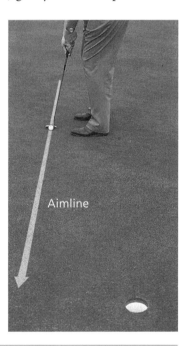

Figure 4.1.3: The Aimline is the desired initial starting line of a putt.

Ball Track

The entire path that your putt takes is the "ball track" (left side of Figure 4.1.4). It may remind you of the "action track" sometimes used on television to show how a ball has traveled. The distances between the balls on the track indicate how fast (relatively) the putt is traveling: Farther apart means it is rolling faster; closer together and it is rolling slower. A detailed ball track provides an accurate understanding of a putt's entire motion—both where and how fast it was going—better even than the same putt recorded and played back on videotape.

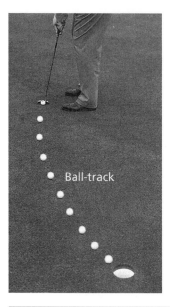

Figure 4.1.4: The ball track (left) shows the path and speed of a putt. The break (right) you play is how far to the side of the hole you aim your putt.

Break

The amount or size of the "break" played on a putt is a measure of the difference between the direction you aim and start the putt rolling, and where you want it to go. We define the amount of break as the distance between the Aimline (up by the hole) and the nearest edge of the hole, measured along a line between the two (right side of Figure 4.1.4). The actual amount the ball breaks (curves) is something different, because the ball track ideally curves into the center of the hole. But golfers refuse to deal with that detail. When golfers say they are playing one inch of break, what they mean is that their Aimline passes one inch outside the edge of the hole, as shown in Figure 4.1.5. Technically, they expect the putt to break 3⅛ inches—one inch plus half the diameter of the hole (2⅛ inches)—but they insist on thinking, and saying, that they are playing one inch of break.

Golfers the world over have made a tacit agreement to think of break as measured from the edge of the hole rather than the center. Unless the putt breaks less than half the width of the hole. Then we refer to it as breaking from somewhere inside the cup, such as an "inside left edge" or "right center," to the center of the hole. Only then do we acknowledge that our target is the center of the hole.

Let's be sure that you understand the terms I've defined so far. You've cleaned your ball on the green and replaced it in front of your mark. Standing behind your ball on the ball-hole line, you realize that if you putt directly along that line it will break to the left and miss below the hole. So you move slightly downhill from the

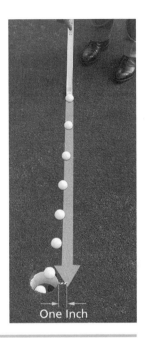

Figure 4.1.5: When your Aimline passes 1 inch outside the cup, and your putt breaks 3⅛ inches into the center of the hole, you have played 1 inch of break.

One Inch

ball-hole line and try to imagine how far uphill to the right you must start your putt if you want to make it. You select an Aimline, which runs about 28 inches outside the right edge of the hole, you walk to the ball, set up perfectly along your new Aimline, and make practice strokes until ready. You execute the perfect stroke and your ball starts exactly on your Aimline. You guessed the right amount of break (28 inches) and gave your putt the perfect speed, so as it rolls it breaks gently to the left and into the center of the cup. Your ball track formed the perfect arc (Figure 4.1.6), the ball entered the exact center of the hole (centered relative to the ball track), and all is right with the world.

4.2 Stroke Definitions

Where are you aiming? Sooner or later I ask that question of every golfer I work with. Aim is a critical aspect of putting (more on that later), and both you and I need to know not only where you are trying to aim (where you *think* you are aiming), but also where you are *actually* aiming your putter, your stance, and your stroke.

Aim

Technically, when I refer to aim, I am referring to a direction. The direction of your aim can be at a place, like the edge of the hole, or at an object, such as a discolored piece of grass, a spike mark, or anything you can see and define. What you choose to aim at can be anywhere along your Aimline, from just in front of the

Figure 4.1.6: The ball-hole line, Aimline, ball track, and break of a beautifully rolled putt.

ball to alongside or even past the hole. Your aim can be one inch, one ball, three balls, a foot, or even 10 feet outside the right or left edge of the cup, or it can be anywhere inside the cup. Only after you determine how much you expect your putt to break and define somewhere or something to aim at can the direction of your aim, your Aimline, be visualized, located, or marked on the green.

Path

The track along which your putter travels is your "putter path." It can move straight back and straight through in-line with your Aimline, it can cut across from outside-to-in or inside-to-out (shown in Figure 4.2.1), or it can loop around your Aimline. Golfers take their putters severely or slightly inside and outside their Aimlines, waver along their Aimlines, and sometimes incorporate a bit of all of the above into their putting paths. I believe there are almost as many distinct putter paths as there are golfers, and I'm sure I haven't seen them all.

Face Angle

A very important consideration is the putterface angle, which we define as the angle between the perpendicular to your putterface and your Aimline (left side

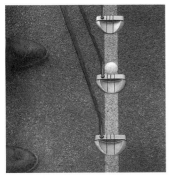
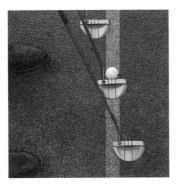
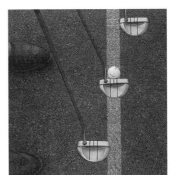

Figure 4.2.1: Putter path can be in-line (left), cutting outside-to-in (center), or inside-out (right) through impact.

Figure 4.2.2). The face angle of your putter can be square (zero angle) to your Aimline throughout your stroke, or it can be open and closed relative to it. When your face angle is pointing to the right of your Aimline, we call that open for right-handed golfers (Figure 4.2.2 right side).

When your face angle is pointing left of your Aimline, it is closed (again for right-handed golfers). The "open" and "closed" terminology reverses for left-handers. You must understand and remember that your putterface angle and putter path are completely independent of each other.

Impact Point

Your impact point refers to the center of the contact area between your ball and putter on the putterface (Figure 4.2.3). For each and every putt, there is one unique impact point, which sometimes centers on a single dimple, but more often several dimples plus an edge of one or more dimples. After many putts, your many impact

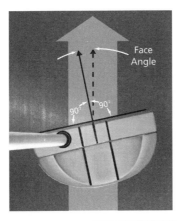
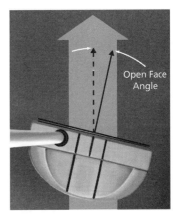

Figure 4.2.2: Face angle is measured between the putterface perpendicular and Aimline directions (left). An "open" face angle points to the right of the Aimline (right).

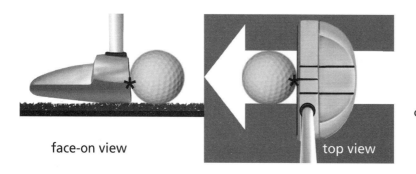

face-on view

top view

Figure 4.2.3: The center of contact area between ball and putterface is the impact point.

points will form your impact pattern (Figure 4.2.4), which is very important to the success of your putting. Aim, path, face angle, and impact pattern are four of the 15 building blocks fundamental to your putting stroke mechanics. They describe and define how you move your putterhead, and how your putterhead moves through the impact zone determines how well you roll your ball relative to your Aimline.

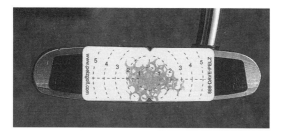

Figure 4.2.4: Multiple impacts show your impact pattern location on your putterface.

4.3 Defining Speed

Putt Speed

The velocity with which a ball moves along the green can be referred to in several ways. Some golfers refer to this as the rolling speed or speed of the putt. Some golfers talk about the pace of a putt, while others talk about how fast a putt is moving. It would be nice if we all could mean and understand the same thing when referring to speed.

Technically, the speed of a putt can be described and measured in quantitative terms as the velocity of motion (in units of inches or feet per second) in a given direction, and the decay or decrease of velocity (the velocity profile) as the ball rolls to a stop. However, since most golfers don't think in technical terms on or off the course, the actual velocity of a putt at any instant is neither very meaningful nor useful. As a result, golfers talk about the speed of their putts as being too fast, too slow, or just about right as they approach the hole.

But if you want to learn more about controlling your putting speed and making more putts, you need to know more about speed than that. In fact, you need to know how the rolling speed of your putts compares to their perfect or optimum speed around the hole. The speed of a putt depends on its length, how fast it started, where it is along its ball track, how fast the green surface is, and the slope (up, down, or sidehill) it is rolling on. For every putt, there is an optimum speed that will optimize the percentage of putts that would both hit, and stay in, the hole. Therefore, in this book, as in my Scoring Game Schools, we refer to a putt's speed (while imagining its ball track) as how it relates to the optimum speed it should, or could be, rolling. For example, as you can see in Figure 4.3.1, the left putt's speed was too much as compared to the right putt's speed, which was virtually perfect. A detailed discussion of putting speed and optimum-speed ball tracks is in Chapter 7.

Green Speed

The speed of the surface of the green, or green speed, affects a ball's roll in speed, direction, and amount of break. I'm sure you have heard greens referred to as "fast," "slow," "quick," "slick," or "sticky." Technically, the speed of the green is determined by the frictional characteristics of the surface of the green, which is controlled primarily by the length, type, density, and moisture content of the grass (more on this in Chapter 7). Golf course superintendents traditionally measure the speed characteristics of greens using a device called the Stimpmeter.

Figure 4.3.1: Too much speed (left) and perfect speed (right) for two putts rolled on the same starting line.

The Stimpmeter, developed years ago by a man named Edward Stimpson, is a crude yet simple way to measure how far a ball will roll on a flat portion of a green when it is given a standard starting speed. The USGA-approved version of a Stimpmeter is a solid, straight piece of aluminum extruded at a 30-degree angle, with an indentation near the top and a beveled bottom (Figure 4.3.2). The beveled bottom allows the Stimpmeter to sit low to the green surface and reduce the bounce of a ball rolling down the channel when it hits the green.

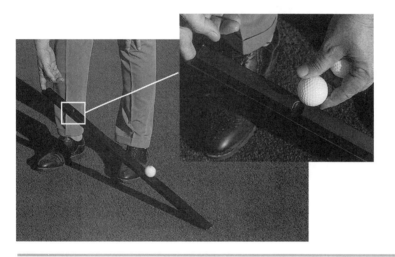

Figure 4.3.2:
The Stimpmeter was designed to release balls onto a green surface with constant initial speed (energy).

Measuring Green Speed

To use a Stimpmeter, a ball is placed in the indentation and the device is raised slowly until the ball rolls free and down the groove onto the green (Figure 4.3.3). Care must be taken to hold the Stimpmeter still as the ball rolls down the ramp, to ensure constant release energy and ball speed at the bottom of the ramp.

To measure green speed, three balls are rolled in one direction on the green, measuring how far each ball rolls (in feet) from the end of the Stimpmeter. The same three balls then are rolled in the opposite direction over the same section of the green, and again the distances are measured. The six distances are averaged to produce a quantitative measurement of the average distance a ball rolls on that green, called the green speed. A slow green is about a 7 (meaning the balls rolled an average of 7 feet), while a fast green comes in at about a 10. Most PGA tournaments aim for green speeds between 10.5 and 11. When greens start rolling at 12 to 13, they are called "Augusta fast," because that's often the speed of the greens at Augusta National Golf Club, home of The Masters every spring.

Longer rolls (from higher green speeds) for longer times mean the friction of

Figure 4.3.3: The average roll distance (in feet) of 6 balls (3 in each direction) on a flat green surface determines green speed.

the green surface is low, letting balls roll farther and longer. A rapidly slowing and short roll off a Stimpmeter means the friction of the green surface is high and the green speed is very slow.

Green speed always affects a putt's speed and direction of roll (except on dead flat greens, where direction is straight no matter what the speed). And the combination of green speed, the amount of energy transferred to a putt, and the influence of contours and slopes on the greens determines the results of your putts based on how much the putt truly breaks, your putt's initial Aimline, and starting speed.

The Seven Building Blocks of Stroke Mechanics

4.4 Aim

Seven of the 15 building blocks of putting deal with stroke mechanics. By the end of this chapter, you should understand them and how they affect your ability to putt. These seven fundamentals (Figure 4.4.1) have the most to do with determining the quality of a putting stroke and its results. They are not the only mechanical factors, but they are the primary ones, and the ones we are most concerned with in our schools. They are your aim, power source, putter path, putterface angle, impact point, flow lines, and putter fitting. If you understand and improve these seven fundamentals, you will roll better putts. If you also can understand

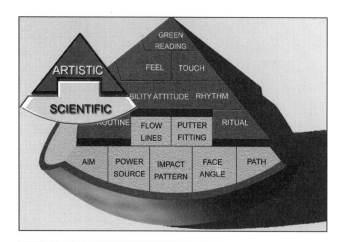

Figure 4.4.1: Seven (of 15) fundamentals of putting are scientific in nature, can be measured and quantified, and relate to stroke mechanics.

how to read greens better and learn to have better putting feel and touch, then there is no question but that you will also make more putts.

It is a fact, proven by testing, that the better you aim, the better you putt. That's why I say aim is the first fundamental of putting stroke mechanics. Most golfers aim very poorly, which is significant because aim can have a direct impact on all the other fundamentals: If you aim poorly, something else in your stroke must compensate to correct for the error.

Aim Is Learned

Aiming is easy. Everybody aims. It is aiming precisely where you want to aim that is more elusive. The fact that most golfers do a poor job of aiming is not surprising, because there's no feedback on a putting green to teach golfers how to aim properly. In the absence of feedback, golfers use two inputs to guide their attempts to aim: First they use their previous putting results (what I call reaction aiming), and second they use the look of their putter relative to their Aimline (what I call position aiming). Further explanations are in order.

Reaction Aiming

The way most golfers aim is to consider past results and then align themselves and their putter to correct for stroke faults and produce the results they want. For example, you miss a putt to the left and think, "I pulled it," or maybe "I aimed too far to the left." Miss several putts left and you think, "I *must* be aiming too far to the left." So what do you do? You aim to the right. Pretty soon, and without realizing, you've learned to aim consistently to the right as a way of compensating for a stroke that tends to pull to the left.

Data taken in my Scoring Game Schools show conclusively that reaction aiming is a learned skill that most golfers develop as a way to compensate for their putting stroke deficiencies. Players who block their strokes to the right of their Aimline learn to aim to the left of the Aimline. Players who pull their putts to the left learn to aim to the right.

Think about it: Have you ever seen golfers who block putts to the right also aim too far to the right? Of course not. They would miss putts so far to the right it would be ridiculous. They learn to aim to the left, and they think this is proper because it produces better results. So the overriding influence on how golfers learn to aim is as a *reaction* to their results. That is reaction aiming.

Position Aiming

Less important to the golfer's overall aim than reaction aiming, position aiming is a golfer's tendency to modify his or her reaction aim, based on the position of the eyes relative to the Aimline. There are valid reasons for this phenomenon.

Figure 4.4.2 is a down-line view of a golfer standing over a short putt. In this example, his eyes are well inside the line (directly over a spot between his feet and the Aimline). From this position, the golfer will look at the putterface and imagine the direction it is aiming, then look to the hole by turning his head (Figure 4.4.3 A), so his view of the hole will be from alignment angle A. Assume he aligns his putter perfectly on that three-footer and makes the putt. On the next hole he faces a 15-footer (Figure 4.4.3 B); if his eye position is again over a spot between his feet and the

Figure 4.4.2: Eye position affects how you aim your putter. My eyes are inside the Aimline in this figure.

Aimline, then he is sure to misalign his putter (and likely miss the putt), because now his view has changed to alignment angle B. The mind can't keep everything properly aimed if it has to deal with constantly changing views of alignment.

Any golfer whose eyes are not consistently vertically above his Aimline will have to change his view of alignment due to the changing angles he sees for putts of different lengths. The result is inconsistent alignment. The only way to align the putterface properly time after time is by positioning both eyes exactly vertically above the Aimline so the alignment angle is always zero degrees for all putts, regardless of length (Figure 4.4.3 C and D).

Detailed procedures for learning how to aim properly will be discussed in section 12.6, where I'll show you how to improve and even perfect your ability to aim. But for now, realize that aim is an essential fundamental of putting, a learned skill you have probably learned incorrectly (without knowing it) based on the results of past putting strokes and the positioning of your eyes (which you should keep vertically above the Aimline, Figure 4.4.4).

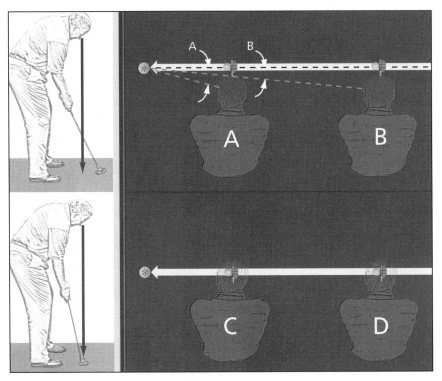

Figure 4.4.3: Eyes positioned inside Aimline (A and B) create different alignment angles for different-length putts. Eyes positioned over Aimline (C and D) create alignment angle of zero for all length putts.

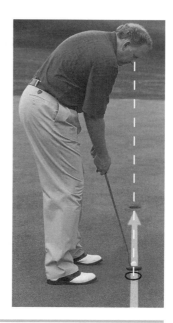

Figure 4.4.4: With eyes vertically above Aimline, there is no alignment angle to compensate for.

If you don't learn to aim correctly, then no one (myself and my Scoring Game Schools included) will ever be able to teach you a good putting stroke. A good putting stroke with bad aim will miss every time, and your subconscious will never let you learn a stroke that it knows will miss every time. Instead, you'll begin compensating. However, once you learn to aim accurately along the Aimline you choose, your putting instincts will lead you to make better, less compensating strokes, and that leads to holing more putts.

4.5 Power Source

Your power source is the part of your body that supplies the power to control and move the putter through the impact zone of your stroke. The muscles you use to control your putter determine your putting power source. The three most common power sources used in putting are: (1) the small muscles of the fingers, hands, wrists, and forearms; (2) the arms and shoulders; and (3) body motion.

Fingers, Hands, and Wrists
Most golfers control their putting with the small muscles of their hands, wrists, and forearms. These are the muscles that control most of the things we do in life—hitting things, twisting things, moving things—so using our hands and forearms in golf is instinctive and, therefore, feels natural to us. But instinct and natu-

ralness don't necessarily mean correct. And, in fact, trying to find a way to putt that is both initially comfortable and natural usually leads to disaster.

Supplying the power, which determines how fast and how far your putts will roll, from the muscles of your wrists, hands, and fingers (Figure 4.5.1) is bad. Wrist motion (hinging) causes putterface angle variations, and hand and wrist muscles tend to tighten up and not work well under even slight pressure. But powering your putts with these muscles also brings an added complication: It's not bad all the time.

Figure 4.5.1: Wrist muscles provide an inconsistent supply of power.

You can practice putting this way for years, and as long as you putt on the course exactly the way you do in practice—relaxed and calm—things will be reasonably okay. But wait until you get really excited. When your heart begins to beat faster because a putt really matters, your body naturally produces adrenaline, which makes all of your muscles stronger. Then all your practice goes out the window, because the muscles that control your putting power are now stronger than they ever were on the putting green. Even if your stroke feels the way it did in practice, the adrenaline-induced extra power will cause it to provide the wrong amount of energy to your putts and produce bad results on the course.

You Can't Avoid Adrenaline

Everybody gets to experience excitement and adrenaline in golf. It's part of why we love the game, and if you want to become a better player, you must learn to deal with it. You must learn to play well when adrenaline is in your system. This is easy in the power game when you want to hit the ball as far you can with whatever club is in your hands. Adrenaline in your system helps you to do this. But putting is altogether different. You can't take one less club on the green when you're pumped up. And you certainly don't want to putt the ball as far as you can.

Luckily, there is a simple way to control adrenaline when putting. Learn to putt in such a way that the adrenaline-affected muscles of your fingers, hands, and wrists don't control how far or fast your putts roll. You'll learn about that in section 13.5.

Forearm Rotation

Just about every shot in golf except putting requires rotation of the forearms through the impact zone. But apply that same rotation to your putting stroke and you'll produce double trouble. First, your putterface will rotate from open to closed, so the likelihood that it is square at the moment of impact becomes very small. Second, forearm rotation supplies unwanted and unnecessary power, and usually a lot of it.

But there's yet another problem with forearm rotation: It feels natural. Even Tour professionals don't realize they're doing it, and when I tell them to stop they usually say, "What do you mean, I'm not rotating my arms!" But, of course, they are. And like the pros, most golfers don't mean to do it, and if you ask them, don't think they are. But they are, and you probably are, too. Which is too bad, because forearm rotation makes putting more difficult, more inconsistent, and less effective.

You'll have to wait until Chapter 13 to learn how to stop rotating your forearms. For now, however, make a mental note that you will stop making this destructive motion. It will be one of your challenges in improving your putting, and a crucial one.

Body Power

In the previous chapter, I talked about body putting, something rarely seen among the pros because it's a bad thing to do. Your body is large, and the big muscles of the chest, back, and legs are strong, particularly when compared to the small amounts of power needed to roll a ball on the fast surface of a putting green. Still, many golfers put too much of their body into the stroke, rotating the lower body, sliding the lower body toward the hole, or moving the upper body away from the hole (Figure 4.5.2). All these motions are unintentional (at least, I hope so), but they still produce unwanted power and directional instability.

For example, I estimate that for every inch the body moves toward the target during the putting stroke, the ball moves an additional foot on the green. And rotating the lower body not only adds power, it also causes the putterface to rotate from open to closed.

Putting is a game in which delicate feel and touch create exactly the right speed and break of your putts. When you're trying to be precise, body power causes nothing but trouble.

Figure 4.5.2:
School students turn (top), slide (middle), and reverse (bottom) their bodies during their putting stroke motions.

Arm Power

The final power source is the best power source, the gentle swinging of the arms (which also involves the shoulders). Think about a grandfather clock, in which the pendulum swings back and forth with a gentle, constant, rhythmic motion. Now imagine your arms are connected at your shoulders at one end and at the putter at the other end, forming a triangle, as shown in Figure 4.5.3. Imagine letting this triangle become the pendulum of a grandfather clock (Figure 4.5.4), swinging back and forth with the same gentle, constant motion. This is what I call a pendulum putting stroke, and it's the best stroke I know because it is the most easily repeatable and predictable (plus additional benefits, as you will soon see).

A pendulum stroke works under pressure because adrenaline-filled muscles don't get to determine how far the ball rolls. In this stroke, putting speed and roll are determined solely by the length of the stroke motion. As a result, if you practice controlling speed this way, you can be sure that it will work on the course and under pressure the same way. And that's what you want.

Figure 4.5.3: Both arms and the line between your shoulder sockets form your putting triangle.

Figure 4.5.4: With putting triangle angles constant, your stroke will swing like the pendulum of a grandfather clock.

4.6 Putter Path Is a Small Factor

I'm fairly sure there are almost as many different putting paths as there are golfers. And it seems there are as many ways to stand over (address) a putt, too. Even for the same golfer, each day's stroke path seems to be different from the last, with some golfers changing their paths from straight to breaking putts, and changing again from a right-to-left breaker to a left-to-right breaker. Common sense should tell you that changing this often can't be a good idea; my putting mantra—

"simpler is better"—guarantees that the more different putting strokes you employ, the worse your problems on the green.

The most practiced putting fundamental is the putter path. However, my testing shows that path is actually one of the least significant factors in good putting. Yet, when I ask golfers on the practice green what they are working on, the most common answer is always "the path of my putter."

The direction that the putter is moving at the moment of impact has very little influence on the starting direction of a putt: Assuming you make contact on the putter's sweetspot, the degree of influence is only about 17 percent (Figure 4.6.1). That means if the putterface is square to the intended starting line and the putter moves across that line at a 10-degree angle as it makes contact, the ball will start only 1.7 degrees off-line (17 percent times 10 degrees equals 1.7 degrees).

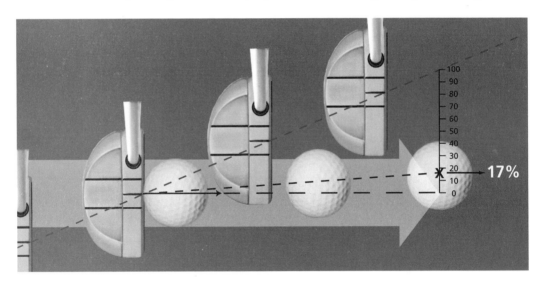

Figure 4.6.1: Only 17 percent of your putter path error is transmitted to the starting line of your putt.

So you can make a large error in your stroke path and see only a small error in the starting line of your putt. Another way to think of it is this: On a dead-straight five-foot putt, your path could travel along a line aimed 13 inches left of the hole center and the ball would still hit the left edge (Figure 4.6.2), assuming you hit the sweetspot and everything else about your stroke was perfect.

As you will see in section 4.8, putterface angle has more effect on the line a putt starts on than does the putter path. But golfers practice putter path because

Figure 4.6.2: Your putter path would have to be awful to cause a miss from 5 feet (if everything else was perfect).

it's easier for them to see, their friends (from whom they take advice) can see it, and they don't know what else to practice. I guess it's not too hard to understand why their putting doesn't improve.

The Screen Door

For many years, Harvey Penick, one the game's greatest teachers, taught that the putter should swing open on the backswing and swing closed on the follow-through like a screen door, as it moved around a player's body (Figure 4.6.3). He believed that the natural stroke path should move to the inside on the backswing (around a motionless body) and back to the inside on the follow-through. He taught many golfers to become great players, including my good friends Tom Kite and Ben Crenshaw, and his screen-door concept has been the generally accepted way to putt throughout most of the 50 years I've been playing this game.

It was how I wanted to putt back when I thought I had a chance to have a playing career. However, despite my tremendous admiration for Mr. Penick and his teaching accomplishments (which are legendary), and my own efforts to copy his opening and closing "screen-door" method, my more recent research has proven that while this stroke can be effective, the screen door is neither the best nor the simplest way to swing a putter.

Three Pendulums

In my first book on putting, *Putt Like the Pros,* which was published about 10 years ago, I pointed out that a pure-in-line stroke path along the Aimline was the easiest, most natural, and best putter path to use (Figure 4.6.4). However, it turns out that many golfers, including some golf professionals, never read or understood the concepts that determined this to be a natural motion, and continue to

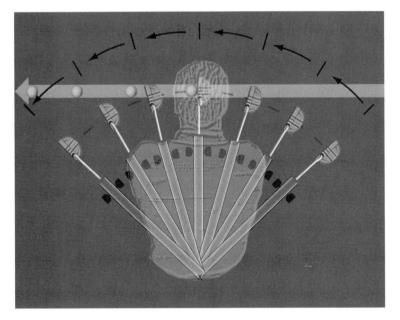

Figure 4.6.3: The "screen-door" stroke opens on the backswing, closes on the follow-through.

Figure 4.6.4: The "pure-in-line" stroke swings straight down the Aimline.

believe and teach that the putter should swing around the body in the screen-door-type, semicircular motion as shown in Figure 4.6.5.

To understand why the in-line stroke motion is the simplest way to putt, you must first understand the mechanics of the way pendulums swing. Three pendu-

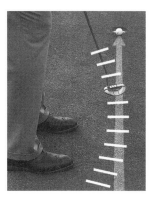

Figure 4.6.5: Some golf professionals still teach the path and face rotation of the screen-door stroke.

lums are illustrated in Figure 4.6.6. Each is swinging from a fixed point, with pendulum A swinging vertically below its suspension point, describing a back-and-forth in-line path along a straight line. Pendulum B is swinging at a 20-degree angle to the vertical, supported by a small force shown by arrow B, and describing a curved path around the spot directly below its suspension point. Pendulum C is swinging at the opposite 20-degree angle, supported by arrow C, in a curved motion in the opposite direction around the spot below its suspension point.

All three pendulums are describing pure pendulum motions (the pendulum

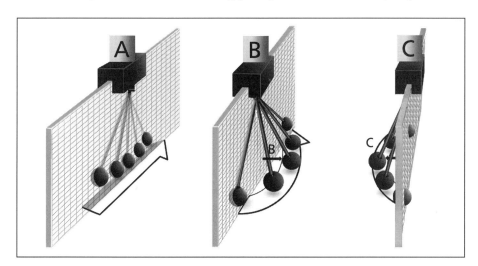

Figure 4.6.6: Three motions: vertical pendulum with in-line path (A), inclined pendulums with curved paths (B and C).

rhythm will be discussed in section 6.3), which occur in a gravitational field such as that found on Earth. But only pendulum A swings with gravity helping to determine its straight in-line path, without any rotation or curvature of the swing path. As you can see, both pendulums B and C require outside forces to keep them moving in circular motions.

Now relate these pendulums to putting strokes by attaching putters to the bottom of each pendulum. Pendulum B is what Harvey Penick prescribed: The golfer's hands hang outside of his shoulder line (the suspension point) at some angle, supported by the force B (shown by Justin Leonard in Figure 4.6.7). This putter will describe a curved path around the body, like a screen door, as long as no hand or arm muscles prevent it from doing so.

In Figure 4.6.8, Fuzzy Zoeller simulates pendulum C by holding his hands in-side of his shoulders and at an angle to his suspension point. This putter clearly rotates from outside the Aimline going back to outside the Aimline on the follow-through (the opposite of the screen-door rotation of pendulum B). Again, this is a natural pendulum motion, but it requires a small force (C) to keep his hands and his 15-degree angle to the vertical below the suspension point.

In these two examples of pendulums B and C, it is clear that small side forces are required to make these strokes acceptable for putting, and both strokes involve curved paths rotating around the golfer's body. Now look at pendulum A as a putting stroke, which involves no side force or curving path.

Figure 4.6.7: Justin Leonard putts with a 10 degree inclined pendulum (hands outside the vertical plane).

Figure 4.6.8: Fuzzy Zoeller putts with a 15-degree inclined pendulum (hands inside the vertical plane).

The Simplest Pendulum

To examine the putting stroke of vertical pendulum A, look at Figure 4.6.9, where the golfer's hands hang vertically below his shoulders. On the left of this photo, the attached putter hangs vertically below the hands, which looks a bit strange. But stay with me. If the golfer now swings his arms straight back along the line of this intended putt, lets them relax, and then swings them through—guided simply by the force of gravity—the putterface would swing perfectly along the line of this putt (Figure 4.6.9A[1]). This path is purely in-line along the Aimline, just like pendulum A, with no side forces or path curvature.

By starting with the putterface square to the line and using this pure-in-line stroke, the ball would have to start rolling on that line. The pendulum swings this way because gravity is the only force acting on the stroke: There are no rotating forces to turn the putterface away from the target line, and no side forces to push the putter off the straight Aimline path.

Now imagine a minor modification to this putter, a lightweight but much longer face (Figure 4.6.9A[2]). With this change, the putter would still swing perfectly in-line beneath the shoulders and there still is nothing to cause rotation or circular motion in the stroke. In Figure 4.6.9A[3], we've added a lightweight, but rigid, connection from the grip to the putterface near its toe. Assuming this connection

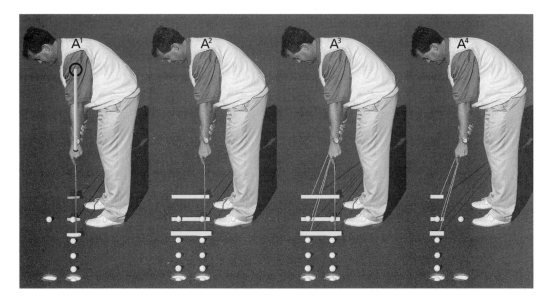

Figure 4.6.9: The vertical pendulum A (shoulders to hands) swings the putterhead "in-line" regardless of shaft or head position.

is truly lightweight and doesn't change the putter's balance, the swing path still would not change, still would not rotate, and would naturally continue to swing in-line along the straight line path beneath the shoulders.

Finally, having seen how this putter swings with both shafts, now look what happens when the vertical part of the shaft is removed in Figure 4.6.9A[4]. By removing the original vertical shaft (which hung under the hands) and the back of the putterface, we have turned this into a normal-looking putter, which still swings in a pure-in-line path as before. This face (again assuming the putter was balanced perfectly) will not rotate open or closed, and will not swing or curve around the body. The natural swinging motion of this putter will be purely in-line along a line exactly parallel to his shoulder line. In other words, this putter path will track right down the Aimline, the intended line of the putt.

4.7 A Pure-In-Line Stroke Keeps the Putterface Square

Section 4.6 should prove to you that a pure, simple pendulum can swing in three different motions, all of which can relate to a putting stroke. The pendulum of a putting stroke (assuming the golfer *has* a pendulum, and doesn't hit with his hands or wrists or move his body) is the pendulum formed between his suspension point (between his shoulders) and his hands (Figure 4.7.1). And it is this position of a golfer's hands, the angle of his pendulum relative to vertical, that determines not only the natural swing path of his putterhead but also the behavior of the putterface angle relative to the Aimline. (Note: your elbows and forearms don't have to be under your shoulders, just your hands.)

As shown on the bottom in Figure 4.7.2, when the golfer's hands (pendulum

Figure 4.7.1: The angle of a swinging pendulum motion determines both its path and face angle rotation: Vertical (A) = no rotation; Inclined (B) and (C) = screen-door rotations.

balls in illustration) are outside his shoulders, the screen-door stroke produces both a curved path around the golfer's body and significant putterface angle rotation relative to the Aimline. This is where the in-line stroke shines, as shown in the top figure: When the golfer's hands (pendulum balls) are vertically under his shoulders, his stroke path is not only naturally in-line with his Aimline, his putterface also stays square to the Aimline at all times. As you will see in section 4.8, this is an incredible advantage, because the face angle is very influential in determining what line the ball starts rolling on in putting.

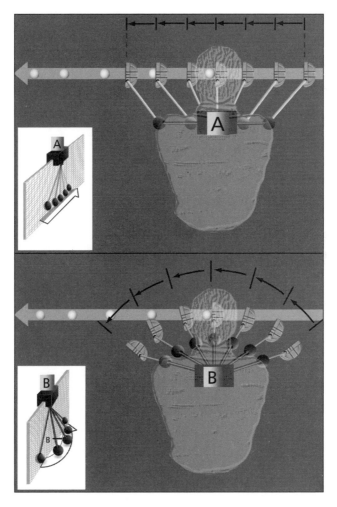

Figure 4.7.2: Vertical pendulum (A) produces a pure-in-line-square (pils) stroke. The inclined pendulum (B) produces a screen-door stroke with face rotation.

Great Putters Are Square

Do great putters rotate their putterfaces, or do they keep them square through impact?

Because I have advocated the pure-in-line-square (pils) stroke for many years, I have often heard from both playing and teaching professionals, "But Jack Nicklaus, Loren Roberts, George Archer, Dave Stockton, and Ben Crenshaw rotate (screen-door) their putters through impact. Just look at this photograph. See, you can see the putterface rotating!"

Then they show me a photo like Figure 4.7.3.

Now I want to show *you* something. Look at the photographs in Figure 4.7.4. On the left you see Perfy, my putting robot, making a pure-in-line-square stroke with his hands

Figure 4.7.3: George Archer's putterface appears to be slightly open at the top of his backswing.

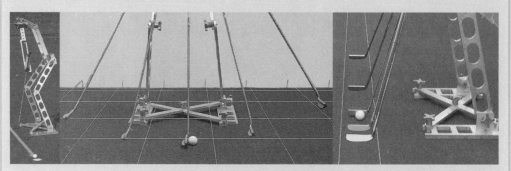

Figure 4.7.4: Perfy's pure-in-line-square (no rotation) stroke.

vertically under his shoulders. In the center photograph the perpendicular gridlines show that his putterface stays perfectly square all the way down the line, and the right side of the figure shows an incoming view of the same stroke (with different lines to show how perfectly on-line his stroke stays). Okay? You agree Perfy makes a pils stroke from this hands-under-shoulders (vertical pendulum) set-up?

In Figure 4.7.5, I put the camera perfectly face-on to Perfy as he makes the same pils stroke, but this time I moved in a little closer and removed the gridlines to emphasize the effect. Now doesn't that putterface look like it's rotating, screen-dooring through impact? I promise you it is not! Perfy's swing was no different; it's only the appearance (an optical illusion) that has changed.

My point is, great putters have their putterfaces square to their Aimlines through impact, what you see in photographs, on TV, or in person notwithstanding. That's one of the reasons they putt so well. If the camera is not on-line or if gridlines aren't present to reference your vision, you can't believe what you see because of the optical illusions. Even standing face-on watching a player putt at a tournament, your eyes (and those of playing and teaching pros) deceive you in the same way. You've got to get your eyes (or the camera) either on-line or vertically above a swing motion to see if it's on-line and rotating or not (as in Figure 4.7.2, where you can accurately compare the rotation of screen-door vs. pils stroke motions).

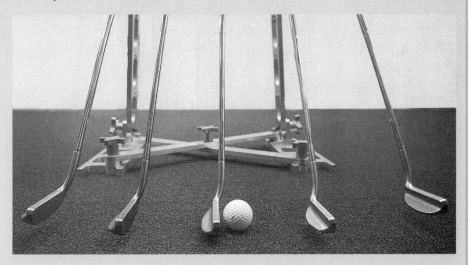

Figure 4.7.5: The pure-in-line-square stroke (no putterface rotation) of Perfy, as it appears to rotate when viewed through a close-up lens from a point face-on to the motion.

It's important to realize that the putter shaft is *not* the pendulum of the stroke, and the lie of the putter shaft does not affect the path of your stroke, unless it makes you move your hands. Figure 4.7.6 shows the path of a vertical pendulum stroke with two different putters with different shaft angles: You can see that both swing in a pure-in-line-square motion all the way.

Figure 4.7.6: A vertical pendulum putting stroke swings all putters, regardless of shaft lie angle, in a pure-in-line-square stroke motion.

Everyone Can Swing On-Line and Square

Away from physics and back to golf. As long as your putting triangle (Figure 4.7.7) remains intact so the elbow and wrist angles don't change during the stroke, and your forearms don't rotate, there is a position of your hands somewhere under your shoulders that will produce a pure-in-line-square stroke. This stroke is perfectly natural, with no involvement of the muscles of your hands, wrists, or forearms. This lack of hand action is what we call a "dead-hands" stroke. (Note: The perfect vertical pendulum hand position can be influenced by the musculature of your shoulders and arms. Golfers with either very muscular or slender arms may find the spot isn't precisely under their shoulders—but pretty close—due to the weight balance of the arms, hands, and putter.)

You've now had it proven that it is not only possible, but also natural, to swing your putter in a pure straight-line motion without any hand or forearm manipulations. And it's equally possible and natural to swing your putter around or away from your body. Which stroke do you think lets you putt best? To me, it's obvious that the pure-in-line-square (pils) stroke is the simplest and best way to putt.

Figure 4.7.7: With the triangle intact, every golfer can find a hand position under their shoulders to produce a natural pils stroke.

It's Natural

Many other accuracy-oriented sports have embraced the pure-in-line stroke motion over a screen-door path, including basketball, bowling, croquet, and shooting pool (Figure 4.7.8). In all of these skills, you could hit or release the ball or object from either a straight in-line or curved (around the body) path. It should come as no surprise that the in-line path is chosen in every case, because the curved path demands perfect timing of the release to achieve the desired result.

Look at the two motions for bowling: Both are perfect pendulums formed by the arm swinging from the shoulder. On the top, the arm swings along the desired starting line of the ball, so whether it is released a little early, a little late, or at the perfect time, it always starts in the proper direction. In the lower figure, the arm is swung out and around the body, so only a perfectly timed release will start the ball rolling in the desired direction. The same comparison for shot accuracy is valid in croquet, basketball, pool, and putting.

So does any golfer want to move the putter or aim the putterface in any direction other than the desired starting line of the putt at the moment of impact? Of course not! Yet some golfers think they can achieve the perfect path through impact by using a screen-door stroke, which rotates around their bodies. They obviously don't realize that the timing of impact (and ball position) must be perfect every time if they hope to have a chance of holing any putts. And they don't realize that the in-line-square stroke motion minimizes the effects of inconsistencies in timing and ball position.

One Negative

I'm not trying to sell you an in-line putting stroke. If this pils stroke seems too

Figure 4.7.8: The pure-in-line stroke motion (above) is superior to the screen-door motion (below) in creating accurate ball direction in many sports.

simple, and you want to make putting more difficult, that's okay by me. I'm just trying to inform you that a pure-in-line stroke is the easiest and best way to putt. But it's not a panacea, and there is one potential drawback to putting with this stroke (it's the same drawback as for the screen-door stroke, too).

To see this drawback, look at how Perfy misses a simple three-foot putt with

Figure 4.7.9: A pure-in-line stroke requires a good parallel-left set-up to produce good putting results.

his perfect in-line-square stroke (Figure 4.7.9). The problem is obvious: If you don't align your shoulders parallel to the desired starting line for the putt, even the perfect stroke path and a square putter blade won't start the ball rolling on the right line.

So if you are going to take my advice and develop an in-line-square stroke, you must be absolutely sure that as you learn this stroke, you also learn to address the ball with your shoulders square (parallel-left) to your putting line. And as you will learn in Chapter 11, setting up parallel-left has other benefits, as well.

4.8 The Importance of Putterface Angle

While putter path has relatively minor influence on the starting line direction of your putts (only about 17 percent), the putterface angle at the moment of impact (Figure 4.8.1) has a tremendous effect, the remaining 83 percent (assuming contact is made on the sweetspot). This means face angle is more than four times as important as putter path. You may find this imbalance in importance surprising (most golfers do), but it's true.

If you are having a hard time believing this, run the following test for yourself. As shown in Figure 4.8.2, aim the edge of a heavy piece of wood to the left edge of a target. Place a ball just outside the wood, about the distance from the heel of the

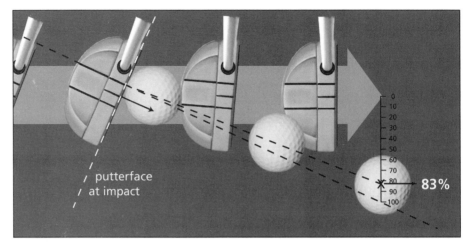

Figure 4.8.1: Face-angle errors at impact transfer 83 percent to ball line.

Figure 4.8.2: With perfect path, a 45-degree face-angle
error produces a 37-degree putt-direction error.

putter to the sweetspot, and hold the putterface open to a 45-degree angle to the target with a piece of cardboard (cut the cardboard with equal-length sides A and B at right angles, then cut side C between the end points, as shown in the inset). Using both hands to hold the face open at that angle and keeping the heel against the wood, slide the putter toward the target to simulate a putting stroke (shown from right to left in figure). If you keep the face 45 degrees open, the ball will start to the right almost perpendicular to the open face (actually, 45 degrees times .83 = 37 degrees), no matter how hard you hit it.

This should convince you that even with the perfect path, poor face angle at the moment of impact will start your putts off-line big-time.

Do you *still* think putter path is as important as face angle? Reposition the piece of wood to produce a path at 45 degrees to the right of your Aimline and hold the putterface square to the Aimline, aiming straight at the hole. Again, use both hands to control face angle and path, and slide the putterface along the edge of the wood. This stroke—with perfect face angle but 45-degree off-line path (Figure 4.8.3)—starts the ball only about 7 degrees off of the Aimline.

So if you are going to make a stroke error of 45 degrees, which result would you rather see? A putt off-line by 7 degrees or 37 degrees? I'm sure you now agree with me that if you want to putt consistently along your intended Aimline, you'd better learn to keep your putterface angle square to that line (the square face angle

Figure 4.8.3: With perfect face angle, a 45-degree
path error produces a 7-degree putt direction error.

Perfectly Square . . . Never!
Trying to get your putterface square at impact with a screen-door stroke is like trying to be "exactly on-time." You can never do it. You're either early or you're late by a minute, a second, a millisecond, or a nanosecond. If your putterface is rotating through impact, it's almost always open or closed, and you will be penalized for being either one at impact (it's just a matter of how much). It will never be square—and certainly never consistently square when you need it!

advantage of the pils vs. screen-door stroke should now be obvious). And if you have some free time, what part of your stroke are you going to practice? Right again: Spend at least four times more time working on keeping the face angle square to your Aimline than you do on perfecting your stroke path (details in Chapter 12).

4.9 The Very Important Impact Point

Putter path is somewhat important to good putting. Putterface angle is four times more important. And guess what? Your impact point—where you make contact with the ball—is even more important still!

The point of contact between your putter and the ball determines how much energy is transferred to the ball at the moment of impact. And the amount of energy your putts receive determines both how fast and far the balls will roll and how much your putts will break. Most golfers believe the distance their putts roll is determined strictly by the length and force of their swing. That's true only if they transfer a consistent percentage of energy from putter to ball at impact. And that is seldom the case.

The Sweetspot

A common term in sports is "sweetspot." Tennis players talk about hitting the sweetspot of the racquet; baseball players like to crack the ball on the sweetspot of the bat. Why? Because when contact is made there, it feels good and maximum energy is transferred to the ball. The same is true for a putter in golf: The sweetspot is that place where contact feels the most solid, which eliminates all rotation and wobble of the putterhead at impact (Figure 4.9.1), and which transfers the maximum energy possible from the stroke to the ball. If you do everything correctly, your impact point will be the sweetspot of your putter.

It is possible to miss the sweetspot either in the vertical plane (hitting the ball too high or too low on the face) or the horizontal plane (making contact toward the toe or the heel of the putter). Any of these misses, by as little as a fraction of an inch, results in a mis-hit and a loss of energy. But you don't need to worry, because in Chapter 12 I will show you how to measure and mark your putter sweetspot and then learn to hit the ball there repeatedly and consistently.

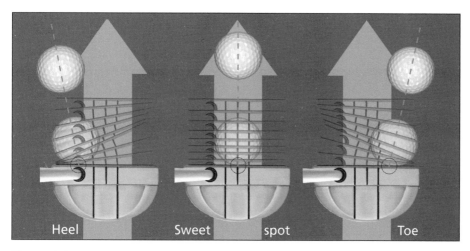

Figure 4.9.1: Impact on the putter's sweetspot transfers maximum energy and eliminates rotation and wobble.

The Quality of Impact

Before we get there, however, I want you to learn how important your impact point is to your putting. Look at the impact patterns shown on the following two pages (Figure 4.9.2). These patterns are all authentic test results made by golfers on the first day in our Scoring Game Schools. Note they are arranged by handicap, with the lowest handicaps at the top left down to the highest handicaps at the bottom right. Also note that the approximate location of the sweetspot of each putter is indicated by the line near the center of each impact tape.

If you study these patterns carefully, the results are clear: The lower the handicap, the smaller—and closer to the sweetspot—the impact pattern. In other words, the better player hits putts closer to the same area of the putterface. And the best players—the Tour pros—have the smallest impact patterns, centered on or very near the sweetspot. In fact, looking at the consistent correlation between pattern size and handicap on these pages, you might think that impact pattern size was the absolute determinant of a player's ability to score. Of course this is not true, but the implications of this data are undeniable.

There's a very simple message here: The more consistently a player transfers energy to the ball, the better his or her putting touch can become. And the better a golfer's putting touch, the more putts he makes and the lower his handicap. Why? Because consistent transfer of energy enhances one's ability to control the speed that putts roll, which controls not only how far and fast the ball travels and how much it breaks, but also the probability of its hitting and staying in the hole.

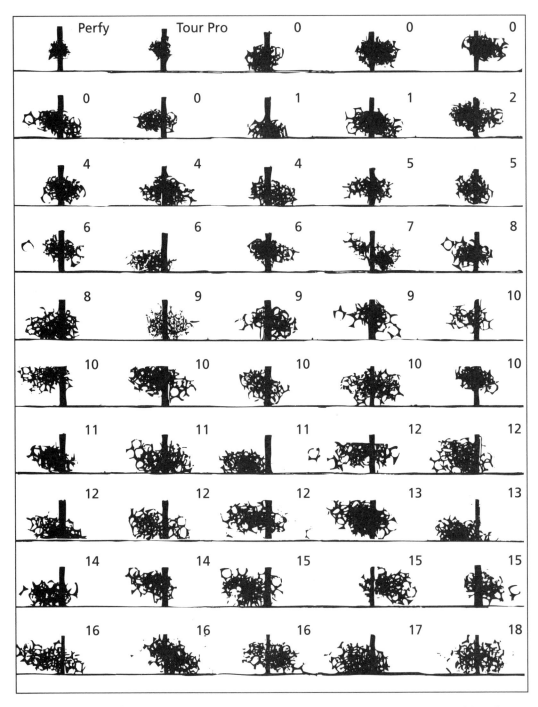

Figure 4.9.2: Scoring Game School students' impact patterns and handicaps.

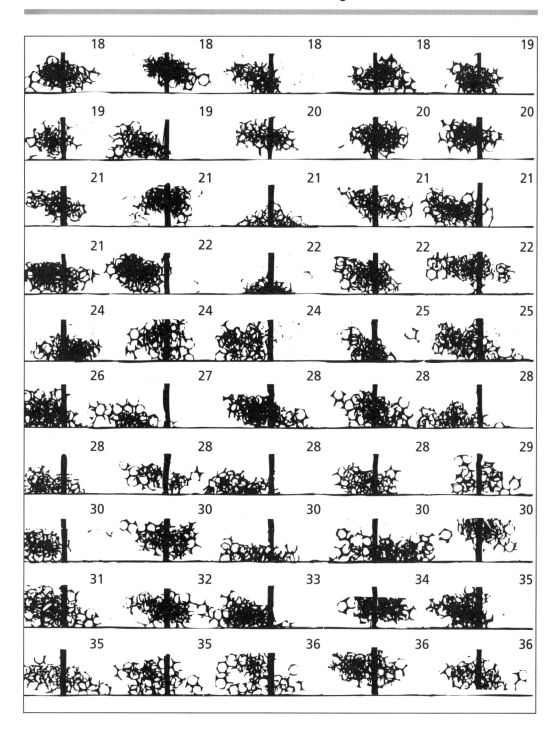

Proper speed also largely eliminates the chance of three-putting. Above all else, good speed control is a requirement for good putting.

The Sweetspot in Two Dimensions

I mentioned briefly that you can miss the sweetspot both horizontally and vertically. So a word about hitting putts high or low on the face. Most golfers habitually make contact at roughly the same height on their putterface. As long as this height is about four-tenths of an inch above the sole, where most putters are designed to be hit, this is good.

But some golfers try to hit up on their putts to produce overspin or topspin, and in doing so usually contact the ball very low on the putterface, near its bottom. This is bad, because it causes hand and muscle control of the putter (subjecting you to the effects of adrenaline), and can even result in some putters rotating over the ball if hit hard enough (Figure 4.9.3). Such rotation can actually impart more backspin on a ball than the hitting-up motion removes. (I prefer back-weighted-low putter designs to eliminate this problem.) Hitting up on the ball also raises the effective putter loft, which can launch a ball up off the green and produce a bouncing, and therefore inconsistent, putt.

Having said this, there is one situation in which I recommend either hitting up on your putts or using a more-lofted-than-normal putter. When you find yourself putting on soft and severely bumpy greens, you might want to try launching your short putts slightly upward to avoid the footprints that would send them squirting left or right. True, this is not a great stroke, but on truly bad surfaces it may be the least bad of your options.

Spinning Putts

Forget here and now the idea of imparting spin as a way to control your putts. Research has shown that the friction of the green removes all spin from rolling balls

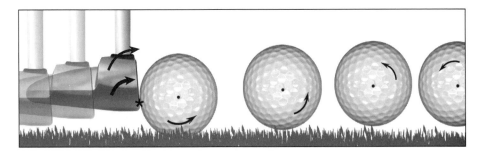

Figure 4.9.3: Hitting up on putts (to impart overspin) can cause backspin.

within about the first 20 percent of their roll. Despite this, golfers think that Ben Crenshaw became a good putter by learning to put overspin on his putts, and that Bobby Locke put "hook spin" on his putts, which made them dive into the hole. Neither of these descriptions is true, but amateur golfers believe them because they sound reasonable and give them something new to try in their own putting. (They also give amateurs an excuse for not putting better. Trust me: Most amateurs don't need any more excuses.)

Still, many golfers, and even some teaching professionals, extol the benefits of "releasing" the putter through impact, rotating the face from open to closed to impart hook spin or overspin. Again, all reasonably well-stroked putts can be shown to be rolling without any spin whatsoever when they reach the hole. So trying to release the putter makes no sense unless it encourages you to follow through in your stroke and eliminates deceleration and instability. However, even in this case, releasing the putter will produce more face rotation and give you more inconsistency in directional control due to increased timing problems.

The Razor-Blade Putter

Because so many people assume that putts can spin all the way to the hole, and are obsessed with the idea of overspin, I built a putter that let me examine and evaluate the benefit of true overspin. I embedded a razor blade just above the center of a putterface (Figure 4.9.4), making sure the sharp edge of the blade would contact the ball above its geometric center and impart true overspin.

I tested the razor-blade putter versus an identical putter with a normal face and counted how many putts each one holed. On very short putts—inside three feet—the razor putter performed pretty well. However, on longer putts it created true initial overspin that caused the balls to "grab" on the green and jump forward uncontrollably.

But there was more. If the grass was damp or I was putting against the grain,

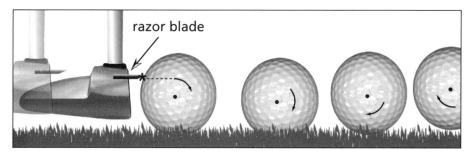

Figure 4.9.4: My razor-blade putter imparted true overspin on putts.

the overspin didn't take and the ball didn't travel as far; when the grass was dry or when putting with the grain, the spinning ball grabbed and jumped forward to roll widely divergent distances. So overspin, if you could create it, causes inconsistency. Which is why I say, "Forget about it!"

Physical and Mental Factors

4.10 Ball Position, Posture, and Flow-Lines

In sections 4.4 through 4.9, the factors discussed are the building blocks involved with the swinging action of your putting stroke mechanics. From here on in this chapter, the factors I'll explain will be ones relating to your body, mind, and equipment. While all of these are less familiar and less popular to work on than the other fundamentals of stroke mechanics, that doesn't mean they won't be important to your success on the greens.

For example, say you employ a very unusual putting posture, but it's one you like and lets you execute a perfect stroke consistently and repeatedly. Then I say it's absolutely acceptable. If it works and you like it, it's okay with me no matter how odd or unconventional it seems. However, if anything about your unusual posture adversely affects one or more of the fundamentals of stroke mechanics, then you should change it. So all of the following are important only in how they influence your stroke.

Ball Position

Any putting stroke that swings in an arc suspended from somewhere around your sternum (or some other spot between your shoulders) will have a bottom to its arc, a low point, a place where the sole of the club is closest to the ground. I have found that the best place to position the ball in your stance is approximately two inches ahead of this bottom point. At this spot you have the best chance of striking the ball on an ever-so-slight upward arc, as your putter comes up from its lowest point (Figure 4.10.1). Striking the ball slightly on the upswing gets putts rolling on top of the grass without lofting them too high, which produces bounce, or hitting them down into the surface of the green so they squirt off to the right or left.

Of course, where your putter contacts the ball also depends on the effective loft of the putterface at the moment of impact. In Figure 4.10.2, the center ball is being struck slightly on the upswing by a putter with a small amount of loft, so it starts on top of the grass with almost no spin. This is the ideal situation. The other

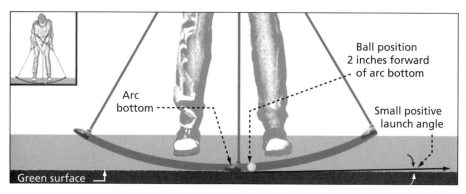

Figure 4.10.1: Perfect ball position is 2 inches forward of your stroke-arc bottom.

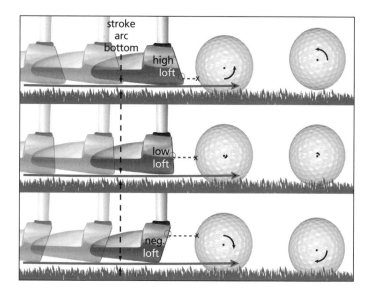

Figure 4.10.2: The best launch angle is just on top of the grass, with minimum spin.

balls in this illustration also are struck at the same point in the stroke, but are launched upward or down, and receive more spin because there is more or less loft on the putterface. Since true overspin, backspin, and bouncing do nothing but make putts roll less consistently, and spin effects are long gone before the ball reaches the hole, there is no reason to try for anything other than rolling the ball on top of the grass with minimum spin.

Again, there is one exception to this, and again, as mentioned earlier with respect to the sweetspot's two dimensions, it is when the greens are very bumpy and soft. In these conditions, I sometimes recommend that players use a more lofted putter, move the ball slightly forward in their stance (increasing the effective loft at impact by catching the putt more on the upstroke), or both. You can see this every year at the AT&T Pebble Beach National Pro-Am, which is held in late winter. The greens are always soft and bumpy due to rain and the large field of amateurs and pros filling three courses every day. By the time our team gets to Pebble for the third round of the tournament, the footprints are really bad.

Despite these conditions, using slightly more loft might help explain why my man, Jack Lemmon (the "human hinge"), always putts so well in that tournament (Figure 4.10.3). (Peter Jacobsen, eat your heart out!)

Figure 4.10.3: Jack Lemmon, the "human hinge," always putts very well at Pebble Beach.

Posture

The angle between your back and your hips should be great enough to provide room for your arms to swing with your hands vertically below your shoulders, but small enough to let you comfortably practice putting at least 10 or 15 minutes at a time (Figure 4.10.4, middle photograph). Your knees should be slightly flexed, enough to give you stability on windy days without making you feel crouched or uncomfortable.

The most comfortable and solid putting posture sets your center of mass (the center of your weight) over a spot between the balls of your feet, as shown in Figure 4.10.5. Leaning too far forward, so your weight gets out over your toes, can cause severe inconsistencies in the impact point of your putts. Leaning too far back, away from the ball, places too much weight on your heels, which leads to instability particularly in windy conditions, again hindering solid and repeatable impact.

Figure 4.10.4: Standing too upright (left) provides no room under shoulders; bending over too much (right) hurts your back.

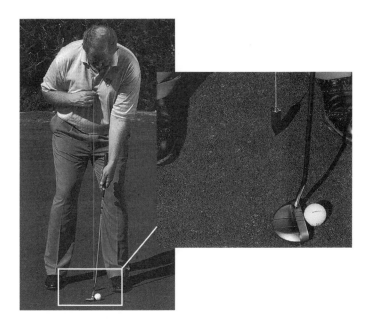

Figure 4.10.5: Balance your weight between the balls of your feet.

Eye Position

Once your posture is correct, as described above, position your eyes somewhere directly over the Aimline of your putt as discussed in section 4.4. Accomplish this by moving closer to or farther away from the ball—not by changing your back angle or leaning over or back. Remember, the Aimline extends behind the ball, so it's okay to set your eyes slightly behind the ball, Jack Nicklaus–style (Figure 4.10.6).

One word of realism here: Positioning your eyes over your Aimline won't

Figure 4.10.6: Eyes positioned vertically above the Aimline, but behind the ball, are fine.

make you aim perfectly, but it will allow you to aim consistently. If you learn how to aim perfectly (in Chapter 11), by eliminating compensations for your stroke faults, then consistently perfect aim will become automatic.

Don't Fight Your Flow-Lines

The easiest way to putt is with the "flow-lines" of your body aligned parallel-left of your Aimline (any line which is parallel to your Aimline, and to the left of it, is defined as "parallel-left" of the Aimline). You're probably not familiar with the term "flow-lines," so look at Figure 4.10.7. The lines of flow through my shoulders, forearms, hips, knees, and feet are all parallel and to the left of my Aimline, which is shown by the shaded white line on the green.

Shoulders

As I mentioned earlier (section 4.7), your putter will tend to swing naturally down the Aimline through impact if your shoulders are aligned parallel to that direction, unless you do something to prevent this move with the muscles of your hands and wrists. So it's very important to start your setup with the flow-line of your shoulders parallel to your Aimline.

To emphasize the power of this concept, my "bad-flow-line" setup is shown in Figure 4.10.8. Look at my shoulder flow-line. From this position, do you expect my putter to naturally swing (flow) down the Aimline? No way! It doesn't do it when Perfy sets up and swings this way, and it won't swing down my Aimline either unless I compensate and use my muscles to make it do so.

Figure 4.10.7: When my body flow-lines are set parallel left, my putter naturally flows (swings) straight down the Aimline.

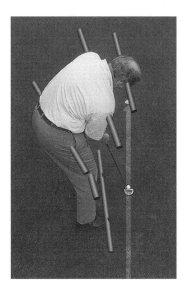

Figure 4.10.8: With bad flow-lines (not aligned parallel left) only muscle power can force this putter to move down the Aimline.

Forearms

Once your shoulders are in place, your attention should turn to the flow-line through your forearms, as they are next most important in determining how your putter will swing through the impact zone. While all of this may sound very simple, and in truth it can be, for some golfers it does not turn out that way. A sure sign of trouble is the golfer who carries his right (trailing) forearm above and outside the perfect forearm plane, as shown in Figure 4.10.9. This is the forearm power position, from which it is difficult for the right forearm to *not* move over and in front of the left forearm through impact. I can assure you that most golfers who putt from this forearm position miss putts to the left when they get excited, anxious, or scared.

Figure 4.10.9: If your forearm flow-line aims left, most of your putts will miss left, too.

Forearm rotation is probably the most frequent killer of putting strokes I see in my schools. The forearm-power position is easy to get into because it feels natural. Well, it is natural, but it's still wrong, and it is something you have to resist.

Some golfers even roll the right forearm over after starting with their forearms level (Figure 4.10.10). This happens because they rotate their forearms for every other shot in golf and it feels like the natural thing to do in their putting stroke, too. Watch out for this trap! There is absolutely no reason to try to supply power or directional control to your putter from the rotation of your forearms. If you let your forearms swing back and through straight down the line, and imagine maintaining your forearms' perfect parallel-left alignment, you'll feel a perfectly natural putting stroke. And the back of your left hand and your putterface will remain square to your intended line at all times.

Eyes, Hips, Knees, and Feet
The alignment of your eyes, hips, knees, and feet flow-lines is important to your putting only in as much as they affect your brain or the orientation of your shoulder and forearm flow-lines. The problem is, they can and do affect them for some golfers.

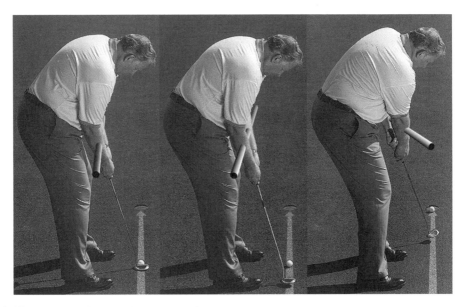

Figure 4.10.10: Forearm (flow-line) rotation eliminates any possibility of maintaining a square face angle through impact.

I say affect your brain because your eyes process information and feed it to your brain at all times. If you perceive that you need to push your putt out to the right because your eye flow-line is aimed too far left, then your brain will make your body do it. When you are trying to perceive distance, your eye-line should be horizontal in the binocular position (the way we usually look at things, with our head up) to enhance depth perception (left side of Figure 4.10.11). However, when you are looking along your Aimline to perceive the flow motion of your putter and ball, along it, your eye-line should be parallel-left (Figure 4.10.11, right).

As for your hip, knee, and feet flow-lines, there is no reason I know of to have them aligned in any direction other than the intended flow direction of your putts. Some golfers tell me they see the line better when they stand open to their putts, but when I test how well they are seeing the line, it is usually pretty poorly. Look at Figure 4.10.12 and decide for yourself: Which setup do you think will produce better and more consistent putter flow down the Aimline?

The Stance

I am a strong believer in taking a narrow stance when chipping or pitching onto the green, because that encourages golfers to use their lower bodies to maintain the rhythm of their swings.

Figure 4.10.11: Use binocular vision (left) to see distance, and down-the-line vision (right) to see alignment.

Figure 4.10.12: Is a putter more likely to swing on-line from the parallel-left flow-line set-up (left), or the aimed-somewhere-else set-up (right)?

And those are the same reasons I strongly *discourage* a narrow stance for putting. A narrow stance makes it too easy for the golfer to move and rotate the lower body. Furthermore, a narrow stance isn't stable enough to resist being pushed around in the wind.

To establish a stable base for your stroke, take a stance width that is at least as wide as your shoulders (Figure 4.10.13), as measured from the centerline of your

Figure 4.10.13: Shoulder-width stance is perfect (left). Wider is okay (center). Narrower is no good (right).

shoes to the center of each shoulder. Even wider stances are okay, but narrower is not.

If stability continues to be a problem, you might borrow something from Arnold Palmer, who established a very solid base for his putting stroke by standing knock-kneed (Figure 4.10.14). With his knees turned in, Arnold absolutely could not move his lower body. However, most golfers I suggest this to seem embarrassed to use it, which is too bad because it works.

Figure 4.10.14: Arnold Palmer's knock-kneed, but stable, putting stance.

Opening or closing your stance by moving your feet off the flow-line is acceptable but not recommended. Because your stance can affect your shoulder alignment, and the line of your shoulders is vital to good putting, I normally recommend setting the feet square. Of course, it is possible to move your feet open or closed without moving your shoulders. Just be sure your shoulder flow-line remains parallel-left to your Aimline.

My measurements also show that many of the world's best putters create a stable lower body by placing slightly more than half—55 to 60 percent—of their weight on their forward foot.

Elbows

Something else to watch out for in your putting stroke motion is any change in your elbow angles. I am told that early in the career of Arnold Palmer, his father, Deacon, told him the secret to putting was to keep his putter low going back and low coming through. However, the only way you can keep the club low to the ground is to extend and contract your elbows: Extend them during your backswing, contract them as you swing through impact, then extend them again on your follow-through. I believe this complex set of motions—plus a propensity to power his putts with a wrist hinge—is what destroyed Arnold's putting in the latter portion of his career.

I don't mean to criticize Arnold or Deacon Palmer, because Arnold putted well enough to be one of the best players of all time. But I'm convinced that with his fantastic imagination, talent, and competitive instincts (he certainly never had the best golf swing), he would have been even more dominant, and for a longer time, if he had used a simpler putting stroke and been a better putter.

The Grip: Light Is Better Than Tight

There are any number of ways to hold a putter. But I think there is only one way to set grip pressure, and that is light and unchanging throughout your stroke. Light pressure is better than tight because squeezing your hands and flexing the hand, wrist, and arm muscles makes them stronger, less pliant, and less sensitive to delicate feelings. And remember, your hands should be dead rather than strong when putting. So the lighter your grip (as long as the putter doesn't slip out of your hands and your wrists don't get floppy), the less likely you are to "hit" your putts and the more likely you will "stroke" them. This applies to all putting grips.

The purpose of your grip is to hold on to your putter as you allow it to move along the perfect in-line path with a square face angle through impact. There is no right or wrong way to hold a putter for all golfers. But there is a best way for each golfer to hold his or her putter. This best way will lead to making the best stroke the greatest percentage of the time.

The grip that makes it easiest for most people to produce a pure-in-line stroke is the parallel-palms grip (Figure 4.10.15). By parallel, I mean the palms and the backs of both hands are parallel to the putterface, which means they are perpendicular to the intended putt-line. Most golfers' arms hang naturally in this parallel position, they find it equally natural to swing their arms back and through perpendicular to their shoulder line (Figure 4.10.16), and this motion is both easy to

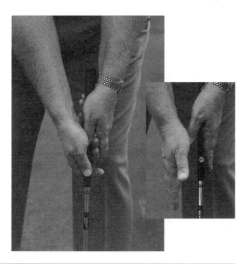

Figure 4.10.15: The most popular putting grip is the parallel-palms reverse (left hand overlaps right) overlap grip.

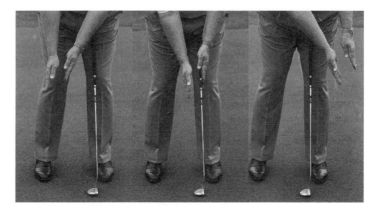

Figure 4.10.16: With both palms parallel to the putterface, the arms swing naturally parallel to the Aimline.

repeat and promotes a consistent position through impact. However, if it proves uncomfortable for you, try putting your hands on your putter shaft in the same positions that they hang naturally (without manipulation) under your shoulders (Figure 4.10.17).

Many other grips are possible, including the "open palm," "left-hand-low," "claw," "fingertip," and "equal-pressure" grips. How to best use these and other grips will be discussed in section 11.6, along with how you can develop the best grip for your putting stroke.

Figure 4.10.17: Relax completely and let your hands hang naturally under your shoulders.

Lower-Body Motion and Looking

Almost all golfers unknowingly move their bodies during the putting stroke. Sometimes a lot, usually just a little, but almost always some, which tells me it must be extremely difficult to eliminate (at least without hours and hours of practice). Try rotating your lower body around your spine in your putting address position and you will see it turns your upper body as well (especially your shoulders, arms, and putter), because your upper body is sitting on the lower (Figure 4.10.18). This also rotates your putterface angle, adding an unknown, uncontrollable, and unwanted variable to the starting line of your putts.

Rotation isn't the only lower-body motion to avoid. Some golfers sway back and forth as they putt (Figure 4.10.19). They probably don't know they're doing it, but the ball doesn't care what you do or don't know. One forward inch of sway during a stroke will move your ball about one foot on the green. And that's a foot you probably did not plan on.

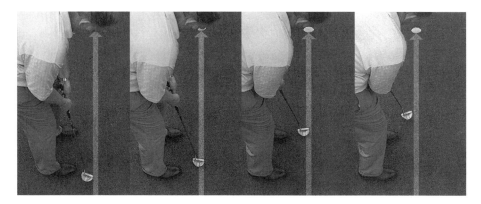

Figure 4.10.18: Lower body rotation causes a screen-door, rotating putterface.

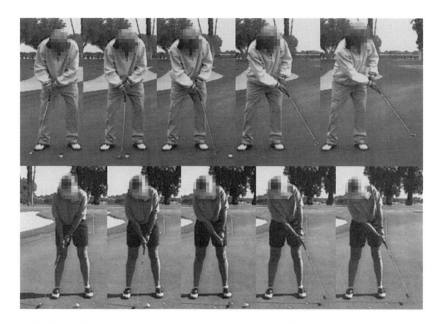

Figure 4.10.19: A sliding forward (top), or rotating back (bottom), upper-body motion degrades the consistency of any putting stroke.

A different kind of move is the "peek," in which the golfer both turns and looks up in the middle of his stroke in an attempt to see the result. Probably the most famous peek was at the 1970 British Open at St. Andrews, when Doug Sanders (Figure 4.10.20) missed a 2½-foot putt to drop into a tie with Jack Nicklaus, who then beat him in the playoff.

Figure 4.10.20: Unbeatable through 71 holes at the 1970 British Open Championship, Doug Sanders "peeked" on his putt to win.

4.11 Putter Fitting

Proper putter fitting is not fundamentally a part of putting stroke mechanics, but there's no doubt that it can help you make better strokes. If the length or lie of a putter is wrong for you, you'll be forced to make compensations in order to putt at all well (Figure 4.11.1). And every characteristic of your putter that is poorly fit to your body size, shape, setup, posture, or alignment is one more card stacked against the odds of your executing a pure, accurate, smooth, and noncompensating stroke.

The truth is that most golfers change their strokes to fit their putters when they should be changing their putters to fit their strokes (Figure 4.11.2). They don't do much in the way of putter fitting, in some cases because all they've been told about choosing a putter is to use one that they like the looks of. In other instances, golfers use whatever putter has been given to them.

Figure 4.11.1: You should never change from your proper eye position, stance, or posture to accommodate a poorly fit putter.

Figure 4.11.2: Bend, cut, adjust, or throw away any putter that doesn't fit you properly.

My belief is that you need to be fit for a putter before you waste too much time trying to work around a bad one. You may or may not end up changing it later, but at least you can make some good improvements until you decide. The details of fitting a putter to your body and stroke will be discussed in section 11.6.

4.12 The Mind's Role in Putting Stroke Mechanics

There is one last ingredient I've yet to touch on in this long list of putting factors. And that is the mind. How important is the mind when putting? You can't move the golf ball even $\frac{1}{32}$ of an inch with just your mind. Your mind doesn't hold the putter. However, that doesn't mean the mind has no power, because the mind can stop your body from accomplishing something in a heartbeat. Your mind must believe you can make a putt, at least that the possibility exists . . . or you won't. You must realize that of course you "can" make the putt. It really is possible. Always remember what one of my favorite putters in the whole world (Dave Stockton) said to me: "I never met a putt I couldn't make."

Your mind controls your body, your body controls your putter, and the way you swing your putter controls the starting conditions of your putt. And controlling a putt's starting conditions is all any golfer can do. None of us can control the conditions on the green, the wind, footprints, or Lady Luck. All we can do is get our mind to let us put the best possible stroke on the ball; then we have to live with whatever happens.

So forget using your conscious mind to help your putting. What you want working for you is your subconscious mind, that part that handles images and memories. Of course, the first time you try something, you need your conscious mind to think about it. But after you've made good strokes and holed putts many times, it can become a habit, totally and completely controlled without any conscious thought. That's when putting becomes controlled by the subconscious mind.

Now how do you do this? By far the most important thing in your mind prior to the putting stroke should be an image in your mind's eye of the stroke you want to make. This should be a clear picture—based on your observations, reading of the green, and knowledge of the conditions—first of what the putt is going to do and then how you are going to stroke it so it does exactly that. The subconscious sees this stroke image and uses it to tell the body what to do. Obviously, you want this image to be of a good stroke, and to be clear, strong, and proper so it gets the right idea to the body about executing a good putting stroke.

The importance of this image is something we deal with in depth in our schools. We go to great lengths to get golfers to see and feel in their mind's eye what their perfect strokes are going to be like *before* they try to make them. Because once you see and know exactly what you are trying to do, and have a clear picture of it in your mind's eye, it is so much easier to do it.

The basic idea is to keep your conscious mind busy seeing your perfect stroke during your practice swings, as a way to build your confidence and form a clear picture in your mind's eye. Once you see and feel how you want to stroke your putt, the trick becomes simply keeping your conscious mind busy and out of the way (for example, thinking about your preshot ritual) so your subconscious can do its thing. Our procedure for developing this skill, and our recommended drills and practice techniques to ingrain it, are detailed in Chapters 11 and 13.

4.13 The Best Way to Putt

A quick review. The easiest way to roll balls at controlled speeds on your intended line is to use a True Roller. Mechanically, the simplest way to swing a putter along your Aimline is to straddle the line and use a croquet-style putting stroke.

But the best legal way to putt is to take a perfectly fit putter and aim it accurately from a square setup with your feet, knees, hips, shoulder, and eye flow-lines aligned parallel-left of your Aimline; put your eyes vertically over the line and your hands vertically under your shoulders; then stroke your putt solidly on the sweetspot with a dead-hands, pure-in-line stroke, keeping your putterface square to the Aimline (Figure 4.13.1). In the next few chapters you'll learn that if you make this stroke in your own body rhythm, following a perfect routine and ritual sequence, with good touch and feel, and play the correct amount of break, then you've got it.

This pure-in-line-square putting stroke is natural, works under pressure, minimizes the critical nature of timing and ball position, conforms 100 percent to the USGA Rules of Golf, and is fundamentally simple to do. I highly recommend it!

Figure 4.13.1: The pure-in-line-square stroke is the best legal way to putt.

CHAPTER 5

Five Nonphysical Building Blocks: Touch, Feel, Attitude, Routine, and Ritual

5.1 Controlling the Ball

The whole purpose of putting is to put the ball into the hole in as few strokes as possible. To accomplish this successfully, you must consistently strike your putts with precision and accuracy, starting them on the correct line and giving them the correct initial speed. If you can accomplish the initial conditions of proper line and speed, the rest of your putting results are up to Mother Nature and the greens.

Starting your putts on your chosen initial line is primarily a function of your stroke mechanics, specifically aiming your putter properly and striking it with a good path and square face angle. That's the easy part. Imparting the proper initial speed is significantly more difficult, because it involves stroke mechanics (making solid contact on the sweetspot), as well as putting "feel" and "touch" for distance, plus your ability to read greens.

Taking a Trip

Stick with me here as I equate the skills of putting touch, feel, and green-reading on the golf course to what you do when taking a Thanksgiving drive to your parents' house. First, to have a nice trip, you need to know how many miles you have to drive and how much of the trip is mountain driving. With that knowledge you can figure out how much gas you need to make it there. This is like having touch in putting, which is knowing how long the putt is, so you can then figure out how much power will be required in your stroke to get the ball to the hole. And you'd better know how much gas you need before starting the trip, because there are no filling stations (putting stroke adjustments) along the way (after you hit the ball).

Once you know how much gas you need, then you have to figure out how hard to step on the gas pedal, and when to step on the brakes, as you drive on your Thanksgiving trip (something you figure out after you are into the trip), to negotiate the stops and turns in the road along the way. This "knowing how to drive" is analagous to knowing how to feel the proper stroke in putting, where you must know in your mind's eye the required size of the swing (or hardness of the hit), as well as how it will look and feel to impart the power, which will provide the proper energy and speed of roll required. So touch is knowing how long the trip is and how much power it will require, and feel is knowing how to apply the power (how to drive) to get you there.

Of course, good touch and feel also require a proper read of the green, knowing what will happen to your putt as it rolls. Think of green-reading as having a good road map for your journey. A good map or good directions can make the trip easy, but a bad map with poor directions can turn the simplest trip into a nightmare.

So you need a map, enough gas, and the knowledge of how hard to step on the gas pedal along the way. You need all these things, in concert, to have a good trip. And you need good feel, touch, and green-reading skills, also working together, to putt well. Leave one out or do one poorly and it will be the same as losing your way on your Thanksgiving trip. Feel, touch, and green-reading are separate skills, essentially different in nature, yet each needs to be developed to provide the best result. And in case I've confused you, that result is to roll the ball into the hole.

5.2 Touch and Feel Are in the Mind's Eye

The skill bases for your touch and feel (green-reading will be discussed in Chapter 7) are intermingled in your mind. They are also intermingled in that they have a combined effect on putting results. But each is a separate skill, which can be learned and developed over time.

Touch is in your head, but it begins with knowing what your putt looks like, and remembering (knowing based on past experience) how much power (the size or intensity of stroke) was required in the past for similar putts. Touch is an acquired skill based on past experiences. It resides in your memory bank, and plays a part in creating the mind's-eye picture of the size of stroke you need.

Before you can develop a good feel for a putt, you need to have a good idea for how long it is and how much power will be required to roll it the proper speed and distance: In other words, you need to have touch. Given that, feel for the putt involves having a good idea of how to apply the power, which will be needed to roll the ball at the optimum speed along that line, to allow it to break into the hole. Having good feel for a putt is having the idea or picture in your mind's eye of how the stroke will look and feel, in both rhythm and intensity, as it rolls the ball to the hole. So a part of feel is in your head. Feel also involves a kinesthetic awareness for the violence (or nonviolence) of your swing and knowing the physical sensation to expect at impact, including the vibrations that will travel up the shaft after the putter strikes the ball. It is based on the feel of your collected experience from thousands of swings you've made on previous putts, and the results they produced. This feel is produced in your nerve endings, fingers, arms, and shoulders, in the muscles of all of these entities, as well as in your brain and memory.

Is one part of feel more important than any other? I don't know. But more to the point, I'm not sure I care. Because I do know that all these factors are necessary for good putting, and the end result, feel, ultimately is experiential. You've got to do it lots of times to learn it and know it.

Feel is knowing how to do it, touch is knowing what to do. A golfer with good touch can have a bad day physically, when his body simply can't execute what his brain knows he should do. On a day like this, we'd say his feel is off. This golfer will be frustrated because he doesn't seem to be able to do what he knows he can and needs to do. Compare that to a golfer with poor touch: He can have great feel and still never make a putt, because if you choose the wrong speed yet roll it perfectly at that speed, the results still won't be very good. So poor-touch golfers are more likely to get bewildered than frustrated (Figure 5.2.1).

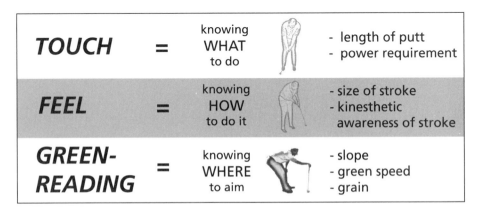

TOUCH	=	knowing WHAT to do		- length of putt - power requirement
FEEL	=	knowing HOW to do it		- size of stroke - kinesthetic awareness of stroke
GREEN-READING	=	knowing WHERE to aim		- slope - green speed - grain

Figure 5.2.1: It's all in your mind.

5.3 Realities of Touch and Feel

Adrenaline Effects

Since touch and feel both reside in the brain, and the brain travels with a golfer's body, it would be logical to assume that both touch and feel would transfer easily from the practice green to the course. Sorry, but that is not the case. In fact, transferring them to the course is often one of the most difficult aspects of the game for golfers at all skill levels (this is true for the short game as well as putting, and, as you'll see, for the same reason). When a golfer feels excited, anxious, scared, or is under any kind of pressure, his heart beats faster and his body produces adrenaline, which causes the muscles to get stronger. This can happen on the first tee, over a two-foot putt to win the Saturday nassau, or on the final hole of the U.S. Open. In all these situations, pressure means stronger muscles. And stronger muscles are certain to affect your putting results if it is your muscles that are determining how far and fast your putts roll.

What happens when you practice putting? The heart doesn't beat faster, you are not excited, and adrenaline isn't produced. No adrenaline, because no matter how hard you practice or how much you concentrate on the practice green, by it's very nature, practice is repetitive and boring. Deep inside, you know that the results don't matter. You can pretend that this five-footer is to win The Masters, but you can't fool your subconscious. If you want to put a little pressure and excitement into your practice sessions, either compete with a friend for more money than you can afford to lose, or when practicing alone, tell yourself (and then live by it) that you can't quit until you achieve some specific goal, such as holing 10 three-footers in a row. We call this "a closer," and I highly recommend it. (More about it in Chapter 13.)

So if you can't practice with pressure, how do you make practice help your putting on the golf course when it really counts? You could try to avoid pressure on the course, but that's not going to happen. The only way to putt well under pressure is to develop a stroke in practice that works both in practice and on the course when the pressure is on and your muscles are strong. I'm not saying you should develop a "pressure stroke," one that's different from the stroke you normally practice and use. What I am saying is that you should be smart enough to use your practice time to develop a normal stroke that is the same as your pressure stroke. This is a stroke that doesn't depend on the strength of your muscles or the speed of your heartbeat. It is a stroke that will work just as well under pressure as in practice. As you'll see below, it's called a dead-hands stroke.

The Hit Stroke

Let me explain what this "dead-hands" stroke is not. It is not your natural stroke, because most golfers' natural instinct is to "hit" a putt with the muscles of the fingers, hands, and wrists. Our instincts are developed in our childhood when we play games that involve hitting things, turning knobs, and manipulating, pushing, and controlling the objects in our lives with our fingers, hands, and wrists. This also is the way most people putt, because they consider it to be natural. But just because it's natural does not make it either the right way or the best way.

But golfers hit their putts (Figure 5.3.1). And when a ball is hit, the distance it rolls depends on how *hard* it is hit. The power of the putt depends on the energy or effort put into the stroke. And therein lies the problem: You can't see or feel the power of a hit before it happens. No matter how much a golfer practices hitting putts the right distance and speed, when he or she gets under pressure and tries to apply the same hit to the ball with adrenaline-filled muscles, the results will be wrong. Once again, as the muscles get stronger, the same feel that produced good results in practice produces a more powerful hit under pressure.

Figure 5.3.1: A Scoring Game School student powering a putt with wrist muscles.

Many low-handicap amateurs fall into this trap. They practice with the belief that the harder and longer they work, the better they'll putt under pressure. They believe that putting well under pressure involves courage, strength of conviction, or some other inner quality of the heart. I suppose these character traits are admirable, but they have nothing to do with how far the ball rolls in good putting. If you insist on hitting your putts and controlling your putt distance with your muscles, then the only way to practice feel and touch is under pressure. The good player can accomplish this by playing in tournaments in which he is likely to face many pressure putts. Do enough of that—and enough is a lot—and you begin preparing yourself for future pressure situations.

Higher-handicap golfers have a slightly different problem. Because hitting with the hands is the natural way to putt, most golfers begin by doing just that. The results won't be very good, but because the golfer is still new to the game, poor putting will seem acceptable. It's later, as these golfers improve their ball-striking and short games, and work on bringing their handicaps down, that their natural (hand-muscle-controlled) putting stroke limits their ability to score.

The Amateurs Proved It

Let me give you one more problem with "hitting" your putts: It's an inaccurate way to control the power transmitted to the ball. We measured this (Figure 5.3.2) when we tested the putting strokes of some 150 amateurs at the DuPont World Amateur tournament by measuring the length of their strokes when they putted. The averaged results show (Figure 5.3.3) that the length of their backswings varied only about 6 inches, while the length of the putts produced varied from 6 to 30 feet (on a flat putting surface of 9.0 green speed). This means their backswing, the power generator of the putting stroke, varied only 6 inches for 24 feet, or about one-quarter inch per foot.

Think of the pressure that puts on every putt. These amateurs must be able to sense and feel a difference of less than one inch—between a 9- and 9¾-inch back-swing—to produce putts of 12 and 15 feet, respectively. And that's not all. They

Figure 5.3.2: Testing at the DuPont World Amateur Tournament (after hours).

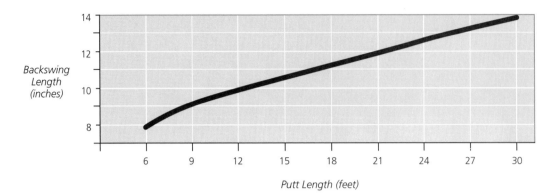

Backswing Length (inches)

Putt Length (feet)

Figure 5.3.3: When putt-roll distance is controlled by "hit" power, backswing length is minimized.

also have to accurately feel the differences in the strength of the hits that produce these two putts of different lengths. As these examples prove, there is not much margin for error when you're trying to control the distance your putts roll with a hit. There is a better way.

5.4 The Dead-Hands Stroke

The alternative to "hitting" your putts is to "stroke" them. And the ultimate stroke is a pendulum stroke, which requires "dead hands" to make it a pure pendulum. A pure pendulum stroke is the weakest, least powerful swing in golf. When you first try it, you will probably feel insecure, as if you can't get the ball to the hole, so you'll probably leave every putt short. You also will feel as if you don't have control of the ball. Of course, no golfer truly ever has total control of the ball: You can only start a putt on the proper line at the proper speed. Thinking you can do anything else classifies you as a dreamer.

So not being able to control the putt is not a negative; rather, it is a truth of the game. Trying to control your putts with a hitting action may make you feel good in the short run, but ultimately it degrades your putting. On the other hand, not trying to control your putting—using a dead-hands stroke—is a positive action because it is pressure-proof. No matter how strong the muscles of your fingers, hands, and wrist become due to adrenaline, if you don't use them, they won't hurt your putting feel or touch.

If you let the length of your swing, starting with the length of your backswing, determine the length of the roll of your putts, and you perform your stroke in your personal body rhythm (more on this in section 6.5), then you can learn excellent putting touch and control of your putts' speed and distance. Look at the putting stroke of Senior Tour player George Archer (Figure 5.4.1). George not only produces a nearly perfect pendulum stroke—as you can see in the consistency of the arm-to-wrists angle in three positions of the stroke (backswing, impact, and end of follow-through)—but he also uses a pendulum rhythm. George's pure-in-line-square putting stroke is one of the best you'll ever see.

The major advantage of the dead-hands stroke is the elimination of the hand and wrist muscles, which leads to the subsequent absence of any adrenaline effects. But there are two more reasons to recommend it. Because it is the weakest swing in golf, it requires much longer strokes for longer putts than the hit stroke. That means it will be easier to learn to control the length of the roll by the length of the stroke. And, since the wrist muscles aren't used for power, they become more sensitive to the feel (kinesthetics) of the stroke.

Figure 5.4.1: George Archer makes the best pendulum stroke.

A Dead-Hands Advantage

Figure 5.4.2 is a graph that shows how Perfy's and my backswings change length to control the distance our putts roll (on a flat green of 9.0 speed). You can see that the lighter dead-hands stroke (of Perfy) has an advantage over my heavier pendulum stroke, judging by the differences in the length of the backswings. But even as imperfect as my stroke is, it still has an advantage over the hit stroke.

Notice the backswing lengths I use to hit putts compared to the hit strokes mea-

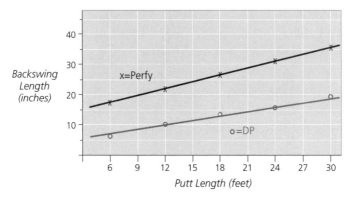

Figure 5.4.2: My pendulum backswing length varies more than a hit stroke to determine distance, but Perfy's stroke is even better.

sured for amateurs in Figure 5.3.3 (page 118). As you can see, there are substantially larger differences in the lengths of my backstrokes using the dead-hands action. This means that there is more room for adjustments when producing putts of different lengths with this stroke, because the roll is a pure product of my backstroke length, and not any hard-to-regulate "hit instinct" of the muscles. You know that if you take the putter back so far, it will produce the same-distance putt (assuming you make the same stroke time and again); take it back a little longer, and the putt will roll a little farther. This also means, assuming you put in the same amount of practice time for both strokes, that you'll develop better feel and distance control using the dead-hands stroke than using the hit stroke. And with the dead-hands stroke, what you practice is what you do under pressure, with no deviation.

The final advantage of the dead-hands stroke is that you can see it, evaluate it, and get comfortable with it before you use it. If, during your practice strokes, your mind's eye sees the proper-length stroke required for the putt at hand, then simply repeating that stroke on the real ball will create your best possible putt. No matter how much adrenaline is flowing and no matter how strong your hand and wrist muscles are, if under pressure you can make a pure pendulum stroke with dead hands, it will be the length of your swing that controls your putting speed, not your level of excitement.

5.5 Putt in Your Personal Rhythm

The power in a golfer's hit stroke is the product of the speed, timing, and muscle strength (adrenaline-aided or not) of the golfer. So what produces the power of a dead-hands stroke? It's simply the length and rhythm of the stroke. So putting this way becomes easier. Not easy, mind you, but easier. In this regard, putting is similar to the rest of golf. If you swing in a rhythm consistent with the way you naturally move your body, then your consistency becomes a function of your talent and technique, which is how it should be. This means putting with a rhythm consistent with your personality, body size, weight, and walking pace. All athletic motions become more consistent and repeatable when performed to a consistent rhythm. This doesn't mean you should swing the putter at a speed that exactly matches your walking pace. But fast walkers generally should have faster putting stroke paces than slow walkers. I'll explain more about your best putting rhythm in section 6.5. Until then, accept that you must putt "within yourself," or at your own body rhythm, to putt your best.

Whether or not you have decided to take the hit out of your stroke, understand that a putting stroke with a repeatable rhythm will always outperform one with an inconsistent, herky-jerky motion. A natural, consistent, repeatable rhythm improves your results regardless of your stroke mechanics. So you shouldn't be surprised to learn that the beneficial effects of rhythm are magnified under pressure. When you are scared and distracted, your subconscious reverts to your most deeply ingrained tendencies, and you want those to be putting with good rhythm. So that's how you should practice. Be sure you aren't rushing your putts or just beating balls, and watch every putt until it stops. And when you superimpose good rhythm on top of a good dead-hands stroke, you'll begin to see improved results both in practice and on the course.

Look at Figure 5.5.1 to see how the feel and touch for distance of several PGA Tour pros I work with compares to that of the amateurs in our schools. Fortu-

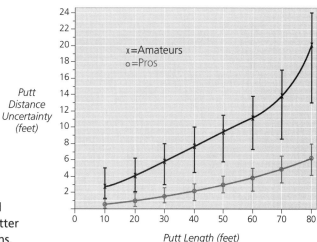

Figure 5.5.1: PGA Tour Pros control their putting speed and distance better than amateurs for putts of all lengths.

nately, there is no law against improving one's putting feel and touch, so with some work, yours can become more like that of the pros'. In Chapter 13, I'll describe excellent learning aids for both of these skills. Once you know your best putting rhythm and how best to practice it, all it takes is a little practice and time to see big improvements in your feel and touch.

5.6 Two Types of Muscle Memory

If you ever learned how to ride a bicycle, even if it was 30 years ago, you will never forget the feeling of how to ride. You may be a little rusty and momentarily forget how to balance your body on the bike, but in just a few moments you can ride away almost as if you'd never stopped. This is a good example of long-term muscle memory, which is stored in your brain and never forgotten.

Everyone has a second kind of muscle memory, called short term—thoughts and sensations that disappear from our bodies and minds at a rate of about 30 percent every eight seconds. Say someone pinches you on the arm: You feel the pinch and it hurts. But it hurts only for a little while, the pain fades away, and in almost no time the pain is gone and you feel better. The memory of how badly you hurt, or what the hurt actually felt like, fades quickly. In eight seconds, about one third of the feeling is lost. In the next eight seconds, another third of what is left goes, and on and on until there is nothing left to feel. Most humans operate with this same eight-second clock, so it is called the "time constant" of short-term memory. It is also a good measure of your loss of kinesthetic awareness involved in the feel of your golf swing or putting stroke.

Both long- and short-term muscle memories are important in putting. Once you learn and know the feeling of your perfect putting stroke, it will reside in your long-term memory and never totally be forgotten. You may not be able to produce it at will immediately after a long layoff, but with a little work you'll do it and, just as important, you will recognize it. The memories of the good stroke will come flooding back, just the way they do when hopping on a bicycle after a long layoff. That's the good news.

The bad news is that the short-term feel for your putting stroke motion is subject to the short-term time constant of eight seconds. When does this come into play? As you are learning and practicing putting touch, and on the course as you make practice strokes in preparation for the real one.

The way you learn what size stroke is required for each length putt during practice is by trying several and seeing how they look. This is what practice swings are for. After each stroke—whether or not it was the right length to roll the ball the perfect distance and speed—your mind consciously and subconsciously correlates your stroke action with the result it would anticipate it to produce. Then when you putt, the ball usually rolls for at least four to six seconds or even longer, and you need to retain the feel of each stroke for at least that long to maximize the learning of the correlation between the feel of your stroke motion and the result it produced (the roll of your putt). This is why you must learn to hold your follow-through until the ball has stopped moving: As soon as you drop your putter or move your body in a motion unrelated to putting, the feeling of the stroke is replaced by the feeling of that motion. Your mind remembers only the body's most recent sensations, and these, too, fade by 30 percent every eight seconds.

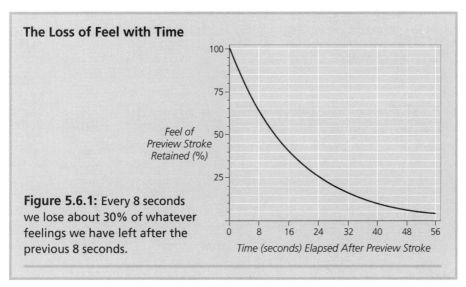

The Loss of Feel with Time

Feel of Preview Stroke Retained (%)

Figure 5.6.1: Every 8 seconds we lose about 30% of whatever feelings we have left after the previous 8 seconds.

Time (seconds) Elapsed After Preview Stroke

Hold Your Finish

Greg Norman understands that he must hold his finish when putting (Figure 5.6.2). Just watch him: Whether he is putting to win a tournament or putting on a practice green, he always holds his finish as he watches the ball roll. He learns a little bit about his putting, his stroke, and the green from every putt.

Compare this to the common golfer's reaction to a putt (Figure 5.6.3). The ball is barely struck, and he is reacting, talking, complaining, letting go of the putter, standing up, and turning away. Before the ball has stopped rolling, he has lost all feeling for the stroke that moved it, and there is nothing left to correlate with the result. Not only hasn't his putt found the hole (a safe bet), but the golfer hasn't learned anything from it. By holding his finish and watching his putts, Norman learns a lot about his putting. By looking away and complaining while the ball is

Figure 5.6.2: Greg Norman watches his stroke result while he can still feel the swing and impact sensations.

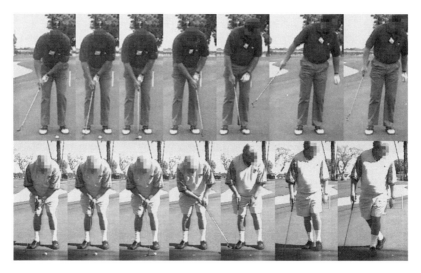

Figure 5.6.3: Amateurs tend to be result-oriented, paying no attention to the feel that produces each result.

still rolling, most amateurs learn little to nothing about theirs. And, by the way, if you ever learn as much about your putting as Greg has about his, you'll probably win lots of tournaments, too.

You can only practice and learn to improve putting touch in the present, in the now. You must be on the green, watching the ball roll to a stop, while retaining the feel of the stroke that caused that result. If you think this requires a lot of attention or is difficult to do, it is not. Simply by making it a habit to hold the finish of every putting stroke and watching your putts stop, you will learn a little about your touch with every putt you make, for the rest of your golf career. Then, as you putt on the course or on the practice green, your touch will become a little bit better with every roll. All it takes is learning what size and feel of stroke make the ball do what you want it to do. And after a few thousand watched strokes and a few thousand little bits of learning, the results start to add up and your putting touch begins to show dramatic improvement.

Don't Think, Repeat

The eight-second time constant of short-term muscle memory hurts most golfers in another way. They spend too much time thinking as they prepare to strike their putts. I have timed many golfers both on course and in my schools, and I'm always amazed to see that they usually stand over their putts for 20 to 30 seconds before starting their strokes. What are they thinking about during these many seconds? Alignment, posture, grip, stroke mechanics, and who knows what else. They usually think about the mechanics of how they're going to stroke this putt, and about exactly where they are aimed. But while they stand there thinking, they are losing the feel of their perfect practice stroke. In only eight seconds, they've begun to forget the touch and stroke requirements they just created in their mind's eye.

Don't let this happen to you. Use your indoor practice time to turn your stroke mechanics into habit, controlled automatically by your subconscious mind. Once this happens, you are free from having to think about them before and during each putt on the course. That time can then be used for focusing on the feel and look of the size of your practice stroke, as you judge its appropriateness for the upcoming putt. Once you feel and see what you believe to be the perfect practice stroke, you have eight seconds to step up to the ball and stroke it exactly that way. Within that eight seconds you still have a vivid memory in your mind's eye of how your "preview stroke" looks and feels, so that's how much time you have to do it again, with the only difference that this time there happens to be a ball just ahead of the bottom of the stroke arc.

Putting within eight seconds of your last, perfect practice stroke is not hard to do. Force yourself to make it a habit. This will not only help you develop better feel and touch for distance, but will make putting under pressure easier, because thinking is taken out of the equation.

Great putters don't think their way through great putting strokes. Great putters make great strokes out of habit, while they focus on the feel and size of the stroke they need to make.

5.7   Attitude

I strongly believe that your mind and your attitude play an important role in your putting success. Not that your mind can move the golf ball, or that "positive thinking" can overcome a bad stroke. But if you have developed a reasonably good mechanical stroke as well as the ability to use that stroke without thinking about it, then you can use your mind to focus on the touch and feel required to putt well. And a good attitude will let your body proceed with the work at hand with confidence.

Experience is required both to learn good feel and touch and the confidence to fully use it. You cannot learn confidence from a book or videotape, although both can teach you how to learn it. Once you learn the size of the stroke that you need, and how it feels to make it, then all it takes is practice to learn to move from the preview stroke to the real stroke in a timely manner. If you have learned to do this and practiced it a lot, you'll develop a quiet understanding, a confidence, a calm, and a focus that allow you to concentrate on the meaningful and controllable aspects of feel and touch.

And your mind is important because it controls all of the above. It controls how you move your body, and how you move your body controls your putter and how your putts start rolling. Your mind orchestrates the symphony—the motions, the rhythm, and the sequence of those motions—it controls the complete motion of the putting stroke. If you use positive self talk—something like, "Okay now, let's make this the most beautiful, rhythmic, and smooth stroke we've ever seen"—before you prepare to putt, and then maintain the presence of mind to prepare properly (making and judging a proper practice stroke, then focusing on repeating it), your mind will allow you to execute the best stroke you know how to make. This is how a confident (positive) attitude helps a golfer putt better.

Some golfers even learn to create positive focus by using a negative image. A few of the professionals I've worked with stand over an important putt and imagine that they've already missed it. This is their way of creating a positive attitude, because they know that they almost always make their putts on the second try.

The point is not how you create a good attitude. Rather, it is that you do create an attitude before you putt that allows you to use a clear mind to see and feel the perfect stroke before you try to make it, and also allows your body to go ahead and execute it without self-doubt.

5.8 The Preview Stroke

Once you see and feel the perfect practice stroke, you must believe that if you re-peat it exactly, you will make the putt. If you don't believe this, make a few more practice swings. Only after you have seen what you believe to be your perfect prac-tice stroke—what I call the "preview stroke"—can your mind's eye know exactly what you want for your real stroke. This combination of vision, feel, and belief will give you the confidence to repeat that preview stroke as your real stroke. And that is how you hole putts.

Jack Nicklaus (Figure 5.8.1) once beat Tom Weiskopf in the final round to win a tournament. Although Tom had hit the ball better from tee to green all day, Jack had holed an unusually large number of putts, including one on the final hole to settle the matter. After it was all over, Tom commented to Jack, "You knew you were going to make that putt before you putted it, didn't you?"

Figure 5.8.1: Classic Jack: "If you don't [believe your stroke will make the putt] . . . then why the hell do you putt it?"

Jack replied, "No, I didn't. But I *believed* I would. That's no different than for all the other putts I hit today and every other day, though. I don't putt until I think I'm ready to make it. Do you? And if you don't, then why the hell do you putt it?"

That's classic Jack, and dead on target. If you don't have a clear idea of the feel and touch of the stroke needed to make the putt, then you aren't ready to putt. It sounds simple and obvious, but of the thousands of golfers I've taught putting to, very few stand over the ball fully believing in their ability to hole the putt. Most golfers are thinking about their stroke mechanics, thinking negative thoughts about missing or three-putting, or doubting their aim. Is it any wonder they miss? Not to me.

5.9 Preparation: The Routine

To get you over any negative or nonproductive thinking and provide a proactive way to approach your putting, you should establish both a routine and a ritual for every putt you face. And by every putt I mean *every* one, in practice and in play, for the rest of your career.

Routine and ritual are not synonymous, but two very different things. Both are important to your putting. First I'll deal with your routine, which prepares you to putt.

Routine is the sequence of actions you perform in preparing to execute your stroke. It starts after you read the green and ends just before you start your ritual (which begins just before you actually make the stroke).

Assume you have walked the green and read the break of your putt. Standing behind the ball, looking along the Aimline, you get committed to that line. If you aren't sure how much break is there or the precise line you want to start on, then you are not ready to begin your routine. So look some more, maybe walk around again, and resurvey the green for its slope, speed, and grain.

In reading the green, you use your touch to imagine what kind of ball track it is going to take to get your ball into the hole. Once the break and line are firmly in mind and you are committed to that read, you are ready to get into your routine, to see and feel which stroke your mind's eye tells you will produce that perfect roll into the cup.

The routine I suggest (detailed in section 11.2) is a five-step procedure that usually takes somewhere between 20 and 40 seconds, at the end of which you should be absolutely prepared to execute your ritual and the stroke you have just seen and felt and believe will hole your putt.

5.10 The Ritual

A putting ritual consists of a few motions, the last few you make before initiating the backswing of your real stroke. Besides being a consistent set of motions, they are all made in a constant rhythm and timing sequence. It should never change. Your ritual sets the tone and timing for the rhythm of your stroke. It is this pattern and timing of motions that provides the trigger—the "one-two-three-go"—for your stroke. Your ritual must take less than eight seconds to execute, so the feel and vision of your perfect preview stroke is still mostly there, fresh in your brain and body.

Once your ritual has begun, there is no turning back unless you are so distracted by something that you must abort the stroke altogether. And once your ritual has begun, there is no thinking other than what it takes to execute the ritual and repeat the preview stroke.

I have simplified my own putting ritual since I wrote *Putt Like the Pros* 10 years ago. It is now slightly shorter and more repeatable, taking only a five-count to execute. This means I can strike my putts within six seconds after committing to my preview stroke.

I haven't changed this new ritual in seven years, and it's not going to change in the future. All of my stroke mechanics have been grooved to this rhythm, and I have committed them to habit. I don't have to think about the mechanics when I putt, so I can concentrate on the feel and touch of my preview stroke. And if I can concentrate fully enough to create a good preview stroke (which can be difficult at times), I can putt every time with the full belief and confidence that I have made the best stroke I can. So I honestly feel that on most putts, with any luck at all, I'll probably make it. That's a great feeling to have.

5.11 Creating the Best Feel for Touch

In building a putting game, things must happen in order. You cannot develop good putting feel and touch if your stroke mechanics are poor. Without consistently good mechanics, which transfer a consistent percentage of energy to the ball, learning to roll a ball the proper speed and distance is impossible. Poor aim or a poor face angle through impact also will prevent the golfer from learning good touch. Because when a putt appears to be off-line, it is so distracting that most golfers cannot hold their finish and focus on how far they rolled the ball. As a result, they don't learn anything from that putt, regardless of how good or bad it may have been.

When you miss a three-foot putt to the right and you know you pushed it badly, do you really think about whether or not you rolled it at the optimum speed? I doubt it. In my teaching, I have found that a good setup, good alignment, and reasonably good stroke mechanics and execution are prerequisites for allowing the brain to move its focus to touch, feel, and the proper control of speed. Also, if you cannot read greens reasonably well, in terms of how fast the ball will roll and how much it will break, then you have little chance of developing your putting feel or touch to anywhere near its ultimate level.

So developing good stroke mechanics comes first. Once that's done, learning good feel comes before touch. Golfers must learn the look and feel of executing good strokes, and what results they produce, before they can focus on reversing that process and learning what kind of putt is required in the various situations they face. Remember, touch is knowing *what* is required, while feel is knowing *how* to produce it.

Assuming you have good mechanics and transfer a repeatable amount of energy in your stroke, then the practice drills in Chapter 13 will provide you with the feedback required to develop good feel and touch in your putting. And once you have developed an undistracted focus on creating and evaluating your preview stroke, your best putting performances will occur when you repeat that preview stroke in a ritual lasting less than eight seconds. Your short-term muscle memory dictates that you must learn to move from your practice stroke setup into your real putt quickly and efficiently. What you do then is simple: You take one last look, execute your ritual, and go.

This means you should practice taking your putting posture just as much as you practice the putting stroke itself. Because if you set up incorrectly, even a great stroke will miss the putt. And if moving into your proper setup takes too long, you lose too much of your feel before you putt.

Great putting comes from trusting your preparation and your ritual, and allowing yourself to stroke putts as you have created them in your mind's eye and your preview stroke. It has nothing to do with the size of your body, your gender, strength, the importance of the putt, or the time of day. Great putting is all about the execution of great-feeling putting strokes, which were chosen with great touch, after a great read of the green.

Big Men Can Putt

A final thought about putting feel and touch. It has always amused me when television commentators say, "He has really good touch *for a big man*." As I just noted, great putting should have nothing to do with the size of the player's body. No, putting touch is the creation of practice techniques, mind-set, feel, and stroke mechanics. Size of one's body should have nothing to do with it. In fact, if I had to guess, I would say that in my lifetime tall golfers have probably putted better than short ones. Perhaps tall golfers tend to have more room to swing their arms naturally under their shoulders. Plus, maybe they've grown up using short (short for them, normal-length for most golfers) putters since that was all that was available, so their arms and wrists tend to be extended rather than bent and cramped (Figure 5.11.1).

Regardless of whether or not this is true, whether or not tall golfers really putt better as a group, if I had to choose a team of the world's best putters and they

Figure 5.11.1: Given the length of most putters, tall kids grow up learning better set-up postures (especially wrist angles) than shorter kids.

all had to be either taller or shorter than six feet tall, I would take the tall team. Just give me George Archer, Bob Charles, Raymond Floyd, Andy North, Brad Faxon, Loren Roberts, the late Payne Stewart, Lee Janzen, Steve Elkington, and Colin Montgomerie, and I wouldn't be afraid to putt against anyone for anything.

CHAPTER 6

Stability and Rhythm:
Two Artistic Fundamentals

6.1 Where Science Meets Art

In the old days, when I started talking in my schools about acceleration, stability, and rhythm in putting, I realized that I had reached the place where science and art begin to meet. Golfers rarely understand how the concepts of stability and rhythm apply to golf, and they think acceleration is something that applies only to race cars.

Even though acceleration is an important aspect of a good putting stroke, I no longer talk about it or teach it in our schools because golfers misinterpret it, then mess up their strokes as a result. It is a fact that a putter accelerating through impact will maintain club-ball contact for a slightly longer time than will a putter traveling at the same velocity but decelerating at impact. It also is true that the greater the force pulling the shaft and the head of the putter through impact, the more stable that clubhead becomes, and the more it resists turning and wobbling if the ball isn't hit squarely on the sweetspot. But while both statements would seem to mean that acceleration should be good for putting, I have found that teaching it only makes golfers putt worse, not better.

It didn't take me long to figure out the reason. When golfers *try* to accelerate their putter through impact, they instinctively do it with the muscles of their hands and wrists (Figure 6.1.1). But as I mentioned in Chapter 5, golfers who control their putters with their hand muscles will have difficulty performing under pressure. And this is exactly what happened when I taught them to accelerate. At first they saw some success and felt that they were making more putts. However, as soon as they faced any real pressure, their adrenaline-strengthened muscles took over and the putts exploded past the hole. As you can imagine, it takes only a few explosions to create a fear of the next one, so they reverted back to

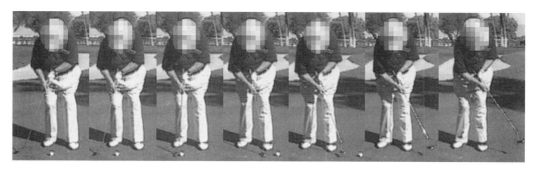

Figure 6.1.1: Golfers instinctively use hand and wrist power when told to "accelerate" through impact.

decelerating, in fact, doing so more dramatically than they had been doing in the first place.

So acceleration is out and we are better putters for it. This is because only gentle acceleration is beneficial or required to produce a stable stroke, and I have a better way to teach golfers to make such stable putting strokes.

6.2 Stability Is the Real Fundamental

For the moment, forget about acceleration and concentrate on stability. First off, what does stability mean in putting? Stability relates to the relative success a putter has in retaining its orientation and motion upon encountering outside forces and influences. A little more simply? If your putter is more stable when mis-hit, it will stay more nearly on its path, twist less, feel a little more solid, and direct your putts a little closer in the proper direction. Conversely, an unstable putter will twist and wobble more when it is mis-hit, and will be less effective in starting your putts in the direction or at the speed you want them to go.

How can you achieve stability in your stroke? A simple suggestion is to try pulling the putter through impact, leading it with your left hand and arm (for right-handed golfers). Be warned, however, that if you do this with your hand and arm muscles, you will become susceptible to adrenaline, and this is not good. The better way is to imagine the stroke as a pure pendulum motion, devoid of any hand or wrist action, with a slightly longer follow-through than backswing. If you think of your forearm and shoulder triangle (Figure 6.2.1) swinging back and through like a pendulum, you will instinctively perform a dead-hands stroke and be completely immune to the pressure effects of adrenaline. Once you can make a smoothly swinging pendulum stroke, simply position it so your backswing is slightly shorter (10 to 20 percent) than your follow-through (Figure 6.2.2), and you have created

Figure 6.2.1: The pure, smooth, rhythmic, beautiful swinging motion of a pendulum . . . produces the best putting stroke.

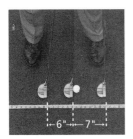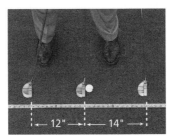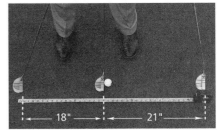

Figure 6.2.2: With the follow-through longer than the backswing, the pendulum stroke is stable through impact.

an accelerating and stable putter without any hands or wrist muscle control. If you keep this stroke smooth and rhythmic, its maximum velocity will occur in the middle between the two extremes (top of backswing and end of follow-through), and your putterhead will be stable through impact (details in section 12.2).

6.3 Perfy Has Rhythm

Near the end of the preceding paragraph, I mentioned rhythm. It's crucial that you understand the importance of rhythm to your putting game.

Back in Chapter 4, I discussed how Perfy, my putting robot, can make a pure-in-line stroke and always keep the putterface square to the Aimline. In Chapter 3,

I explained how the stroke mechanics of a pendulum motion are simple and well adapted to a putting stroke. However, there is an additional benefit to Perfy's pendulum motion, something that makes Perfy's stroke the one to emulate. That would be its rhythm.

Look at the three strokes Perfy is making in Figure 6.3.1. Obviously, each stroke is a different length, and if you imagine Perfy putting, you can also imagine that the putts rolled farther as his stroke motion got longer. As I've mentioned several times already, this is a fundamental principle of a smooth, rhythmic putting stroke: The longer the length of the stroke, the longer the roll of the ball.

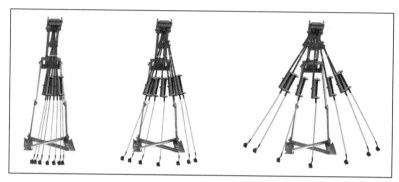

Figure 6.3.1: The pendulum stroke: short swings for short putts, long swings for long putts.

There's nothing new about this concept: Golfers expect a longer stroke to produce a longer roll. But what golfers don't expect is that all three of Perfy's strokes—regardless of their length—take the same time from beginning to end. From the top of the backswing to the end of the follow-through, all three strokes took exactly 0.70 seconds.

If you're surprised, you either don't understand putting or you don't understand physics. The rhythm of a pendulum—or the length of time needed for each complete swinging motion—is the same regardless of its swing length. That's why we use grandfather clocks to tell time, because as the lengths of their swings decay, the timing of their swing motions remains constant. If it were possible to produce a pendulum motion, swinging from a friction-free suspension point in a perfect vacuum (no air to create resistance), it would swing in the same rhythm (take the same amount of time) forever, no matter how long the swing.

How does this relate to your putting? Simple. Your stroke should always take the same amount of time and should always move at the same rhythm, for all putts, regardless of putt length (Figure 6.3.2) or the length of your stroke.

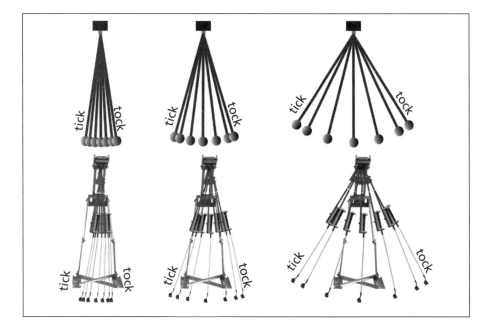

Figure 6.3.2: Whisper tick-tock-tick-tock to yourself, at the same rhythm, as you look at all of the pendulum swings and putting strokes in this figure. That's right, they all take exactly the same amount of time to swing from one extreme to the other.

6.4 Rhythm Has Benefits

Imagine that your putting stroke always moved at the same rhythm out of habit, so you never had to think of it. Now the relationship of feel and touch to distance becomes simple. If your stroke always takes the same amount of time, the only way to cover longer stroke lengths in that time would be to move your putter faster. Therefore, longer swing lengths produce faster motions, which roll putts farther. In other words, the longer you swing your putter, the longer your putts roll. There is never any thought of how "hard" to hit your putts or how "easy" to roll them. The only judgment required during your practice and preview swings is to judge the length of your stroke as it compares to the length of your putt.

Look at my two putting strokes in Figure 6.4.1. If you imagine the actual motion of these strokes, can't you just see each stroke rolling the ball distinctly different distances? I assure you, both strokes took exactly the same amount of time. That time is based on my rhythm, and if you measured it—from the top of my backswing to the end of my follow-through—you would find it swings at a

Figure 6.4.1: Both strokes, regardless of backswing length, should take "exactly" the same amount of time.

cadence of 80 beats per minute, or three-quarters of a second per through-stroke.

The results of this system—vertical-pendulum stroke mechanics swinging in a pendulum rhythm—are staggering in the simplicity they bring to putting. They reduce the complexity of calculations to judge the feel and touch for distance, and completely eliminate the need to guess how hard or fast a stroke is necessary to roll your putt the perfect speed. They eliminate the forces required to keep the putter blade square to the Aimline. And perhaps best of all, they eliminate the need for golfers to think about their strokes, about what they should and shouldn't be doing. Learning the mechanics of a vertical-pendulum motion, then learning to use that motion at a rhythm compatible with your body, eliminates most of the variables that screw up most golfers' strokes.

Before finding your rhythm, a proviso. Having that rhythm won't do you much good if you don't first develop a putting ritual (see section 5.10), because the two must work together: The ritual is performed at the cadence of your body rhythm, so the ritual is a warm-up for the stroke rhythm. Your ritual is put to a count (based on the rhythm), and practiced often enough that you can perform it even when the pressure is on. So if you can remember how to count, you can putt, no matter what the circumstances.

6.5 Find Your Body Rhythm

The rhythm of your putting stroke should be compatible with who you are: your size and weight, your personality, your metabolism, and the rhythm that already governs actions like the way you walk and talk. (Rhythm is easier to see than read about, so if you have difficulty visualizing what I'm saying in this section, I recommend you watch a videotape I made called "Developing Great Touch" to understand what rhythm is and how it influences putting.)

Golfers come in all different sizes, shapes, and speeds. I'm generalizing, but small people usually walk at a faster pace than large people, just as short people take quicker steps than tall people. And what controls the natural rhythm of a pendulum? Its length and weight: Longer, heavier pendulums swing at slower rhythms than do shorter, lighter ones (imagine how fast a wristwatch tick-tocks back and forth compared to a five-foot-long grandfather-clock pendulum). And while pendulums don't have metabolisms, people do, making them either more tightly wound or laid-back: Tightly wound people talk and move faster than laid-back people. So shorter, lighter, faster-moving golfers naturally swing their putters at a faster rhythm than taller, heavier, slower-moving golfers.

Of course, there are exceptions to what's written above. But I actually measured the rhythms of the world's best golfers, the players on the PGA Tour. Figure 6.5.1 shows the walking rhythms in steps per minute of some of these players as a

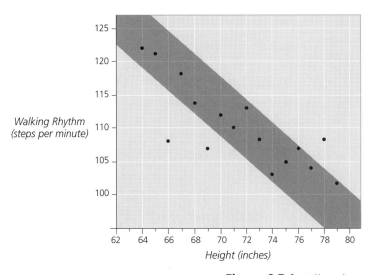

Figure 6.5.1: Taller players move and walk more slowly than shorter players on the PGA Tour.

function of their height. These are all averages taken under normal, pressure-free playing conditions (like a practice or early tournament round) and represent what I believe to be each player's natural walking pace.

I also measured these players' putting stroke rhythms and found a strong correlation between the speeds at which players walk and putt. As there should be. While this makes good sense, most golfers have never thought about their putting in these terms. Many golfers, amateurs and pros alike, have tried to emulate the game's great putters despite having a different body size, metabolism, and temperament. So their failures should come as no surprise. I don't expect anyone can putt like Ben Crenshaw better than Ben Crenshaw can. So try to be the best you that you can be. That starts by learning to putt at your own best rhythm. (I'll show you how to find yours in section 11.3.)

Once you learn to putt at your own cadence regardless of the length of your putt or stroke, you'll be forced to develop a dead-hands stroke. And if you develop your preshot ritual in the rhythm of this cadence, you'll become more consistent in all aspects of putting. By conforming to your natural putting rhythm, you'll have to do less thinking as you putt. So not only is this good for your putting, it's probably easier to do than the way you putt now.

6.6 Learn from Perfy

I think at this point, after all this talk about pendulum-stroke mechanics and pendulum rhythms, we should step back and look at the big picture. Perfy, the perfect pendulum putter, who uses no muscles and is totally immune to the effects of adrenaline, can putt very well. But even his pure-in-line stroke, with no putterface rotation and perfect rhythm and timing, cannot make putts when he is not set up properly in his address position (Figure 6.6.1).

However, set his shoulders square to his Aimline, place the ball exactly at the sweetspot of his putter in his address position, and give him the proper-length backswing, and Perfy can putt as well as any man, woman, or child alive. In fact, he can putt *better* than any man, woman, or child.

What I'm trying to do is teach you how to putt as much like Perfy as humanly possible (and "humanly" is key here, because you'll never putt that well, at least not time after time after time, which Perfy is capable of doing). And in teaching you the key factors of this kind of putting, you will be able to become your own teacher, watching and monitoring your progress, keeping yourself moving forward, spotting and correcting mistakes before they become too serious—doing for yourself the things a good teacher would do.

Figure 6.6.1: Perfy does a lot of things right. But set him up wrong to a putt, and he'll miss it every time.

What I'm *not* trying to do is take all the challenge out of the game and ruin golf. I want to help you learn to putt better, to make more putts, and to enjoy your golf more by improving your putting skills. If you realize that the pendulum motion illustrated by Perfy is the simplest way to putt mechanically, and that the pendulum rhythm is also the greatest (and simplest) rhythm concept in golf, then you should be willing to give these concepts a try. Once you have determined your own best body-rhythm cadence, and have worked your preputt ritual into that cadence, you'll find yourself automatically staying in rhythm as you execute your real stroke. And there is nothing that will allow you to putt better than staying in this rhythmic, repeatable, thinking-free system.

Rhythm and Repetition Eliminate Thinking

Watch any good athlete, and even more than the skill, you can't help but notice the same attribute over and over: rhythm. It may seem natural—and in some cases I think it is—but it is something they continually must work on (repeat), and something that anybody can develop and make his or her own.

Rhythm is more than the fluidity of the athletic motion. Rhythm is a way for athletes to suppress thinking and obtain consistency and accuracy. Basketball players create and use a rhythm to help make more free throws: They bounce the ball three times, position the ball, breathe deeply, cock their arms, and fire, all in a sequence and rhythm practiced (repeated) thousands of times. Tennis pros set up the rhythm for their serve in the last few seconds before they begin: They bounce the ball, rock their body, swing their arms, then cock, toss, and fire. It's all set up, through a preshot routine and ritual, to be as rhythmic as possible, then habitualized through repetition for the most consistent and accurate results possible.

So you need to putt with practiced rhythm to allow your body and subconscious brain to "do what it knows how to do." Because nowhere in sports is accuracy more important than putting a golf ball.

6.7 All Good Putters Have Good Rhythm

There's nothing good about "hitting" your putts. Using a hit is disastrous under pressure, while trying to control distance with a hit stroke requires providing a different amount of force and a different rhythm to every putt, totally eliminating consistency. There is no way a player can anticipate executing a different stroke on every putt on every green as well as an equally talented person can learn to execute the same stroke at the same rhythm, changing only the length of the swing.

Look at the color photographs (see insert in the center) of some of the best putters in the world. From George Archer and Ben Crenshaw, probably the two best ever, to Brad Faxon, Loren Roberts, Lee Janzen, Dave Stockton, Bob Charles, and Phil Mickelson, each has a beautiful, smooth, flowing, and—most important—rhythmic putting stroke. Each one has a rhythm that tends to be the same day after day, week after week, year in and year out, for all of their putts.

If you think these guys are just lucky when they putt, then you haven't watched them. They all have reasonably good mechanical stroke actions (although none are perfect), so their putters remain stable through impact. And they all have great rhythm. Even on their bad putting days, they *almost* make most of their putts, burning the edges of the cups. The reason for their consistency? Rhythm.

Rhythm is the glue of these great strokes, but these guys don't own the patent on rhythm. As you will see in section 11.3, anyone can improve his or her rhythm, and I've never seen anyone who hasn't putted better for it. Good setup, alignment, touch, feel, green-reading, and stroke mechanics are all necessary for good putting. But without a constant and repeatable rhythm, preferably one that is in sync with the natural cadence of your body, you will never become a great putter. Never. And that's a fact.

CHAPTER 7

Green-Reading, the 15th Building Block

7.1 Houston—We Have a Problem

When the world-famous phrase "Houston—We have a problem" was transmitted from the *Apollo 13* spacecraft back to earth, it signified one of the most profound understatements of all time. It came as a calm voice from a spacecraft on its way to the moon, to the Houston ground-control command center, from an astronaut who, while petrified with fear, understood that he had a real problem (there had been an explosion on board his spacecraft; Figure 7.1.1). However, no one on Earth understood the magnitude of the problem. Ground control had lost all normal monitor and status signals, and nothing they saw on their control-system panels made any sense. They were sure the crazy array of warning signals and lights, out-of-tolerance levels, and emergency-warning systems had to be some malfunction of their ground-control systems. The ground controllers thought, "This can't be real, because for these readings to be correct the spacecraft would have to explode."

I'm not an astronaut, but I did work for NASA during the years of the Mercury

Figure 7.1.1:
An explosion aboard *Apollo 13* crippled the spacecraft halfway to the moon, almost costing the lives of three astronauts.

and Apollo space missions. I was a research scientist at the Goddard Space Flight Center in Maryland, studying the aeronomy (physics and chemistry) of Earth and our near planetary atmospheres, involved in launching satellites and then trying to figure out what the returning data meant (Figure 7.1.2). In 1975, I turned the focus of my research from outer space to golf, and I have been studying, testing, and teaching the game ever since. Today, as founder of the Pelz Golf Institute, which is designed to study and understand the game so we may teach golfers to play better and enjoy it more, I say, "Golfers—We have a problem."

All right, maybe this isn't quite as serious as a crippled space capsule halfway to the moon. But for the 27 million golfers in this country (and the millions more worldwide), the problem is very real. I feel like the astronaut who knows there's a serious problem but nobody believes. So I'll say it with details. "Golfers—We have a problem because you don't know how to read greens, you are consistently under-reading the break, this is causing you to miss many putts you could otherwise make, and it's screwing up your putting strokes, too."

This is not the first time I've said this. After researching this problem for five years, I reported the problem to the World Scientific Congress of Golf in St. Andrews, Scotland, in July 1994, then published a 1995 cover story in GOLF MAGAZINE titled "The Amazing Truth About Putting" relating some details. But the golfing public has neither understood nor solved the problem. Only the PGA and LPGA Tour professionals, and some of our school students, have fully understood the problem, learned how to get around it, and improved their putting as a result.

Figure 7.1.2: As a young research scientist at NASA's Goddard Space Flight Center, I spent 15 years preparing for my lifework of research in golf.

Now, once and for all, I want you to understand:

1. You are almost certainly under-reading the break in your putts.
2. You are probably doing it consistently.
3. If you learn to read them correctly, you will make a lot more putts.
4. If you don't listen up and pay attention concerning this problem, improving the other 14 building blocks of putting discussed in this book won't do you much good.

You must know where to aim your putts if you are going to make them with any consistency. So here and now, it's time to solve this problem.

7.2 Golfers Don't See the True Break

Golfers—and by this I mean all golfers, of high, low, and zero handicaps—don't see the true (correct) amount of break in their putts. Exactly what do I mean by break? The true break of any putt is the distance from the edge of the hole to the point (called the true break point) at which the putt's extended starting line (Aimline) reaches the putt distance (as shown in Figure 7.2.1). In other words, the break is the distance the putt had to be started off-line from the hole to allow it to curve into the hole.

When the amount of break is less than half the width of the hole (2⅛ inches), we measure it from the center of the hole and refer to our break point as a point inside the cup, such as left center, left edge, or inside right edge (Figure 7.2.2).

Figure 7.2.1: Break is the distance from the true break point to the hole, the distance your putt will curve (at perfect speed) by the time it gets to the hole.

When the break is greater than 2⅛ inches, we measure it from the nearest edge of the hole outward and don't bother to mention the other 2⅛ inches to the center of the hole. So the three breaks shown in Figure 7.2.3 would be referred to as three feet left to right, one inch outside the left edge, and six inches outside the right edge.

They All Under-Read the Break

Knowing how break is defined is definitely not the same as being able to see and predict how much a putt will break (curve) on a real green for a real putt. Most

Figure 7.2.2: This putt has a left-center break.

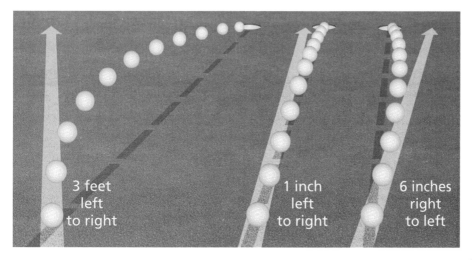

3 feet
left
to right

1 inch
left
to right

6 inches
right
to left

Figure 7.2.3: These putts (left to right) break 3 feet, 1 inch, and 6 inches, respectively.

Almost All Putts Break

Almost all putts break one way or the other. Measurements show that about 98 percent of putts have at least some break or curvature in their roll to the hole. This occurs because greens are built with slight inclines to shed water. There are no dead-flat greens, as they would create small depressions where water would pool after rain, inhibiting grass growth and subsequent play. The only putts that don't break are those that run straight uphill or straight downhill, along the pure "downhill" or "fall line" direction of a green (as shown in Figure 7.2.4). Only about 2 percent of all putts line up purely along these lines.

Figure 7.2.4: Water overflowing from a cup will always run in the downhill (fall-line) direction.

putts break, and golfers know it. Yet in testing more than 1,500 golfers, including 50 PGA Tour professionals, I discovered an amazing truth about putting. Not one of these players was reading as much break as actually existed on any one of their putts. In fact, most didn't even come close to reading anywhere near the true break.

As shown in Figure 7.2.5, when I asked them to tell me how much break they saw, or point to how much break they were going to play on a putt (where their Aimline extended as it passed the hole), most golfers saw only about 30 percent of the actual true break that existed for that putt. Think about that: If the real break was three feet (and I'd measured it with the True Roller), they saw only about one foot; or if it was one foot, they saw a little less than four inches. The PGA Tour pros were a little better, reading slightly more break, but even they saw only about a third, or 33 percent, of the actual amount of true break. Both those percentages have changed slightly since I first reported them, because we changed how we

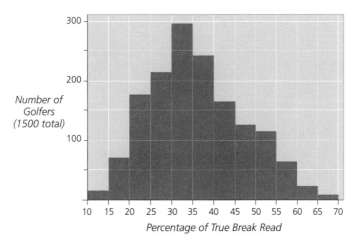

Figure 7.2.5: Golfers read or "see" only about one-third of the true amount of break in their putts.

defined break (as measured at the hole distance instead of perpendicular to the ball-hole line).

Is it any wonder that of all the putts missed by amateur golfers, 80 to 90 percent miss below the hole? Even Tour pros miss 70 to 80 percent of their misses on the low side. Obviously, you would expect that if golfers under-read the break, they should miss their putts below the hole. But that isn't quite the whole story.

7.3 The Subconscious Knows Better

While golfers don't recognize the true amount of a putt's break in their conscious minds, their subconscious minds do better. How do I know? After asking these 1,500 golfers how much break they were playing, I asked them to putt at the same holes. But before they hit any balls, I measured where they were aiming their bodies, putters, and strokes. Again, I was amazed at the results.

While they told me they were playing break values that were less than a third of the real value, they were aiming to play breaks much closer, to between 65 and 75 percent of the true break values. So if the true break was 40 inches, they said they were putting at a spot 12 inches above the hole, then actually *aimed* at a spot between 25 and 30 inches above.

Possibly the most incredible aspect of all this was that not one of the golfers was aware of doing this. They didn't realize they actually were playing far more break than they thought they were or would admit to playing. Test this yourself:

Stand on a putting green with your friends and ask one of them how much break he is allowing for; then watch as he tells you one thing but does something completely different. You don't need any sophisticated equipment to see it.

The Subconscious Fights

I believe this battle between the conscious and subconscious minds is the reason golfers feel uncomfortable standing over many of their putts. Consciously they're thinking about playing three inches of break outside the left edge, while subconsciously they are aiming their putter and body for a putt that breaks at least 6 inches.

Now, playing 70 percent of the break is much better than playing 30 percent, but it still isn't enough. Yes, the subconscious compensation corrects for a major portion of most players' inability to read greens, but even correcting to 70 percent means most golfers still should miss their putts on the low side of the hole.

But again, this is not the end of the story.

7.4 The In-Stroke Correction

Now take a look at what happened when these golfers actually made their strokes. Remember, they professed to playing less than a third of the true-break, then stood over their putts and aimed for 65 to 75 percent of the true-break value. Then, believe it or not, as they swung their putters, they subconsciously made in-stroke compensations to pull or push their putts onto a starting line at between 85 and 95 percent of the true break (Figure 7.4.1).

It was amazing, but it happened almost every time, and still happens whenever I run the test. When I first started researching this behavior, I thought, "How could golfers not know they are doing this?" I've since learned a very important lesson: *In golf, the subconscious always wins.* Golfers do many things they are not aware of. They don't swing the way they think they swing (for proof, watch someone's face the first time he sees his swing on video), and they don't play anywhere near the same break they think they're playing when they putt.

It Is Amazing

Take a look at the in-stroke compensations. If you tried to think about them, consciously trying to turn or correct your putterface angle and path during your stroke, I don't think you could do it. Yet there's absolutely no question that your subconscious can and does do it all the time. And actually does it pretty well, all things considered, rerouting the putter so the starting line of your putt is almost (but not quite) on the 100 percent correct line.

Figure 7.4.1: When I measured 1,500 golfers, they read, on average, less than a third of the true break, set-up to about two-thirds of the break (dashed line), then in-stroke compensated to start their putts almost on the true-break Aimline (white wide line).

Now here's a final mind-blowing thought: Almost every putt any golfer makes is the result of this series of mistakes. If there's any break at all (and I've already told you that almost every putt breaks at least a little bit), and if it's more than a tap-in, then no matter what your intentions or how much time you spend sizing it up, the putt that goes in is not a conscious result but a subconscious one. I'm not saying it's lucky, but the fact that a putt went in the hole is as much the result of forces you don't recognize as those you do.

Let's go through the steps again. When golfers read a putt, they under-read its break. When they address a putt, they subconsciously add more break to the read. When making the stroke, they add still more break, subconsciously making compensations that pull left-to-right putts and push right-to-left putts (for right-handed golfers), so the ball begins rolling on a line that almost gets it started on a line headed toward the true break. Now the ball is rolling, and if they get lucky and it hits a footprint or two, or if it's stroked a little too hard (reducing the amount the ball actually breaks), there is a chance that the putt will find the hole.

This Makes Big-Breakers Tough to Make

This domino effect of mistakes has many consequences. One of the most prevalent is the serious problem many golfers have putting on very sloping and undulating greens. As the amount of true break increases, the amount of "net underread" (the 10 percent of the true break that is never compensated for; see Figure 7.4.2)

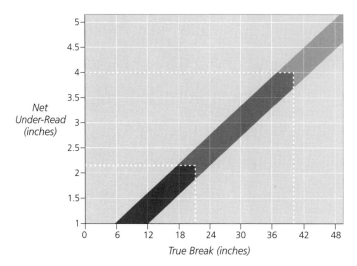

Figure 7.4.2: The more putts truly break, the more golfers miss the hole below the cup, and the more 3-putts that follow.

becomes so large that the only chance of a putt finding the hole comes from hitting it much too hard (because a footprint providing a slight nudge from the lumpy donut is no longer enough to knock it in). After a while, the subconscious thinks that it needs to hit all big-breaking putts too hard, and so begins doing it all the time. This is why golfers have so many three-putts on undulating greens, especially on downhill putts, when rolling the ball just a little too fast can have disastrous results.

Let's Ignore It

It sometimes amazes me that golfers make as many putts as they do. Even though most golfers see or read less than 30 percent of a putt's true break, they never miss by the other 70 percent. In fact, most golfers come pretty close to making most of their putts. Their compensations, therefore, are very good, and since they are subconsciously controlled, seem very easy.

Which explains the response I often get from the golfer who is beginning to understand the problem, which is "I don't want to deal with it." He says, "If I'm compensating so well, and my subconscious is doing such a good job, why not let it be?"

The answer is simple. If you learned to read the proper (true) amount of break, you'd make more putts. You could use the same noncompensating stroke for all your putts. And learning to repeat one stroke for the rest of your golf career is much simpler and easier than trying to execute a different stroke, with a different in-stroke compensation, on every new putt. The truth is, the more you compensate—that is, the larger your compensations become—the less accurate your putting results will be.

Let me say it again: By under-reading putts, you are requiring your subconscious to compensate by a different amount on every putt. That means your body must make a different stroke on every putt on every green. And there is no way you (or any golfer) can learn to properly execute a different stroke with different compensations on every putt nearly as well as you can learn to groove and repeat one stroke (one with absolutely no compensations) for all of those putts.

Remember? Simpler is better. And simpler tends to be the stroke with the fewest compensations.

7.5 It's Hard to Believe

Golfers find all of this hard to believe. (I don't blame you. I also found it hard to believe until I proved it scientifically over and over.) Golfers think that if they read a five-inch break and then make the putt, the five-inch break is justified. They say, "See, I played five inches and it was perfect." They don't recognize—and they don't *want* to recognize—that although they read five inches of break, they set up 12 inches to the left of the hole, pulled the ball another four inches to the left, and the ball broke 16 inches into the cup.

In my Scoring Game Schools, having proven to our students that they are significantly under-reading, we measure the true break accurately by rolling putts at the optimum putting speed with a True Roller (Figure 7.5.1). With the True Roller

Figure 7.5.1: In our Scoring Game Schools, we prove how much putts truly break to every student.

evidence, they can see, and begin to understand, how much true break there is. Then we mark the true-break Aimline and ask the students to actually putt along that line and try to make the putt. What happens? They usually miss high.

The read was perfect; we marked the correct Aimline. How could the students miss high? Blame the subconscious. The player's subconscious doesn't trust this new read, so it sticks with its habit of pulling or pushing to a spot higher than whatever the player thinks is the proper line. Now our students, having missed several putts on the high side, say, "See? I knew that was too much break." They revert to their old green-reading ways, continue to under-read the break, and continue to miss 90 percent of their putts below the hole.

My Frustration

Ever since writing the article "The Amazing Truth About Putting" in GOLF MAGAZINE, I implore my students on the putting green, "Please pay attention. You need to see how much your putts are breaking. Would you please focus on how your putts break?" But I couldn't give them a way to see the true break other than to tell them it was there. I pleaded with them to play more break, but it was a battle, and one I usually lost. They didn't "see" the true break when they looked (even when the location of the true-break Aimline was shown to them on the green), and they couldn't stop making compensations for their under-reading. So despite my best efforts, too many students were leaving my schools with their green-reading skills about the same as when they arrived—not reading enough break. This has been one of my biggest frustrations as a teacher, which we are now ready to eliminate. Please read on!

7.6 There Are Three Problems

Now that you understand you don't read greens properly, there are three problems you must solve if you are going to learn to read them accurately.

Problem 1 is that at the present time you can't see the true breaks as you stand on greens and survey their contours. Problem 2 is that even if you are told how much your putts truly break, you can't produce the proper noncompensating strokes on the true Aimlines to make the putts, so you miss them above the hole when you try. And problem 2 causes problem 3, which is that you can't stay with a program of playing true breaks long enough for your previously ingrained compensations to go away.

Problem 1, your inability to see how much putts truly break, has been with us for a long time. Many golfers still don't realize it exists, and until recently, I never understood why golfers couldn't see the true break even after I told them where it was. But I understand now, and know how you can learn to see true break after your exposure to the proper knowledge, information, experience, and feedback. We will provide you with this information and knowledge later in this chapter, and the "how" to solve the problem in Chapter 13.

Problem 2, your inability to make noncompensating strokes, comes about simply because it's very difficult (in putting as in all swing changes) to make two corrections at the same time. When we change golfers' minds so they begin reading greens perfectly, they immediately begin missing putts high. Always. The compensations they've been making for under-reading greens over the years don't disappear right away. This is normal and understandable, and we've learned it can be handled by some new training techniques (in Chapter 13) developed for just this situation.

Problem 3, missing consistently high, has always been difficult to accept, especially when you are trying to make yourself play more break (which causes you to miss high again). At this point in the past, it was too painful to wait for deeply ingrained subconscious corrections to go away, so golfers reverted to their old under-reading ways. But this is no longer going to be a problem. We now understand how to take away the "missing-high" problem, and have both the learning tools and a system for staying with them (again in Chapter 13). So this is all very good news. Your green-reading problems are solvable. We have discovered a solution that works for golfers willing to give it a try. However, as in most situations we face, once you realize you have a problem, it helps to understand its "whys" and "hows," making it easier to internalize your solution to it.

In the remainder of this chapter, I will give you the information you need to prepare yourself to learn to read greens better, which you will learn how to do in Chapter 13. I advise you not to skip to that chapter immediately, however, because without this information, your chances of success are significantly diminished.

7.7 Visible (and Invisible) Break

For the last two years, the Pelz Golf Institute has been using tilt greens (putting greens) on which we can control the surface slope (Figure 7.7.1). By keeping the speed constant and adjusting the slopes, we can study and measure how putts break based solely on the slope of a green.

We currently use two greens, one indoors (at our headquarters in Austin, Texas), the other outside (at our teaching facility in Boca Raton, Florida), and

Figure 7.7.1: An outdoor tilt-green (with canvas wind curtains) at our Boca Raton teaching facility, and an indoor tilt-green at the Pelz Golf Institute in Austin, Texas.

both have helped us make a very important discovery that's relevant to your putting. The discovery is that golfers can't see either the true break in their putts or their Aimline (the perfect line they're supposed to start their putts on), because true break is invisible. That sounds silly, but it's true. It's also important.

Figure 7.7.2 (left) shows the actual ball-track of a nine-foot putt on a fast, sloping green. The same putt and ball-track along with the putt's initial starting line (the Aimline) and true break point are drawn in on the right. The important point to see here is that while the ball started rolling exactly along the Aimline toward the true break point of this putt, 36 inches above the hole, the ball itself (rolling along its ball-track) never got more than 12 inches above the hole.

You Can't See What Is Invisible

This maximum departure from the ball-hole line is what we now understand to be the "visible break" (Figure 7.7.3 left). It's the amount of break the golfer actually sees as the ball rolls toward the hole, because all he sees is the ball, and that's where it rolls. Golfers never see their putts rolling along the lines they start them on,

Figure 7.7.2: A nine-foot putt rolling through the hole bridge at optimum speed (left), and showing the Aimline and true break point (right).

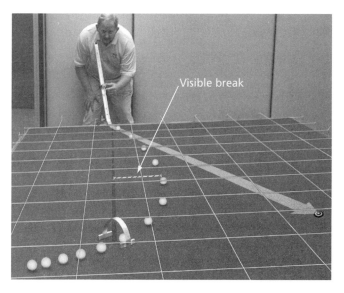

Visible break

Figure 7.7.3: Visible break is the maximum distance the ball track departs from the ball-hole line (left). On big-breaking putts, the ball gets pulled below the Aimline by gravity early in its roll (right).

because the balls don't stay on those lines long enough to be seen there; gravity immediately pulls the ball down the slope to the ball track. Please notice here, and this is important, that this putt did start correctly on the perfect Aimline, as if a golfer had putted it perfectly on a line aimed 36 inches above the hole (a close-up view of the initial roll is shown on the right). But even when putts start rolling perfectly, playing for the correct amount of break (in this case, 36 inches), gravity pulls them down to roll along their ball tracks, showing golfers only 12 inches of visible break above the ball-hole line. So the golfer, even when he compensates perfectly and putts it perfectly, never sees how high he actually started the ball rolling, and thinks he started it 12 inches above the hole.

So this is the key point: Putts never stay on the line you (or the True Roller) start them on; they always get pulled downhill and show you only the visible break, which you wrongly assume is where you putted them.

There will always be a theoretical line, called your Aimline (aiming at the true break point), on which you want to start your putts. But as soon as you do, gravity will pull them off that line and down the slope. No balls will ever roll up to, or even near, the true break point. The only way a putt ever continues to roll in its initial-starting-line direction is if the green is dead flat and the putt rolls dead straight. No breaking putts stay on their initial Aimlines (starting lines) long enough for golfers to see those lines. Even when their subconscious (by pulling or pushing) starts putts on the correct line (true-break-point Aimline), golfers never see them there. Golfers assume they start their putts on the lines they think they aimed at (where they see them), which we call the "visible-break ball track" (Figure 7.7.3). And because no balls ever roll along the true break Aimline and there is nothing to show us its location, true break is, for all intents and purposes, invisible to golfers. With nothing to mark it, we don't see it. It's invisible.

I Never Realized This Myself

I'd done all the research. I'd known for years that golfers were under-reading the true break in putts. I'd been pleading, begging my students to look at their putts and watch how much they broke, to learn they needed to play three times as much break as they used to think they were playing. I promised that if they did, they could stop their subconscious compensations and they would make more putts. But I'd been asking them the whole time to putt along a line they had no chance to see, because it is invisible to them.

It was a day in the fall of 1999. As I watched putts roll over and over through our hole bridge, which marks the hole for putts without affecting their roll, as shown in Figure 7.7.4 (on left) on a perfect ball track, I realized that no ball ever came close to the true break point. At that moment I saw (in my mind's eye) the true break and the visible break for the first time at the same time. When I saw both breaks simultaneously, I was almost paralyzed. I realized that I'd never truly understood how balls curve as they break along their tracks. I had always imagined that they moved rapidly after first being struck, rolling along the line they started on for a good distance up to their apex, before curving quickly down to the cup as they lost speed toward the end of the roll (Figure 7.7.4 right). But that is clearly not the case. In fact, if you look again at the real ball track on this 9-foot putt, and compare it to my previously imagined ball path, you can see how bad my imagination had been. Can you see why I (and perhaps you) thought these putts broke less? If you are an apex putter (you imagine and aim at an apex) and you look up and see the ball at what you assume is its apex (but is really only its visible break), rolling down into the hole, the next time you see a putt on a slope like this, you'll under-read it for sure.

I immediately measured and learned that the visible break of most putts is only about a third of the true break. A third! I finally understood why my students couldn't see the true break even when I was beating on them to look for it. It's hard to see something that never appears before you (the true-break Aimline), especially when something that looks so real (your ball rolling on the visible-break ball track) is right in front of you. So the eyesight of the 1,500 golfers I tested was

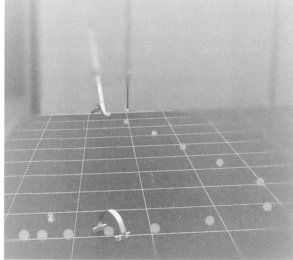

Figure 7.7.4: What a 36-inch break putt really looks like (left), compared to what I had always (previously) imagined a 36-inch breaking putt would look like (on right).

not so bad after all. The amateurs had seen most of the visible break, and the Tour pros had seen all of it. The problem was, they thought the visible-break apex was where they had aimed and stroked their putts. They were totally unaware of their subconscious compensations to pull or push their starting lines up near the true-break Aimline in order to get their putts to roll there!

7.8 Gut-Feel Putting

You now should understand why most golfers under-read break. The only break they ever see is the visible break, and they assume the visible-break apex is the line they *started* their putt on. They never realize that their subconscious is fighting, compensating to get their putts high enough to have a chance to find the hole (although it doesn't quite make it all the way, so 90 percent of their misses are below the hole).

When I ask golfers how they read the break of their putts, what they are looking at, or how they do this, they often can't answer. Those who do sometimes say they pick the spot they want the ball to roll over, then aim at it. Many of them tell me they just feel the break in their "gut," and putt "out there" somewhere. If you think about these answers, and compare them to the situation detailed above, you can understand why golfers miss most of their putts below the hole: Your putt needs to start on a line aimed at the true-break point to roll over the visual-break apex; but you don't have a chance of rolling over the visual-break apex if you start your putt rolling at it, because gravity will pull it down the hill every time.

If you just "trust it," "go with your instinct," "go with your gut," "trust your first read," or "listen to your caddy," you are a "gut-feel" putter. You're probably trying to aim at the visible-break apex, thinking it's the true break, and probably missing about 90 percent of your breaking putts below the hole. Most golfers are "gut-feel" putters. It's the easiest way to putt, because it's comfortable (it's the way you first learned) and your subconscious keeps you from being embarrassed. Unfortunately, it's not the best way to make putts. But that's the way it's been for over 400 years, and it's likely to continue that way for another 400 if you don't start playing more break.

Test Your Ability to Compensate

If you feel that letting the subconscious do all the work by compensating is the easiest way to putt, I want to ask a favor. But first we must establish some facts:

1. You believe trusting in your "gut feel" to read break, then letting your subconscious do the rest (compensating for your under-read), is the best way to putt.

2. I believe the more you ask your subconscious to compensate, the less accurately it can perform those compensations and the worse you will putt.

There is a test that will show which of us is right, and the favor I ask is that you run that test.

Play an entire 18-hole round aiming your body and putter straight at every hole for every putt. Read the break as you normally would, so you know how much break you think there is, but then instead of aiming for that much break, aim straight at the hole. Set up in your normal address position, as if every putt were dead straight. Then try to make your putts by letting your subconscious and conscious minds work together, pulling and pushing (loop-stroking) to compensate for the break you read but didn't set-up to play for (Figure 7.8.1).

My bet is that you will say at the end of this round, "This is making putting too difficult. It's really hard to make breaking putts this way."

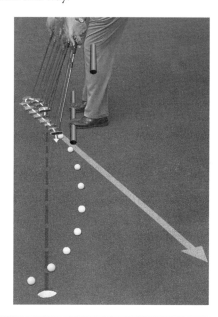

Figure 7.8.1: Test this for 18 holes: Set-up and aim straight at every hole. Then let your loop-stroke compensations pull or push putts enough to play for the break.

Larger Compensations Are More Difficult

In the past, you've been depending on your subconscious to compensate for the two-thirds of the break above your normal under-read (about 30 percent of the true break). This test adds the original break you read (the visible break you believe is the true break) to the 70 percent of the break you don't believe is there anyway, to see if your subconscious can handle that, too. I think you'll find, as I have, that the farther you set up and aim away from the true-break Aimline, the worse you'll putt. The bigger the compensation, the more difficult it is to make it accurately. The simpler the better . . . again.

7.9 Facts About Break

You need one more bit of insight into how balls roll on greens before you start to reconstruct your green-reading abilities. The true amount any putt will break depends on the slope of the green, the green speed (determined by the type, length, and grain of the grass; the moisture content of the soil; and the humidity), the length of the putt, and how fast it is rolled, among other things. Among those "other things" are the lumpy donut (explained in Chapter 8), the wind, and the balance of your golf ball (both Chapter 9). At this point, however, I want to show you some of the basic fundamentals of how generic balls behave on the surfaces of generic greens. The slope on the green surface is the primary determinant of how much, if at all, a putt will break. As you can see in Figure 7.9.1, if the surface is flat and level, there is no side force due to gravity, so a putt will roll straight. But as soon as a slope provides a downhill component from the force of gravity (Figure 7.9.2), a putt will start to break downhill. At any given speed, the greater the slope of the green, the more the putt will break down the hill.

Speed Affects Break
The faster a ball rolls, the less it will break on its way to the hole; the slower it rolls, the more it will break. That's an oversimplification, but the concept is true. Here's why:

Force
of
Gravity
|
G
↓

Figure 7.9.1: On flat, level, horizontal green surfaces, the force of gravity (G) has no side force component, so putts roll straight.

Figure 7.9.2: On sloped greens, the vertical (down) force of gravity (G) creates a side force component (A), which pulls putts downhill.

If the slope on a green is constant, then the faster a ball rolls between its starting point and the hole, the less it will break. This occurs because the faster a ball rolls, the less time gravity has to act upon it (Figure 7.9.3). But there is a caveat to this situation. If you are going to roll your putt faster so you can play less break, you'd better make the putt, because it's still going to break later, on the other side of the hole as it slows down. And while it is slowing down, it will be

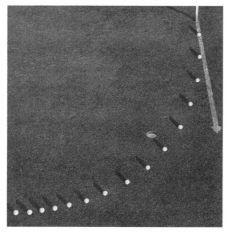

Figure 7.9.3: Rolled on identical Aimlines, the faster rolling ball (left) will break less by the time it gets to the hole. But if it misses, it will still break more later on.

rolling away from the hole. This can be a problem when you attempt to make the putt coming back.

This rule—the faster the roll, the less the break (on any given slope)—holds whether the faster ball speed is caused by the golfer initially rolling the putt faster because the green is slow, or rolling it faster on a fast green to minimize the break. And while that rule is true, so is its opposite: The slower you roll a ball to the hole (as long as you still get it there), the more it will break.

The High Road Is Best

There is more than one possible Aimline (initial starting line) along which every breaking putt can be made. Roll the ball at different speeds and it will need different Aimlines to find the hole. For example, roll the ball faster and it will take less break, so the Aimline doesn't need to allow for as much break; conversely, roll the ball slower so it breaks more and the Aimline must feature a larger break allowance.

And so there are the extreme Aimlines. At one extreme is the "highest-possible-true-break" Aimline. This works if the ball is rolled at its slowest possible speed, with just enough pace for the ball to die (on its last bit of turn) downhill into the front edge of the cup (Figure 7.9.4 left).

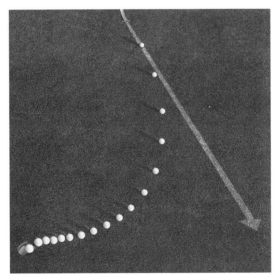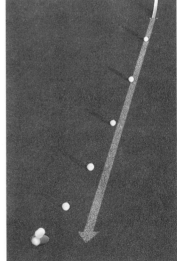

Figure 7.9.4: There is always a highest (left) and a lowest possible (right) Aimline (with slowest and fastest possible rolling speeds) for holing a breaking putt.

At the other extreme is the "lowest-possible-true-break" Aimline (Figure 7.9.4 right). This works with the highest possible speed the ball can roll and stay in the cup (when it hits the back of the hole dead center). Any putt started on a lower Aimline or rolled at a faster speed will miss on the low side of the cup, or jump over, bounce off the back edge, or lip-out due to excessive speed.

Figure 7.9.5 illustrates how these Aimline extremes relate to the "optimum-true-break" Aimline (optimum meaning the most likely to make the putt). Note that the optimum Aimline is *not* in the middle of the two extreme Aimlines. It's usually higher than the exact middle between them, for one reason because more near-edge putts lip-down-and-in from above than lip-up-and-in from below the hole (see sidebar, page 164). We refer to this as the "high road" for putting, and our testing shows that the high road provides the best statistical probability for making putts.

So there is an optimum-true-break Aimline, which is the Aimline combined with a putt rolling at the optimum speed that will allow you the highest percentage chance of holing the putt.

This is an important concept, so let me repeat it: Every putt has an optimum speed, which works with an optimum Aimline, which is aimed for the optimum amount of true break, to find the hole with the highest probability conditions will allow. Ultimately, what I hope to teach you are the skills in reading greens and rolling putts that will help you to hone in on this perfect duo whenever you stand over a putt.

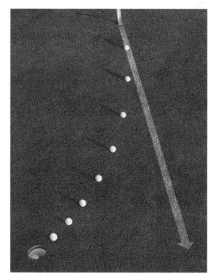

Figure 7.9.5: The optimum Aimline allows putts rolled at optimum speed to be holed at the highest percentage conditions will allow.

Fudge on the High Side

You're standing over a putt, sure that it's going to break, but unsure whether to aim it 6 or 10 inches above the hole. Whenever you have doubts about the true break, fudge toward the higher break. If you are going to make an error judging break, it's always better to play slightly too much than too little.

The reasons are simple: (1) A putt is more likely to catch the high edge and lip-down-and-in than it is to catch the low edge and lip-up-and-in (Figure 7.9.6). (2) Balls that hit spike marks or footprints bounce downhill more often than uphill (gravity causes this). So bad-bounce putts go in more often if they start a little high. (3) When your subconscious thinks you are aiming too low, it tends to hit your breaking putts hard. When this happens on a downhiller, look out for the three-putt. (4) While the chance of the ball wandering into the hole from the high side might not be near 100 percent, the chances from the low side are near zero.

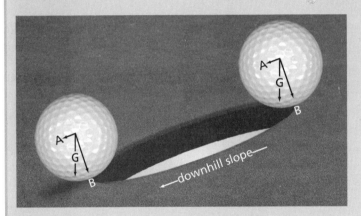

Figure 7.9.6: The side force component of gravity (A) helps putts above the hole lip in, but pulls putts below the hole downhill and out.

Downhillers Break More

Another putting fact you should be aware of is that given the same sidehill angle on a constant-slope green, downhill putts break more than uphill putts. To help you see this, imagine a perfectly flat green with a constant-slope, with a hole at its center (Figure 7.9.7) and a clock overlay.

Putting straight uphill from the bottom of the clock is defined as putting from 6 o'clock. Putting straight downhill along the pure downhill or "fall line" of the green (the direction water will flow when running off the green in that area, Figure 7.9.8), is putting from 12 o'clock.

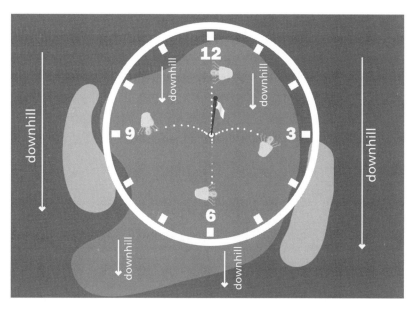

Figure 7.9.7: Imagine a clock overlay centered on the flagstick (hole) of every green, with the 12 o'clock to 6 o'clock direction running straight downhill.

Figure 7.9.8: Overfill any hole with water and it will run downhill toward the 6 o'clock position on the green.

It should be clear that putting a left-to-right breaking putt exactly across the slope would be putting from 9 o'clock, while putting right-to-left breaking putts in the opposite direction would be putting from 3 o'clock.

Now look at the ball tracks in Figure 7.9.9 relative to the fall-line and this clock, for putts rolled on one of our Boca Scoring Game School greens. You can see that the putt from 10:30 breaks a lot more than the putt from 7:30, even

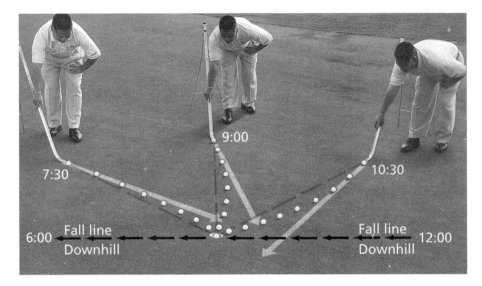

Figure 7.9.9: On a constant slope, downhill putts from above 9 o'clock break more than uphill putts from below 9 o'clock.

though both putts are at a 45-degree angle to the pure downhill direction of the slope. Of course, the putts would break from the opposite side of the hole by the same amounts, in opposite directions.

Beware of Downhill Sliders

Most real greens have a nearly constant slope near the hole, so this clock can be superimposed in your mind almost perfectly over most holes on any golf course. Remember these break relationships (from Figure 7.9.9) the next time you are trying to read a breaking putt. Don't expect putts to break exactly these amounts (all breaks are relative to the slope severity and green speeds). But simply by seeing the relative break in these ball tracks, you should understand putting and reading breaks better than you did before, because it will help both your conscious and subconscious decisions on the greens later on.

In the future, using this clock image, if you perceive you are above the 9 o'clock or 3 o'clock positions on any green (relative to the downhill direction), be careful, because you are looking at what we call the downhill slider, the most dangerous putt of all. Most golfers under-read the break on a downhill slider and then subconsciously hit the ball too hard trying to keep it on-line. It should come as no surprise that the most frequent three-putting in golf follows downhill-slider first putts.

The Subconscious Is Awesome

The more I understand the way golfers under-read the break of their putts, the more I am in awe of our subconscious minds. It is truly incredible the way the subconscious figures out how to compensate for our inadequate green-reading abilities, to push and pull putts without letting us know what we are doing, even letting us occasionally make a few putts almost in spite of ourselves.

Just imagine, now that you know the relationship between true and visible break, if you can somehow read greens well enough to get your subconscious mind working with you (rather than make it fight your green-reading and compensate for it), you might really be able to improve that 15th and final building block of your putting, your green-reading. I'll show you how to make it happen in Chapter 13. Until then, let's keep learning how to deal with it. So far, you have seen that these indisputable facts about your putting will never change:

- The force of gravity is, was, and always will be constant.
- Water runs downhill, putts break downhill.
- The greater the slope, the greater the break.
- The slower balls roll, the more they break (in a given distance).
- Pretending putts break less than the true break doesn't make them easier to make.
- Your subconscious mind knows more than your conscious mind, and will always win over your conscious mind in golf.
- The better you read the true break, the less your subconscious will have to compensate and make in-stroke corrections as you putt.
- True break is about three times greater than visible break.
- Downhill putts break more than uphill putts on the same slope.
- The smaller your compensations, the more accurate your putting strokes.
- The smaller your conscious-to-subconscious fights over break, the more comfortable you will feel over your putts.
- An optimum-true-break Aimline exists for every putt. The question is, can you see it?

So let's move on, and learn more about the realities of the grain of grass, plumb bobs, and how your mind works in your putting.

7.10 What about the Grain?

Something else to factor into your green-reading is the grain of the grass. To many amateurs who don't understand grain and don't consider it in their figuring of how their putts will break, grain may sound like a dirty word, but it needn't be.

Grain is nothing more than the direction in which grass grows. While you may say, "I thought grass grows *up*," only rarely does it grow *straight* up. The roots of grass grow down to their source of nutrition and moisture, while the blades grow up and toward their source of moisture and light. Figure 7.10.1 lists the conditions that affect how grass blades grow, assuming other surrounding factors are normal.

Grass (Grain) *Growth Priority*	1) Toward water source 2) Toward sunlight 3) With predominant wind direction

Figure 7.10.1: Grass seldom grows straight up.

Grass first seeks out a consistent source of moisture (the most consistent being from a nearby lake, pond, or ocean). Since most greens are watered by sprinkler systems, most grain follows local downhill slopes toward low areas where water will collect. On greens with excellent irrigation systems and drainage (which distribute water equally), the grain tends to follow the direction of the afternoon sun (when it doesn't pass directly overhead). In locations where there is no moisture or sun-angle bias, grass will grow in the direction of the predominant wind, providing the wind blows often and strong enough.

Due to the sun, wind, rain, surrounding land features (mountains), and other influences, grass usually grows to one side or another at least to some extent, sometimes in more than one direction on the same green. Since your ball will roll on the grass for the majority of every putt, this growth direction can have a noticeable effect on its movement.

For example, if the grain between your ball and the hole is running from left to right and the slope of the green is also downhill left to right, then the break will be even sharper in that direction than if there were no grain. The putt also will roll farther, because as it breaks more, it begins to roll more with the grain. If the grain is strong and running from right to left and the slope is left to right, the grain will minimize (and depending on the degree of the slope, perhaps cancel or even override) the severity of the break and slow the putt a little.

Sometimes the most significant grain effects occur on putts that go directly with or against the grain, by changing both the amount of the break and the over-all distance your putts will roll. If you putt against the grain (that is, the grass is growing directly into the rolling ball), its speed will be slowed, your putt won't roll as far, and all breaking putts will break a little more than normal (right side of Figure 7.10.2). Putting with the grain not only gives the ball extra speed and distance, but also keeps it rolling more on-line and breaking less than normal (center ball track). On long putts, the difference in rolling distances can be quite significant (Figure 7.10.3).

If you've played in the southern tier of the United States, you've probably putted on Bermuda grass, which has broad, bristly leaves and a sparse grow-ing pattern, and can be especially grainy. But bent grass, which is found predomi-nantly in the northern part of the country, has grain, too, just not as strong. Wherever you play, try to learn about the strength of the grain before you venture onto the course.

There are a few quick ways to judge the way the grain is running on any green. First, look to see if it's obvious—that is, if you can see that the blades of grass lie all

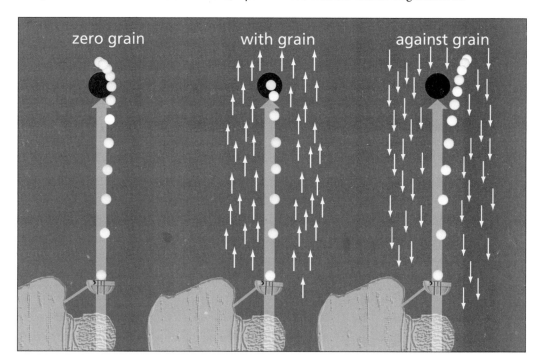

Figure 7.10.2: A slight push stroke error (left) can be minimized when putting with grain (center) and maximized when putting against the grain (right).

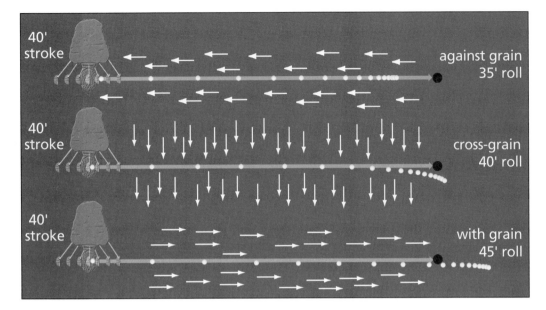

40' stroke — against grain 35' roll

40' stroke — cross-grain 40' roll

40' stroke — with grain 45' roll

Figure 7.10.3: Grain of the grass can cause a roll difference of 10 feet or more on a 40-foot putt.

in one direction. Remember, grass tends to grow toward water and the sun, so look that way first. Then check if you can see the sun's reflection on the grass: If the grass appears whitish or shiny, it means the grain is growing away from you; if the grass looks darker, you're seeing a little shade under the blades as you look into the tip ends, which means the grain is growing toward you.

Grain will have the greatest effect on a putt near the hole, since that's where the ball rolls slowest. So check how the grass is growing around the hole. Also examine the edges of the cup: One side may look cleanly cut while the other is ragged, which indicates how the grass is growing. A clean edge means the grain is growing from that side toward the hole; the ragged edge is on the side of the cup that lost its roots when the cup was cut (that's why it is ragged, because some blades died during the day after having their roots cut off), so the grain runs away from the hole on the ragged side.

Then there's the "drag test"—simply dragging the leading edge (bottom) of your putterface firmly across the grass to see what happens. If the grass continues to lie flat, your drag is in the direction of the grain; if the grass bristles up, that's the against-the-grain direction, as seen in Figure 7.10.4 (you may have to drag in a circle to find the pure "against-the-grain" effect). While dragging your putter

Figure 7.10.4: Grass stands up and bristles when you scrape against the grain, lays down flat and smooth when you scrape with its grain.

provides the best test of grain, it is illegal under the Rules of Golf to check this way during play or anytime on the day of play. But you can always do it on the practice green and compare the conditions—notably, how the different grains look—out on the course. If you're playing in a tournament and there's a practice round, by all means conduct the drag test and mark the prevalent grain direction on each part of each green in your yardage book or on a scorecard (a typical Tour pro's yardage book markings are shown in Figure 7.10.5). It's legal to gather the information beforehand, just not on tournament days.

A last word about grain: Don't become obsessed with it. Note the direction and learn to make it a small modifying factor in your choosing of the correct true break. It will rarely do more than add or reduce the break (due to slope) you read by 10 percent (unless the putt is dead-straight, and you know that there aren't many of those). A larger effect will be when you have to read putts that are with or against the grain, then modify your touch and feel to lag your putts the proper distance (be aware that distance can be affected by 25 percent or more).

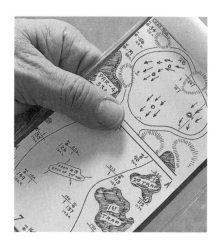

Figure 7.10.5: Grain direction indicators (arrows) for four expected pin positions in a Tour Pro's yardage book.

7.11 Plumb Bobs Don't Work

One practice many golfers use that they think helps them read greens is plumb-bobbing. I've studied this procedure and have learned some interesting facts.

Approximately one out of every seven golfers plumb-bobs in some manner while reading break. However, most of those who plumb-bob have no grasp of the scientific principles behind a plumb line, and cannot explain how they're using their putters even as they hold them (Figure 7.11.1) in front of their eyes.

Figure 7.11.1: Most golfers can't explain how they plumb bob putts. They say they stand directly behind the ball from the hole (and then don't), and let their putters hang vertically (which they don't).

The reason they can't explain how their plumb-bob works is that it doesn't. The principles of a plumb-bob or plumb line are violated by the way golfers use them to read putts, which is an interesting phenomenon.

First, I'll show you the extremely rare conditions (which don't exist in golf) under which a plumb bob *could* indicate the slope of a green and the break direction of a putt. Plumb-bobbing a putt could work only if:

1. The green surface between the ball and hole is flat and at a constant slope angle to the horizontal.

2. The flat green surface and constant slope extend back past the ball on the ball-hole line at least to the point where the golfer is standing.

3. The golfer stands with his feet straddling the ball-hole line, and holds his body perpendicular to the slope so his head and eyes move downhill relative to being vertically above the ball hole line (Figure 7.11.2 A and C).

4. The golfer holds a vertical putter shaft in front of one open eye, so the bottom of the shaft appears to be positioned over the ball.

Figure 7.11.2: If a golfer moves his head downhill from the ball-hole line (by standing stiff-legged and perpendicular to the slope as in A and C), a vertical shaft above the ball will appear to be on the high side of the hole (B and D).

Only when these four conditions are met will the plumb line appear to be on the upper side of the hole, indicating that the putt will break from the upper to the lower side of the hole (as seen by the golfer in Figure 7.11.2 B and D). And even then, under no condition will the plumb line indicate the *amount* of break.

The Conditions Are Not Right
But look closely at these four conditions. In 1 and 2, green surfaces are seldom truly flat and at constant-slope angles all the way from where the golfer stands behind the ball to the hole. Even less often do they meet these conditions along the actual path of the ball track.

More important is condition 3, which is almost never true. On sloping ground, humans tend to stand with one knee bent (Figure 7.11.3 A and C), subconsciously correcting for the slope to hold their bodies vertical. Standing vertically eliminates any chance for the plumb line theory to work for putting.

The plumb-bob technique that most golfers use simply does not work. It never has and never will. In fact, if a golfer stands exactly vertical with his eye on the ball-hole line and holds a true vertical plumb line in front of his eye so it passes over the ball, then all putts, no matter how the green slopes between the ball and the hole, will appear to be straight (Figure 7.11.3 B and D).

Condition 4 is similarly seldom true. Golfers use putters, which seldom hang

Figure 7.11.3: When a golfer stands vertically on a slope with his shaft vertical over the ball (A), the putt plumbs to be straight (B). When the golfer stands vertically on the opposite slope (C), the putt still plumbs to roll straight (D).

vertically (Figure 7.11.4 shows how several popular putter models hang at angles to a true plumb line).

What Are They Looking At?

So what are golfers who plumb-bob doing? What are they looking at? Do these golfers—and I'm talking about some very good players (Figure 7.11.5)—have any idea what they're doing?

After questioning several hundred plumb-bobbing golfers and measuring how they read break, I've determined that they all violate the third rule of plumb-bobbing listed above. They don't really stand behind the ball exactly on the ball-hole line. They say they do, but if you measure where they stand, they really don't. Rather, they instinctively stand below (on the low side of) that line. Then, when they hold the putter over the ball in front of one eye (and that eye is now on the low side of the ball-hole line), the top of the shaft appears to be on the high side of the hole (giving them the view shown previously in Figure 7.11.2 B and D), confirming a break from the high side down the slope.

All this means is that the subconscious knew where to stand, and which way the ball would break, before the golfer ever lifted the putter to eye level. So, in truth, golfers who plumb-bob to read their putts, stand (position themselves) so they see what they already (at least subconsciously) know.

Figure 7.11.4: Few (none of the four shown here) putter shafts hang precisely vertically like a true plumb line.

Figure 7.11.5: I don't know what Ben Crenshaw and Hale Irwin are looking at when they plumb-bob.

I'll say it again: The plumb-bob doesn't work in putting.

Now here's the scary part. My measurements show that golfers who plumb-bob don't read the break any better or worse than golfers who don't (they still see only about 29 percent; pros see 33 percent of the true break). That should tell you something about the state of green-reading in the world today.

One Thing a Plumb Bob Can Do

Let's give the plumb bob some credit. It can do one thing that's productive if you use it properly. Find a putter that truly hangs vertically (so the shaft forms a true vertical plumb line). Then get your eyes close enough to the ground, so the round hole looks more like a slit (or line, as shown in Figure 7.11.6). To do that, you'll have to crouch way down or lie flat on the green.

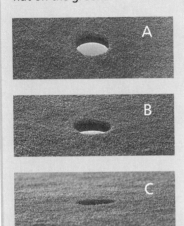

Figure 7.11.6: As you crouch down and get your eyes closer and closer to the green surface (from A to B to C), the hole will look less like a circle and more like a line.

Now when you hang a truly vertical shaft over the hole, you can see the slope of the line of the hole relative to vertical (if the green around the hole is sloped, as in Figure 7.11.7). Do this from behind the ball on the ball-hole line and you'll see which way your putt will turn downhill as it dies around the cup. This won't tell you how much the putt will break along the way, just the direction it will turn as it dies near the hole.

Please note: This slope is valid only if your putter shaft is truly vertical, and applies only to the slope of the green immediately around the cup. Don't depend on this read to tell you how the ball will break on its way to the hole. Only the slope of the green along the ball track determines that.

Figure 7.11.7: If you can see a slope angle between the slit of the hole and a true vertical, you can know which way (downhill) the putt will turn as it dies.

Learning WHAT to learn . . .

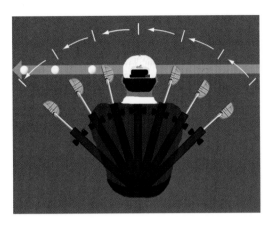

Screen Door (CHAPTER 12)

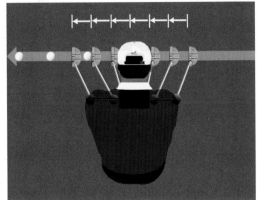

In-Line-Square (CHAPTER 12)

and HOW to learn it . . .

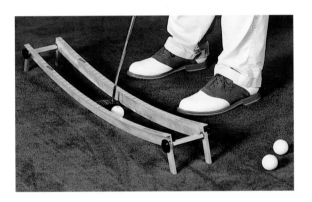

Putting Track (CHAPTER 12)

Truthboard
(CHAPTER 12)

Teacher Clip
(CHAPTER 12)

makes
LEARNING
so much
EASIER!

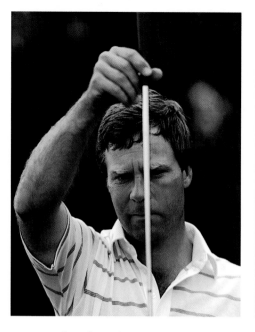

Plumb Bob (CHAPTER 7)

Break vs. Speed (CHAPTER 8)

Tick-Tock (CHAPTER 11)

I Learn from the Master (CHAPTER 7)

Quality Mechanics (CHAPTER 12)

Cut Stroke (CHAPTER 3)

Stability (CHAPTER 4)

Speed is 4 times more important than line.

Dave Pelz

The Jones Method (CHAPTER 3)

The CONDITION of your PUTTING GAME

determines your THRILL of VICTORY . . .

and your AGONY of MISSING short ones.

Long Putter
(CHAPTER 3)

Backyard
(CHAPTER 13)

*"I never met a putt
I couldn't make."*

DAVE STOCKTON

Ritual (CHAPTER 5)

Footprint (CHAPTER 2)   **Aiming** (CHAPTER 11)

A Different Game (CHAPTER 1)

Organization (CHAPTER 10)

Short Strokes for Short Putts . . . Long Strokes for Long Putts

tick

tock

Rhythm (CHAPTER 6)

Sidesaddle (CHAPTER 3)

Putting Is Ageless (CHAPTER 1)

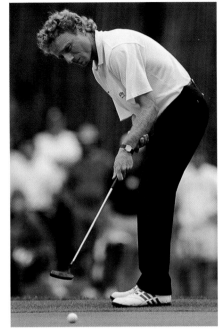

Lead-Hand-Low (CHAPTER 11)

*If you don't
BELIEVE
you'll make it . . . you won't.*

Impact
(CHAPTER 12)

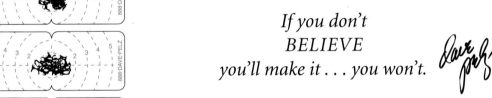

Fundamentals (CHAPTER 4)

GREAT PUTTERS . . .

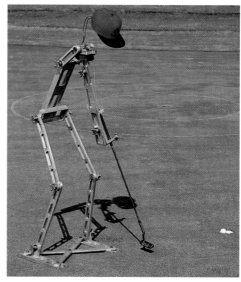

. . . WIN CHAMPIONSHIPS!

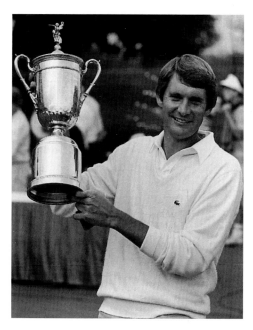

*Good putters
have more fun.*

Dead-Hands
(CHAPTER 5)

Six Games (CHAPTER 1)

Testing (CHAPTER 1)

*Trying to get the putter square with a screen-door stroke
is like trying to get somewhere on time.
You can never do it EXACTLY!*

Attitude (CHAPTER 13)

Cured Yips (CHAPTER 14)

Hold Your Finish (CHAPTER 5)

Elk's Key (CHAPTER 12)

Speed control is the essence of good putting.

Dave Pelz

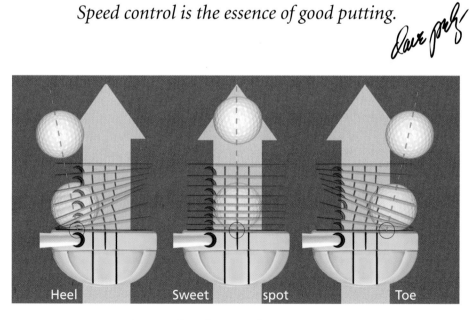

Heel   Sweet   spot   Toe

Impact Fundamentals (CHAPTER 4)

Croquet (CHAPTER 3)

Downhill (CHAPTER 7)

$$\frac{True}{Break} = \frac{Visible}{Break} \times 3$$

Dave Pelz

Chiputting (CHAPTER 14)

Flow-lines (CHAPTER 11)

**Great Putters Are Made,
Not Born** (CHAPTER 15)

Setup (CHAPTER 4)

**Make Friends with Great Putters
(and Players)**

Wind (CHAPTER 9)

Barton Creek

Practice facilities designed for learning
(CHAPTER 15)

Boca Raton

The Homestead

Pinehurst

PGA West

Centennial

Cordillera

Speed (CHAPTER 8)

Eye Alignment (CHAPTER 11)

PRACTICE MAKES ~~PERFECT~~ PERMANENT

Down   **Look**   **Look**   **Back**   **Through**

(CHAPTER 5)

"MY PUTTING HEROES"

Dave Pelz

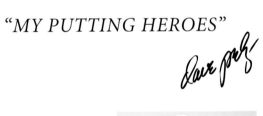

7.12 The Mind's Role in Green-Reading

Your most important tool for green-reading is your subconscious mind. I hope by now you see that I'm doing everything I can to educate and inform your subconscious so you will not only be ready but also able to learn to read greens by the time you get to Chapter 13. Your ability to read greens accurately—to predict future ball tracks and putting speeds before they happen—is a skill that must be developed. It is experiential in nature, and requires good feedback, a keen mental focus, and many repetitions before it becomes accurate and reliable.

The more times you see the same putt on the same green roll the same way, the more sure you become that it will do the same thing in the future.

In the last few sections, you learned that:

- Grain is easy to determine by the drag test.
- Grain usually affects break by less than 10 percent.
- Grain can affect roll distance by more than 25 percent.
- Plumb bobs don't accurately read break.
- Plumb bobs don't hurt your green reading, other than taking extra time.
- A vertical-hanging putter shaft can show you the slope of the green at the hole, and that's all.

It's time to move on, from describing and discussing the 15 building blocks of putting to explaining a few other influences. But I want to warn you of something. If you go out and try to put all I've said in this and the last few chapters to work immediately, before you finish reading this book and start a putting-improvement program, you might become confused and give up, reverting to your old "gut-feel" putting. I don't want that to happen.

I want you to keep reading and learning, preparing yourself to understand putting well enough to make it simple.

Learning to read greens is much more important than improving your ability to make a few more putts. If you never learn to read greens properly, you can never use a pure-in-line-square, noncompensating putting stroke, because it will miss every time if you don't know how to read greens and where to aim.

Only by learning to read putts properly will you be able to benefit from improving the first 14 building blocks of putting. If you spend the time to practice and improve those fundamentals, it makes no sense to throw it all away because you didn't improve your ability to read greens.

Think about it this way. You have three possibilities:

1. If you don't improve any of the first 14 fundamentals but do improve your green-reading, you'll make a few more putts because your compensations will be smaller and more accurate.

2. If you improve some, or even all, of the first 14 building blocks (the ones that were adversely affecting your putting) but don't learn to read greens, you may never make another putt.

3. If you improve the building blocks that help your stroke mechanics, feel, and touch, and *also* improve your green-reading skills, you may begin to hole almost everything.

Your mind is the key. It controls your body, which controls your putter, which controls the starting line and speed of your putts. And your mind reads the greens. Let's keep learning. The more you understand, the simpler it gets. And as always, simpler is better.

ADDITIONAL INFLUENCES IN PUTTING

CHAPTER 8

Speed Is More Important Than Line

8.1 Speed Kills (and Speed Saves)

How important is speed to putting? If you roll your putts at the wrong speed, nothing else matters. You won't make many, and you'll have far too many three-putts. Speed is so important that it could be the foundation, the first fundamental, of putting. However, it is neither a foundation nor a fundamental, but rather a characteristic of putting. Speed is not something you buy, or own, a technique you learn or take out of your bag for use on the course. It is a concept, one you need to think about, understand, and learn to control—because speed has more effect on putting results than most golfers could ever imagine.

As discussed in Chapter 5, feel and touch for distance are the skills you must develop for speed control. But that was just a taste for speed. Now I'll give you a much broader perspective, along with ideas of how you should think about it and deal with it in putting.

Most golfers don't think about speed quantitatively—that is, how much speed they created—unless they've missed a putt so badly (running it far past the hole or leaving it way short) that they are afraid of three-putting. But even then their thoughts are nothing more than assuming that they hit the putt either too hard or too easy: They don't know why they did it and go only so far as to hope they won't do it again (Figure 8.1.1). Their mistake is not understanding that controlling speed is a skill, just like all the others in golf, that can, and should be, worked on and improved. So rather than think about practicing speed control the next time they're on the practice green, they call themselves stupid, give themselves a mental slap on the wrist, and go practice their setup, alignment, or grip.

That's what most golfers think about instead of thinking about speed. They think about controlling the line (what we now refer to as the ball track) of their putts. However, this doesn't mean their aim, setup, posture, or the orientation of their flow-lines. It means that they think about "making" their ball roll on the

Figure 8.1.1: Why me?

proper ball track to the hole. While this may not sound bad, it really is a way to ensure that your putting never improves. It goes back to what I said at the very beginning of this book: Trying to "make" a ball do anything usually involves a mechanical response of the hands, fingers, and forearms, none of which are helpful in executing rhythmic, repeatable putting strokes.

Speed Rules

Golfers simply don't know how to think about speed. They assume their ball track (or line or direction, whatever you call it) is independent of speed. Nothing could be further from the truth! In fact—and this is something you must never forget— everything about your ball tracks (their shape, size, and direction) is a function of the speed. You can start with the same Aimline but produce very different roll distances, ball tracks, and results simply by changing speeds.

Look at the three ball tracks in Figure 8.1.2. These are three different putts, each started on the same optimum Aimline to roll into the center of the hole. However, each putt was started at the wrong speed for that Aimline, so the balls rolled through the break on the high side, lipped out on the low side, and missed significantly low. On the course, these misses probably would have been blamed on misreading the break, pulling it just a little, and hitting the putt poorly (giving it a weak roll), respectively. The truth of the matter is that there was no misread, no pull, and no mis-hit. All three misses were simply the result of rolling the ball the wrong speed.

Blaming the wrong factor has two bad results. First, it encourages golfers to

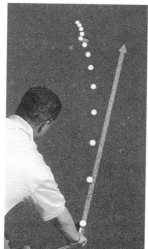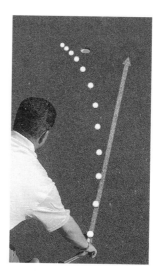

Figure 8.1.2: Three putts started on the same Aimline to the same hole, at different speeds: too much speed (left); slightly too slow (center); way too slow (right).

work on the wrong parts of their game, usually playing with their stroke path, grip, follow-through, or something else that's easy to see. Second, they never work on the real problem, which is learning to control speed.

It's true: Speed itself can be hard to see. And the results of bad speed are difficult to diagnose, and often go misdiagnosed. Let me show you just how big a problem this is. In testing that provided amateur golfers with the perfect aim direction on 12-foot putts that broke 4 inches, we determined that 80 percent of all those that missed were due to improper speed (their line was good enough to go in with good speed). The other 20 percent of the misses were due to pushing or pulling putts far enough off-line to miss. Based on this data, we teach that speed is four times more important than line. But what do golfers work on? Our research goes on to show that most golfers spend more than 90 percent of their putting practice time working on controlling their line.

8.2 Line Is Instinctive

This is another one of those times when I sympathize with golfers, because their instinct—to work on line rather than speed—seems to make sense. Why? Because it is easier to see errors in line than errors in speed. Figure 8.2.1 shows three ball tracks for a straight putt rolled at the same speed but started on different Aimlines. Most golfers with any experience would probably correctly diagnose these three putts as

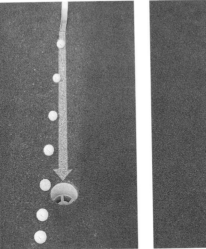

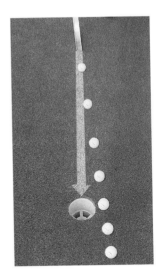

Figure 8.2.1: On straight putts it's easy to see and diagnose a push (left), a perfect roll (center), and a pull (right).

a push, one struck perfectly, and a pull. It's instinct, because it's easy to see: Ball goes right of the target, it's a push; ball goes in, it's perfect; ball goes left, it's a pull.

While realizing that you pulled or pushed your putt off your intended line is an instinctive and natural reaction, golfers take it too far. They get overconcerned and overfocused on the direction, thereby becoming what we call "line-locked" over their putts. They get so concerned about line that they forget how fast or how far the putt needs to roll. As often as not, they leave putts short of the hole, rolling them on-line but at the wrong speed.

Getting "line-locked" is a serious problem. And the best way I know to correct it is to prove to you that there are always several Aimlines your ball can follow and still find the hole. Why is this true? Because the hole is 4.25 inches wide, the ball is only 1.68 inches in diameter (Figure 8.2.2), and different putt speeds will always give you a choice of ball tracks (unless it is one of those few dead-straight putts, in

Figure 8.2.2: Balls are much smaller than holes, resulting in many acceptable entry points over a 4-inch range.

which case it will roll straight at any speed). Because the ball is much less than half the size of the hole, even straight putts offer a choice of makable Aimlines, since you can aim a little to the left, a little to the right, or dead in the middle and still find the hole (Figure 8.2.3).

There are even more Aimline choices on breaking putts than on straight putts. As explained in Chapter 7, starting on any Aimline, the faster you roll your putt, the less it will break; and the slower you roll a putt, the more it will break. So you can choose a very high line and roll the ball so slowly that it breaks madly down the slope and just dribbles over the top edge of the cup. Or you can play a low, closer-to-straight Aimline and drill your putt into the cup, hoping to catch the back edge squarely to avoid the chance of a lip-out (Figure 8.2.4). And then there are countless combinations of Aimlines and speeds in between: a little higher with a little slower roll; a little lower with a little more speed. The choices are almost endless, even on a relatively short putt.

So there are choices, and lots of them. But what you will learn in section 8.6 is that for every putt there is always one optimum speed and one optimum Aimline (which means one optimum ball track, Figure 8.2.5) for holing the maximum percentage of putts from that distance on that green.

Here's a piece of advice to remember as you keep reading. When you're looking at a putt, which element do you consider first? Line or speed? Since line is the more instinctive, it would make sense to choose line first and then determine the correct

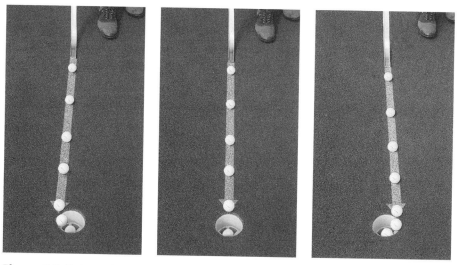

Figure 8.2.3: Straight putts can be aimed plus or minus two inches (4-inch total range) from the center of the hole, and still go in on successful Aimlines.

Figure 8.2.4: The slower the roll (left), the more a putt breaks. The faster the roll (right), the less it breaks.

Figure 8.2.5: For every putt there is an optimum Aimline and speed that produce the optimum ball track.

speed for that line. That's fine, you certainly can do that. But if you do, be aware that you have to perform both judgments—first line, then speed, and you cannot forget to determine the speed (which many golfers don't even know how to do). Having figured your line, you must turn your focus to the proper speed for that line. What if the line feels comfortable but the speed doesn't? Or what if the speed feels good but you know it isn't right for the line you've already picked? There are a lot of opportunities for subconscious conflict. There must be a better way.

And there is. Rather than focusing on line or speed, I've found that the best way is to imagine neither the Aimline nor the speed but the entire ball track you expect your putt to roll on. Because you can't correctly imagine a ball track without your mind including *both* line and speed. That's what the ball track is—the path of your rolling ball that results from the combination of line and speed that you give it (in a real putt or your imagination).

So just as in Chapter 7, where I encouraged you to look for ball tracks in your green-reading efforts, ball tracks again are the answer, this time to seeing speed. Because I assure you, if you can imagine the ball track you want, starting on the Aimline you have chosen, your subconscious will include the speed.

8.3   Green Speed Affects Ball Tracks

The speed of the putting surface is something else to consider when seeing a ball track. Green speeds are measured every day around the world with the "Stimpmeter" (see section 4.3 for details). Most greens in the United States roll between 7.0 and 11.0 on the Stimpmeter, meaning that balls released down this ramp (Figure 8.3.1) roll on average between 7 and 11 feet on the flat portions of these greens. This measurement is a simple way to approximate the frictional force the green's surface exerts on rolling balls, which is what primarily slows them and brings them to a stop.

The faster the green speed (i.e., the higher the Stimp reading), then the less energy or initial speed you have to give to your putts to get them to roll the perfect distance. So putts on a fast green actually will be rolling more slowly, giving

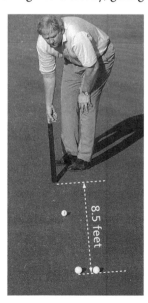

Figure 8.3.1: The average roll distance of 6 balls (3 in each direction) released from a Stimpmeter on a flat portion of the green is a measure of green speed.

gravity more time to influence the ball and pull it downhill, so it will break more. That's why it's important to know the green speed when reading the slope and trying to determine how much a putt will break. Of course, the opposite is also true, that a slower green speed means more friction, so you have to roll the ball faster, which decreases how much it will break.

Green Speed Can Be Seen

Unfortunately, you don't see many signs at golf courses that read "Warning: Green Speed 12. Putts Will Be Very Fast and Break Excessively." But a trained eye can detect and evaluate green speeds within a very small tolerance. If you don't believe me, ask any golf course superintendent or PGA Tour pro. Both make their living knowing how fast their greens roll. How do they know? The superintendent regularly takes measurements with a Stimpmeter, and the pros talk to the superintendents, then correlate what they're told with their experience of watching their putts roll.

But don't think you can ask your superintendent the green speed at your course and automatically be an expert. Appearances can be deceiving. Fast greens usually look brownish, with short grass and firm surfaces. Most slow greens have long, dark green grass, and tend to be softer (Figure 8.3.2). Also, the thicker the grass, even when cut short, the slower and greener it looks. So you always should roll a few putts at any new course to check the green speed, because a green that looks slow can be "sneaky fast," and vice versa.

Grain (see section 7.10 for details) also affects a green's speed. Because Stimpmeter ratings are taken in more than one direction, grain is averaged into the green-speed reading. But grain still can have a dramatic effect on how putts roll and break. I've measured grain's effect on numerous occasions: On a 40-foot putt, putting against the grain can mean a difference of 10 feet versus the same putt rolled with the grain (Figure 8.3.3). So you must learn to recognize green speed in the direction you are putting.

Figure 8.3.2: Greens must be cut every day to maintain a consistent green speed. The shorter the grass, the faster the green speed.

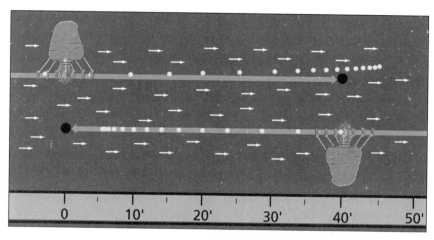

Figure 8.3.3: From identical 40-foot putting strokes, the ball rolls 45 feet with the grain (top), but only 35 feet against the grain (bottom).

8.4 The "Optimum" Putting Speed

Up until now, I've talked a great deal about visible break, true break, Aimlines, and green speeds. Those have all been terms referring to the conditions found on the green you're playing. Now that you understand those concepts, I want to give you another one that applies to all putts and does not change from green to green.

There is an optimum speed that applies to every putt in golf. By optimum speed I mean the best speed for rolling a putt that will optimize its chances of coming to rest in the bottom of the hole. I first reported this finding years ago after extensive testing with the True Roller, and I wrote about it in my first book, *Putt Like the Pros*. It is such an important concept that I must discuss it here again.

Section 8.2 says that there are many possible Aimlines for every putt, many starting lines on which you can roll a putt and still find the hole. And for each of these Aimlines there is one best putting speed as well as many that are a little too fast or too slow (but that will still allow the ball to hit the hole). If you were to take every makable Aimline and roll 1,000 putts on each one at its best speed, one Aimline would stand out as the one on which you holed the greatest number of putts. That would be the optimum Aimline for that putt, and the best speed for that optimum Aimline would be the optimum speed.

Because speed and line are intertwined, you can look at this situation in the opposite way. There are many speeds at which any given putt can be made, and for each of those speeds there is a most desirable, or optimum, Aimline. By rolling thousands of putts, one speed would prove to have the greatest rate of success, and that would be the optimum speed for that putt. The Aimline associated with it would be the optimum Aimline. Just as important as knowing that there are many makable Aimline/speed combinations, realize that there are many more combinations that have no chance of finding the hole. For example, any line/speed combination that leaves a putt short is no good. And any combination that had enough speed to roll the ball more than approximately eight feet past the hole is similarly out of the question. (The exact distance varies due to the green speed, the condition of the back edge of the hole, and the slope.) Suffice it to say eight feet past is roughly the maximum speed at which any Aimline can work.

8.5 The Lumpy Donut

If lots of speed/Aimline combinations roll the ball into the hole, why is one better than all the rest? Why does one produce a higher percentage of putts made? Blame the greens.

The surfaces of most putting greens are not perfect. Unless you're in the very first group of the day (and even that doesn't guarantee perfection), the greens will be covered with footprints, pitch marks from incoming shots, and spike marks that can, and will, knock rolling balls off-line. Furthermore, the edges of the hole often are worn down, beat up, or improperly cut. All of these imperfections get worse as the day goes on (more footprints, more spike marks, more pitch marks). That's why whenever I watch a Tour event and see a player in one of the last groups make an important putt, I applaud the player for both his (or her) good putting and good luck in negotiating the minefield of bad conditions between the ball and the hole.

The most influential of these imperfections, without a doubt, are the footprints made by golfers near the hole. Golfers can't help it. Most miss their first putt, so they must putt a second time, usually from within six feet of the hole. Then they have to get within six inches or so of the hole to retrieve their ball. As a result, there is a high-density ring of footprints around every hole. But at the center of this ring is an area with no footprints at all; it's within six inches of the hole, and golfers know never to step that close. So around every hole is something that looks like a donut—a few feet of high-density footprints surrounding a raised circle one foot in diameter that is absolutely clean. Years ago, I started referring to this area as the "lumpy donut" (Figure 8.5.1).

Every golfer should be aware of the lumpy donut, because it can influence every putt that has a chance of finding the hole. I've run countless tests through the lumpy donut, rolling putts at different speeds to see how they were affected. What I found was that the slower a ball rolls as it approaches the cup, the more often and more severely it is deflected to one side or the other and misses the hole. On the other hand, the faster a putt rolls, the more likely it will maintain its line to hit the cup, but the more likely it will lip out due to excessive speed. What does this mean to you? If you like to die your putts at the hole, understand that the lumpy donut significantly lessens your chance of holing the first putt. If you prefer jamming putts at the hole to minimize the break, realize that the extra speed you are adding can negatively affect the chances of your putt staying in the hole (if you take it too far). Figure 8.5.2 shows the middle ground between these two extremes, the dependence of the "make" percentage on speed.

Figure 8.5.1: Every foursome putts on average 8+ times (left), half from within 6 feet. Their footprints form the "lumpy donut" (right) on each green.

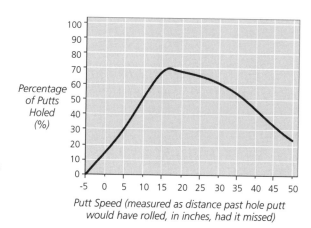

Figure 8.5.2: Optimum putting speed is 17 inches past the hole: lower speeds produce more deflections and misses; higher speeds produce more lip-outs.

Percentage of Putts Holed (%)

Putt Speed (measured as distance past hole putt would have rolled, in inches, had it missed)

8.6 17 Inches Past Is Key

Go back to what I said a few pages ago about there being an optimum putting speed for every putt. Your next questions probably are: (1) What is this optimum speed? and (2) How do you learn to roll your putts at that speed?

Let's start with finding it. I've tested for optimum speeds on different putts and different greens all around the country. Using the True Roller, I've found the line and speed that make the highest percentage of putts, then covered the hole (as shown in Figure 8.6.1), rolled more putts at that speed, and measured how far these optimum speed putts roll past the hole. What does measuring this distance do? It produces a quantifiable and visual result that you can use to evaluate the speed of your putts on any green anywhere, relative to the optimum speed that has the best chance of holing putts.

Figure 8.6.1: After finding the Aimline and speed that made the highest percentage of putts, I covered the hole and found that optimum speed putts roll about 17 inches past the back edge.

It's important to note here that I'm referring not to a speed but a distance past the hole. As I mentioned earlier, golfers don't relate to speeds (velocities), which change from green to green depending on the conditions anyway. But what does not change (at least not very much) is the distance the optimum speed putts roll past the hole, which is, in a general way, a measure of how fast the ball was rolling when it reached the cup after passing through the lumpy donut. That distance is 17 inches. Years of experiments have shown me that the optimum speed for making putts is one that would, if the hole were covered or missed, roll the ball 17 inches past the back edge. That extra 17 inches of speed is enough to keep the maximum percentage of putts on line through the lumpy donut yet not so fast they won't stay in the hole when they hit it.

Something Extra for the Technically Oriented

Understand that 17 inches is an average. The actual optimum distance past varies a little (an inch or two) with almost every putt on every green, depending on its surface conditions. Uphill and downhill putts have slightly different optimum speeds, although not by as much as you might expect. Because downhill putts have gravity helping them stay on-line as they roll through the lumpy donut, their optimum speeds tend to be a little lower as they reach the hole, so they still roll close to 17 inches past (when they miss the hole) before they stop. As explained earlier, uphill putts are being pulled off-line by gravity every time they hit an imperfection. To keep them on-line, the optimum speed tends to be faster, but because they are rolling uphill, if they pass the hole, they also stop about 17 inches past.

Larger variations in the 17-inch distance occur on different grasses. On seaside greens, where the grain of Bermuda grass is very strong, I have seen optimum putting speeds roll balls as much as 36 inches past the back edge of the hole. Compare this to U.S. Open greens, which I've measured with optimum speeds that roll balls only five inches past the cup. But don't worry about these variations.

Every test I've ever done, with all levels of golfers (including Tour pros), proves that one of the most difficult tasks in golf is rolling putts the proper speed. The best you can do is train yourself to get very good at having one consistent touch for rolling putts at the hole. And that best speed is—you got it—17 inches past.

We teach 17 inches in our schools, and we find that it helps students learn the right touch for distance when they practice. Again, this isn't really a speed but a distance. However, as more and more golfers have learned about 17 inches, they've begun referring to it as a putting speed, so "17 inches past" has become known as the optimum putting speed that produces the optimum ball track and makes the most putts. It's a terribly important number to know.

There's another advantage to rolling putts at the 17-inches-past speed. Simply put, it's that by learning to roll the ball a little long, you're much less likely to leave putts short. It's an old joke, but true: Putts that don't make it to the hole have very little chance of going in.

I have test results that back up this finding. Look at the two putt-scatter patterns, both for 20-foot putts, in Figure 8.6.2. The one on the left is the typical first-day pattern made by amateurs at our schools: Before they learn anything about putting, they leave roughly half of their 20-footers short. The pattern on the right is typical of the Tour professionals I work with, putting the same 20-footers on the same green. Notice that the pros roll virtually all of their putts past the hole, giving them twice the chance of making these putts over the amateurs, simply because they've learned a better touch for the 17-inches-past speed.

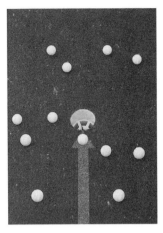

Figure 8.6.2: Typical 20-foot-putt patterns for amateurs (left) and Tour pros (right).

8.7 The Mind's Roll in Speed

Until now, every one of the 15 building blocks I've discussed is something that, once you've worked on it in practice, should not require much thought on the golf course. They are all skills that, once practiced, get into the subconscious and begin to work automatically.

Finding the correct line can become an instinctive result from green-reading; stroke mechanics can be grooved in practice so they become automatic; and your setup should be committed to habit and become automatically controlled by your subconscious also.

But speed? Well, that's different. Every putt is a new experience. You've never putted this exact putt, under these conditions, at your present age at this exact moment before. You've never faced exactly this break on exactly this green, at this green speed, at precisely this distance from the hole. And because everything is new, controlling the speed of your putts will always require every bit of your focus and attention. In fact, ball tracks (which include your Aimlines and speeds) are just about the *only* thing you should think about when putting.

At the beginning of this chapter I said that speed is important enough to be the number-one principle in putting. Now you know why. It is the one element that you should think about with intense, full-bore, flat-out focus in the form of ball tracks every time you putt.

CHAPTER 9

Wind, Lopsided Balls, Dimples, Rain, Sleet, and Snow

9.1 Are You a *Real* Golfer?

I'm not asking how well you score or anything about your handicap. What I want to know is, how much do you enjoy playing the game? For example, when I lived in Abilene, Texas, about 15 years ago, I played with a group of friends, all of whom could be characterized as *real* golfers. We had a regularly scheduled game that went on come rain, wind, sleet, or snow. The only time we didn't play was when the wind conditions of the day failed the "chain test" (Figure 9.1.1): If the wind wasn't holding the chain horizontal to the ground, we played. We are *real* golfers who love to play the game.

So let me ask you again. Are you a *real* golfer? If not, you may want to skip this

Figure 9.1.1: The chain test: In Abilene, Texas, as long as the wind wasn't holding the chain horizontal to the ground, we played!

chapter, because it may tell you more than you want to know about putting. I'm going to discuss how the wind, your golf ball's balance, and even its dimples can affect your putting.

9.2 Does Wind Affect Putting?

For years I wondered how much, if at all, wind affected a ball rolling on the green. And if so, at what speed would those effects begin to occur? Would a putt be affected by winds of 40 miles an hour? Thirty? Twenty? How about a 10-mile-an-hour wind—could that possibly affect my putting? Would it matter if I were putting on a really fast green? I pondered these questions for years and then put them to the test—the "Wind Test" conducted by the Pelz Golf Institute.

I also asked a lot of golfers what they thought the results would be. Many thought it would take some pretty high winds—30 to 40 miles an hour, at least—to have any noticeable effect on putting. Their rationale was that it takes relatively high wind velocities above ground before the wind becomes significant at ground level. In other words, just because there was enough wind to knock down a 7-iron shot didn't mean it would influence a putt.

Your Questions

If that's what you think, I have a question or two for you. You're playing on a windy day (say, 20-mile-per-hour gusting winds), and your hair, jacket sleeves, and pants legs are whipping in the wind. Have you looked down at the cuffs of your pants to see what's happening two inches above the ground? Or have you ever noticed leaves blowing across the greens or fairways? If your cuffs are flapping and the leaves are tumbling across the greens, don't you think that means the wind velocity just above the surface of the ground is significant?

One more question. You've seen that even when the wind is blowing fairly hard, balls sitting on the green don't often get blown into motion or completely off the putting surface. So that must mean the wind won't blow rolling putts off-line, right?

My Answers

We recently purchased some wind velocity measuring equipment and measured average wind profiles, which showed that wind speeds do, indeed, drop as they get closer to the earth's surface. However, we found that they don't get to zero until they reach absolute ground level. And at the height of a golf ball—1.68 inches above the ground—the wind can be blowing at a relatively rapid pace. When we saw wind speeds at 1 inch above ground level within 20 to 30 percent of those speeds measured at 6 feet, we realized that our pant cuffs and leaves are not moving on their own.

And yes, it's true, balls sitting stationary on the green don't move, even when the greens are pretty fast, until wind speeds reach about 25 to 30 mph an inch off the ground, at which point you would call it a very windy day. But the force of friction between a green and a ball at rest (static friction) is different from the friction between the same green and a moving ball (rolling friction) by a significant amount, with rolling friction being lower.

Armed with these ideas and statistics, I decided to look into wind's effects on rolling putts. The intent was to learn how much the wind has to be blowing before you should be concerned about its effects on your putting.

9.3 Scoring Indicates Yes

Let's look at an extreme wind effect from the PGA Tour. Figure 9.3.1 shows the full-field average scores in The Players Championship at Sawgrass over five years. The scoring average was 71.8 on calm days. But on the infamous "Black Friday" in 1977, when the wind blew at an unprecedented strength, scores were significantly higher, averaging 78.3. What happened that Friday was this: After missing the greens in regulation, the pros couldn't make their putts to save par, either. As you can imagine, when wind blows balls away from the greens on the course, putting on the greens also suffers dramatically.

Reviewing the highest-scoring rounds on the PGA Tour over the last few years, we find that essentially all occurred on high-wind days. That won't come as a surprise to professionals, who know that playing in strong winds has a much greater effect on scoring than rain, cold, long rough, or hard greens. But again, while golfers assume that most of this difficulty comes from the wind blowing balls in the air, leading to missed greens and found hazards, the data indicates putting performances also suffer on these windy days.

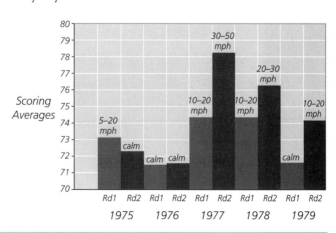

Figure 9.3.1: The harder the wind blows, the more greens-in-regulation, putting, and scoring statistics suffer on the PGA Tour.

9.4 Simple Experiments Say Perhaps Yes

You probably could be pushed to agree that it is reasonable to expect golf balls rolling on smooth, fast, low-friction surfaces (such as a desktop) to be blown sideways by wind. Prove it to yourself by running the "desk wind test," shown in Figure 9.4.1. Roll a golf ball across your desktop five times to get the feel of where the ball rolls on its own. Then roll it five more times, blowing on the ball from the side each time as it passes your face. On at least one of the rolls you'll hit the ball with your exhaled breath (you'll miss above or below a few times, too) and see it pushed off-line. Once you get the hang of hitting the ball with your breath, you can prove to yourself that winds with, against, and quartering across the line of the rolling ball can have an effect, too (Figure 9.4.2).

In the examples and figures above, my breath wind speed was about 10 miles per hour, which shows that even a relatively low-velocity wind influences the roll of the ball dramatically on a low-friction surface. So what does that mean for your putting on fast and slow greens?

Figure 9.4.1: A 10-mph wind will completely change the roll direction of a putt on a desktop.

Figure 9.4.2: With a little practice, you can learn how different winds affect rolling putts on really fast greens.

To help you understand what really happens to a ball rolling on a flat putting green surface, look at Figure 9.4.3. You can see the forces that control the motion of the ball, and a simple evaluation of the strength of those forces will tell you where the ball is going to go.

On a windless day, a putt rolls forward with the momentum you provided by putting it. As it rolls toward the hole, friction against the green surface and air resistance (which is small but does count) slows it down. On a flat green, there is no force pushing the ball sideways, no downhill component of gravity, and no force preventing it from being pushed sideways.

Now look at what happens in the wind (Figure 9.4.4). The ball is rolling toward you (out of the page); there is a side-wind force, but no force in opposition except the very small force of rolling friction. This explains why wind can significantly affect your putting results without you even realizing it.

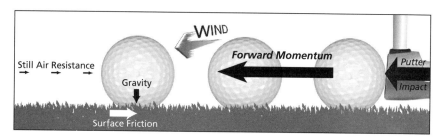

Figure 9.4.3: Impact energy moves your putts forward, air resistance and green friction slow them down, while wind forces and slopes (gravity) can move them sideways.

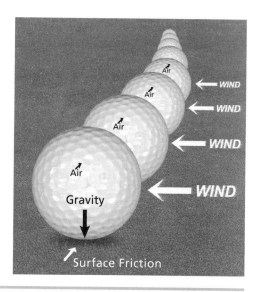

Figure 9.4.4: A side-wind force *will* move a rolling ball sideways. It's only a question of how much or how far.

9.5 Detailed Experiments Prove It

We set up our indoor tilt-green for wind testing, making it dead level with a Stimp speed of 9.5. We rolled nine-foot putts through a 20-mph crosswind field (left side of Figure 9.5.1). With a near-ground wind speed of 20 mph, the putts were moved about 12 inches off-line by the time they reached hole-high. When we rolled putts through the same wind field on the green Stimping at 10.5, putts were blown approximately 38 inches wide of the hole (that's more than three feet on a nine-foot putt). But, you say, golfers don't play in winds this strong. Yes we do, because a 20-mph wind just above ground level is roughly a 30-mph wind at eye level, and we play in gusts that strong frequently.

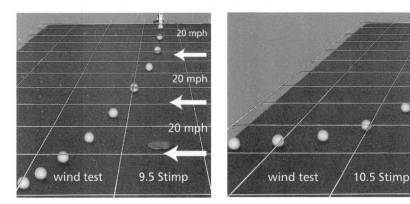

Figure 9.5.1: On our level tilt-green, 20-mph crosswinds moved putts dramatically off-line.

So why don't we see our putts blow three feet sideways? Because we don't get precisely these circumstances very often. Rather than a 20-mph wind blowing constantly for the full roll of the putt, what you might encounter on the course is a wind that gusts to 20 mph, quartering across your ball track for just a second or two, pushing your ball two inches left of the cup. Under this kind of circumstance, you probably would never notice the wind effect, and blame your left-edge miss on a pulled stroke instead.

That's what happens in a 20-mph gust. What about a fairly consistent 5-mph wind, something you probably play in all the time? It can move the ball 2½ inches off-line on a nine-foot putt (on a green measuring 9.0 on the Stimpmeter), and again that's enough to miss the hole (Figure 9.5.2). The 5-mph breeze you enjoy so much as it caresses your face and makes you think golf is the greatest game ever is the same SOB that just blew your ball out of the hole and cost you a stroke.

Look at one last ball track (Figure 9.5.3), that of a putt on a slight sidehill

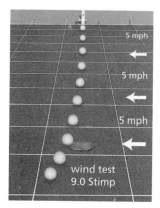

Figure 9.5.2: A constant 5-mph crosswind can blow a perfectly rolled 9-foot putt out of the hole.

Figure 9.5.3: A 3-mph crosswind by the hole can cause your perfectly rolled left-edge putt to lip out.

slope. Now, wouldn't that blow your mind, to enjoy the light (3-mph) breeze as you prepare to putt and then have that same lovely breeze blow your left-edge putt just enough uphill to keep it outside of the hole after you stroked it perfectly? It would if you knew enough to let it, but you probably wouldn't realize that it was the breeze that was at fault, and think you pulled it.

No Doubt

Let there be no doubt in your mind that wind can and regularly does affect how balls roll on greens. Like the lumpy donut, it's part and parcel of the game we love, something we need to be aware of and sometimes even consider in our putting calculations. At what levels do wind's effects become significant? How do they affect your scores? What can you do about them?

I don't yet have all the answers. We're still testing. But I had to share with you the best information we have as I write this, with the understanding that there is more to come.

9.6   What Wind Means to You

While we don't have complete test results, we do know that even fairly low wind velocities can affect putting, especially on really fast greens. And that's not only when the wind is blowing across your line. A 5-mph wind (at ball level on a flat green) blowing straight into or behind your putt can change the distance it rolls by more than a foot either way. Obviously, on longer putts or in stronger winds, these effects will be magnified. So you could do everything right, stroke your 30-foot putt perfectly, and still have it stop more than three feet short of the hole solely because the ball was rolling into a light breeze. Or on what you used to call a windless day, you could roll your slightly downhill, downgrain 30-foot putt 15 feet past the hole and off the green simply because that pleasant 5-mph breeze quietly urged your ball along in the downwind direction.

Since I'm still compiling data, the best wind advice I can give you now is what I hope will be helpful hints. Expect and accept that your putting will be slightly less effective on windy days. And when I say windy, I mean days that most golfers would describe as "breezy" or "fresh," with wind speeds of only 5 to 10 mph. On serious-wind days, when wind speeds above the ground are 15 to 30 mph, expect some serious changes in your putting. And if the winds are really gusting, just smile and enjoy the day, because there is nothing else you can do. A good attitude and the knowledge of what's happening will give you the edge over your competition.

The J.D. Test

If you feel the wind blowing in a constant direction at a nearly constant speed, here's an unscientific test that may give you a slight advantage over your friends. Don't take this too seriously (I don't have enough data yet), but it seems to have some validity, and it's fun. It's a simple way to estimate wind strength, and we call it the "J.D." test after my youngest son, because he thought of it.

In Figure 9.6.1, Eddie, my oldest son (J.D. was not available for a photograph), is releasing grass clippings from about three feet off the ground (the length of a standard putter), and watching not only the direction they blow, but also the distance. For every putter length the grass clippings land away from the bottom of the putter, J.D. calculated the wind speed will be about 10 mph. So if the grass lands nine feet away, the wind at knee height is blowing 25 to 30 mph.

Figure 9.6.1: Eddie runs the "J.D." wind test: Every putter-length the grass clippings blow away indicates 10 mph of wind speed (watch for both speed and direction).

The Short-Game Advantage

If you're smart, you will accept the wind rather than fight it. Tom Kite used a smart wind strategy to win the 1992 U.S. Open at Pebble Beach. The wind gusted to 40 to 50 mph the entire final round, and no one could hit the greens in regulation. Kite tried to keep his shots low and safe up to the greens, then used his exceptional short-game skills (14 wedge shots to 14 different greens) to shoot even par. He played strategically, getting himself into positions from which he could hit relatively easy short-game shots that would leave very short putts.

As is the case in all weather conditions, what is fair for one is fair for all. In high winds, rather than try to fly shots onto the green and stop them, take the smarter "low road" approach. Bump-and-run your shots to the fronts of the greens. A good chip shot and short putt can save par from there.

And yes, I realize this is a putting book, but understand that nothing sets up an easy putt like a good finesse shot.

9.7 Use Your Wind Stroke

Although you can't expect to putt as well in the wind as you do on calm days, you should always try to putt your best. There are compensations you can make to improve your wind putting. Widen your stance to create a more stable base. Grip down on your putter since, with your feet farther apart, your entire body is slightly closer to the ground. And extending your arms down the putter shaft (Figure 9.7.1) will give you more control over the putterhead.

When the wind is blowing across your line, play for a little more or less break. How much? The best you can do is guess how much based on previous experience. But don't overdo it: Don't change your line if the wind is gusting. Instead, play the normal amount of break and make the wind beat you, because you don't know if the wind will blow or not as the ball is rolling. (Wind usually blows much less than 50 percent of the time, and usually not only in the direction that will make your putt miss.) If it blows and makes you miss, that's okay—that's golf in the wind; but if it doesn't blow and you played for it, then you'll be even more disappointed by having given a stroke away for something that might have been, but wasn't.

In really difficult wind conditions, lag your long putts (from over 15 feet), while rolling the very short ones (from less than 3 feet) firmly. On long putts, focus on leaving yourself the shortest possible next putt. Rely on your short game to save strokes by setting up putts that are short enough to make even in the wind. And putt quickly (execute your ritual, just don't waste time); this will minimize the chance of the wind changing between your last practice stroke and your real stroke.

Finally, don't let the wind beat you before you get started. It's easy to overthink or get psyched out by possible wind effects, when, in fact, most putts won't be affected, or if they are, the effects will be small. So work on everything else about your putting—stroke mechanics, aim and setup, feel, touch, and green-reading—before you start worrying about the wind. Become a great putter first; then you can worry about becoming a great wind putter.

Figure 9.7.1: On really windy days: 1) widen your stance; 2) grip down on your putter shaft; 3) lag your long putts; 4) roll your short putts firmly; 5) allow for only "partial" wind effects (you'll rarely if ever see as much as our wind test results).

9.8 Balance Matters in a Putted Ball

Have you ever chipped or putted a ball that had a lump of mud that didn't come off when you hit it? (Figure 9.8.1) If so, you know the ball can do some pretty funny things as it rolls to the hole, even if you hit the shot properly. Funny but understandable things, because golfers accept that the mud would make the ball unbalanced and cause it to roll off-line.

Now imagine what would happen if that same blob of mud, or a very small piece of metal, were inside the ball, just under the cover. This weight (unobserved by the golfer) would unbalance the ball the same way the visible blob of mud did, so this ball, too, would move oddly across the green.

Finally, imagine a third ball, perfectly round and perfectly balanced except for a very tiny piece of metal inside the ball, just off its geometric center (Figure 9.8.2). This "almost-balanced" ball would probably roll almost straight (assuming you putted it straight) on a flat, smooth, level green.

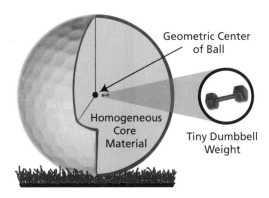

Figure 9.8.1: A lump of mud stuck on the side of your ball will throw off its balance.

Geometric Center of Ball

Homogeneous Core Material

Tiny Dumbbell Weight

Figure 9.8.2: A slightly off-balance ball will roll better than a mud-lump ball, but still not precisely straight and true.

If you haven't figured out where I'm going with this, let me be as blunt as possible: Very few golf balls today are perfectly balanced. Where and how much off-balance a ball is controls in what direction and how far the ball will roll off-line. Sometimes, the amount can be significant.

Most Balls Are Pretty Good

This isn't *Consumer Reports,* and I'm not writing a ball-by-ball evaluation of the golf ball industry. My tests show that most name-brand balls on the market are very nearly in balance. But they're not perfectly balanced. And when you are as concerned as I am about putting, then something needs to be done, because these balls can affect your putting.

Before going on, you should understand that I'm not writing this to criticize ball manufacturers. I know how difficult it is to make anything perfect in this world, particularly a golf ball. The balls of today are far better than the balls of 10 years ago, and the ball manufacturers deserve credit for that. Still, most of their balls are not yet perfect.

How can this imbalance affect your putting? Figure 9.8.3 shows the ball track recorded for the "mud-lump" ball stroked by Perfy with a perfect nine-foot stroke. The green had a Stimpmeter rating of 9.5, and the putt was straight, as evidenced by the roll of the perfectly balanced ball beside it. This was the worst-case scenario

Figure 9.8.3: Given two identical strokes by Perfy, the off-balance, mud-lump ball (left) rolls well off-line, compared to the perfectly balanced ball (right).

for this mud-lump ball, as we positioned it the worst possible way, with its off-balance axis positioned exactly horizontal and perpendicular to the direction of the roll. You can see how far off-line several more reasonable, but still off-balance, putts roll (predicted by our theoretical model) in Figure 9.8.4.

To compare the off-balance effects of real balls to the theoretical predictions, we measured and marked a number of new balls bought off the shelf from local golf shops. Most of these balls rolled within a few inches of straight on nine-foot putts, even when positioned for maximum off-line roll. Which means you shouldn't be too upset by our "mud-ball" results. But how often do you miss a nine-foot putt by less than a few inches? It happens. A lot.

| Putt length (feet) | CG offset distance (inches) | | | | |
	.001	.002	.003	.004	.005
	Distance putts miss center of hole (inches)				
1	0.07	0.13	0.20	0.26	0.33
5	0.46	0.92	1.39	1.85	2.32
9	0.86	1.71	2.57	3.44	4.30
13	1.25	2.50	3.76	5.02	6.29

Figure 9.8.4: When a ball's center of gravity (CG) is offset from its geometric center, it will roll off-line (off-line values greater then 2.13 inches mean the ball would miss the hole on a straight putt, and are shown shaded).

9.9 Measure and Mark Your Balance Line

If you're not a good putter, off-balance balls won't hurt your putting. In fact, they might help by rolling some of your off-line putts back to the hole. But if you start your putts rolling on the correct Aimline, then off-balance balls can only hurt you. If you're likely to be adversely affected, there is a way to minimize these effects. You have to measure the Balance-line of your balls, mark them, and set them on the green so the Balance-line will roll along your Aimline (Figure 9.9.1). Aligning the Balance-line with your Aimline not only eliminates the effect of any ball imbalance, it also may help you aim your ball and putterface more accurately

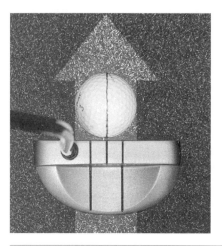

Figure 9.9.1: When the Balance-line is marked and set on the intended line of roll (Aimline), off-balance roll effects are eliminated. The Balance-line also may help you aim your putter better.

Figure 9.9.2: A Balance-line machine (left) or a jar of heavy water (right) can be used to measure the off-balance aspect of a golf ball.

(as detailed in Chapter 11.7). There are two easy ways to measure golf-ball balance: spinning your balls in a Balance-line machine (Figure 9.9.2), or by floating them in a solution of heavy water. The B-line machine is quick and clean; you set the ball in it, attach the cover, push a switch, the ball spins, and you mark it.

If you float your balls in heavy water, they must be marked with a permanent marker as they float heavy side down; then you apply your Balance-lines separately (Figure 9.9.3). The heavy-water method makes more of a mess, and makes finding and marking your desired Dot-spots and Face-lines (details in Chapter 11.7) a little more difficult, but it is significantly less expensive.

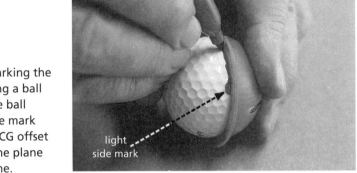

Figure 9.9.3: Marking the Balance-line (using a ball mask) around the ball through light side mark ensures that the CG offset of the ball is in the plane of the Balance-line.

How to Measure the Heavy Side of a Ball

Once balls are marked, always putt with the Balance-line aligned exactly with the Aim-line, so balls roll in-balance and along the intended ball track.

How to Measure Golf Ball Balance

Supplies

1 wide-mouth container (8 oz. Cool Whip container works well)
2½ cups lukewarm water
12 tbsp. Epsom salts (available at most grocery stores)
2 drops Jet Dry (a dishwater-despotting agent available at grocery stores)
1 permanent-ink marking pen

Procedure

1. Fill container with water.
2. Gradually add Epsom salts and stir to ensure all salt completely dissolves. Place a ball in the water. If it floats, you have enough salt. If not, add more salt and observe buoyancy of ball changing. Ball will eventually float when enough salt dissolves.
3. Add two drops of Jet Dry and stir. Solution is now ready to measure ball balance.
4. To measure, place ball in solution at bottom of container. Carefully release ball without spinning. Let ball float to surface. After all motion ceases, mark center of exposed ball cover with permanent marker. This mark identifies light side of ball (gravity pulls heavy side down).

Figure 9.9.4: How to measure the heavy side of a ball

9.10 Golf Balls Have Weird Feet

The game of golf was originally played with a smooth ball. However, once the old Scots saw that scuffed balls flew farther, the dimple race was on. The aerodynamic effects of dimples are well documented. Modern balls fly farther and straighter than ever before, in part as a result of the size and patterning of these dimples. However, dimples have a downside: They make it a little more difficult to roll short putts straight.

Imagine, if a golf ball had feet, how off-line it would roll if it were placed and putted as shown in Figure 9.10.1. If your putter hit a foot first, the ball would roll very oddly indeed. Now look at a close-up of a modern golf ball (Figure 9.10.2).

Figure 9.10.1: If contacted on a foot, a ball with feet would roll more oddly than a football.

Figure 9.10.2: Modern balls are mostly covered with dimples, leaving very little of the true spherical surface exposed.

To optimize the aerodynamics, the dimples consume most of what was originally the spherical surface of the ball. It used to be that balls featured substantial dimple-free areas, where you could make contact with your putter on the surface where it was perfectly spherical. It is much less likely that you'll contact a spherical surface on a modern ball.

Dimples and Direction

There are two ways dimples can affect how—and where—a ball rolls. First, if the putter makes contact on the edge of a dimple rather than the smooth, spherical surface, the ball can rotate and start slightly off-line. This effect can be significant on short putts, but is negligible on long putts when the cover material compresses (as a result of the greater impact velocity). Second, balls that are rolling very slowly can wobble along the edges of the dimples as they slow to a stop. This wobble effect is particularly noticeable just before balls stop, especially on fast, hard greens, since this is when they are rolling the slowest (to see this effect greatly exaggerated, watch a ball roll to a stop on your smooth, hard desktop).

The dimple patterns of six popular brands of balls are shown in Figure 9.10.3.

Figure 9.10.3: The surfaces of six modern balls are mostly dimple area.

The larger the dimples and the harder the cover material, the more likely contact made on an edge will affect a putt's roll. Remember, on normal putts, when the cover material compresses substantially, there is essentially no dimple effect. However, on putts as short as three or four feet (and anything less) on super-fast greens, there can be a measurable effect.

Look at the two ball-putter impact diagrams in Figure 9.10.4. The Dot-Spot (defined as an area of dimple-free spherical surface on the ball) on the left shows perfect contact. The illustration on the right shows contact on the extreme edge of a dimple, which would cause a direction error if the ball were hit gently enough that its cover didn't compress enough to eliminate the effect. Depending on how hard such a putt is hit, the directional error could vary from $\frac{1}{16}$ inch to $\frac{7}{8}$ inch on a four-foot putt on a fast green (Figure 9.10.5).

Those errors might not seem like very much, but it helps to get this effect into perspective. Impact patterns for a number of putts (hit specified distances, as marked) are shown in Figure 9.10.6. These patterns were recorded using Teacher Putter Tape (discussed in section 12.3). The patterns show that as the velocity of the putterhead increases (i.e., as putt distances get longer), the cover of the ball compresses more at impact, eliminating the chance of making contact on a single dimple's edge.

So the dimple-edge effect is only significant for short or downhill putts on super-fast greens (when impact velocities are low). As for the ball wobbling off-

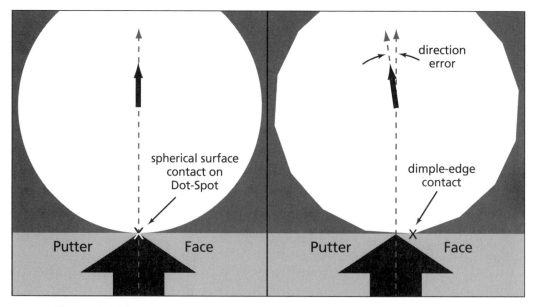

Figure 9.10.4: For identical putting strokes, contact on a ball's dimple edge (right) will roll the ball in a direction different from when contacted on its spherical surface (left).

	Percent compression of cover dimple diameter (%)					
	37.5	50	62.5	75	87.5	100
Putt length (feet)	Distance off-line putts have rolled when hole high (inches)					
0.70	0.54	0.44	0.33	0.22	0.11	0.00
2.11	1.64	1.32	0.99	0.66	0.33	0.00
3.52	2.74	2.20	1.65	1.10	0.55	0.00
4.94	3.84	3.08	2.31	1.54	0.77	0.00

Figure 9.10.5: Dimple edge contact can cause perfectly stroked putts to miss the hole (values greater than 2.13 inches in shaded boxes) only on short or downhill putts on fast greens.

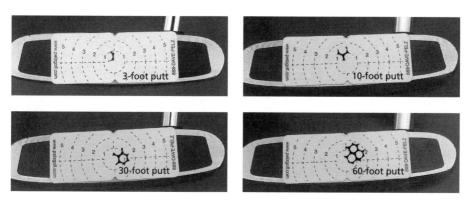

Figure 9.10.6: As putt length increases, single dimple edge contact is eliminated.

line just before it stops, there's nothing you can do about that except to keep the ball moving more briskly as it nears the front edge of the cup. In other words, don't die your putts to the front edge and expect to get a dimple-free last turn; roll your putts at the optimum speed (the 17-inch-past speed), which is fast enough to eliminate wobble near the hole.

Mark Your Dot-Spot, Too

Yes, dimples can affect putting. Or, more precisely, making contact on the edges of dimples can affect your putting. It's not a large effect, and it's even less significant the harder you strike your putts. Also, the effect doesn't occur every time, because if you place your ball down on the green in random orientations, you're more likely to strike the ball somewhere that won't have an effect—on the spherical surface, across the flat of a dimple, or close to the flat of the dimple. Still, the possibility does exist, and there is a simple way to avoid it altogether.

Having marked your ball with its Balance-line (see section 9.9), rotate it until you locate the largest spherical surface (non-dimple) area on the Balance-line, then circle it: This becomes your Dot-Spot (Figure 9.10.7). Set your ball so the Dot-Spot is at the back of the ball (away from the hole, where it will be struck by the putter) when your Balance-line is aimed precisely along your Aimline. That way, when you make contact, there will never be a dimple effect.

Figure 9.10.7: Circle the largest dimple-free area along your Balance-line (usually where it crosses the cover seam) to mark your Dot-Spot. Then strike your putts there.

9.11 Rain, Sleet, and Snow: Are We Having Fun Yet?

As I warned you at the beginning of this chapter, the information here truly could be more than many golfers want to know. But please don't think that I'm trying to make putting seem more difficult. You don't have to carry any of this information with you onto the course. You don't have to think about it ever again if you don't want to. But someday, the fact that you read something about putting in the wind may help you. Or perhaps you'll think, "Maybe I'll try that Pelz tip and turn the ball so I don't hit the edge of a dimple." It can't hurt.

You've been putting all these years without thinking of any of these effects I've mentioned. So why do I bring them up? So you will stop beating yourself up every time you miss a putt. Golfers usually blame themselves for a miss even when it isn't their stroke that's at fault. I want you to stop doing that, because this game is hard enough without it. Save the self "butt-kicking" for the errors you really *do* make and deserve!

HOW TO IMPROVE
YOUR PUTTING

CHAPTER 10

The Improvement Process

10.1 First Comes Understanding

Before you can improve your putting and become the best you can be, you must fully understand the 15 building blocks of the putting game, then understand your personal performance (what you do right and wrong) in each block. I say this from my experience working with so many golfers. The physical act of putting is not difficult to do, and the putting stroke itself is not difficult to execute, but many aspects of putting are difficult to *learn* to do. Most golfers try to work on their putting strokes with little or no feedback, while many others work with bad or inaccurate feedback. As I said earlier, putting is the simplest physical swing in golf, but it also is the most frustrating for most golfers because when they practice to get better, more often than not they get worse.

You can practice, develop, and improve the wrong aspect of your putting (that is, an aspect that is not causing your problems) for the rest of your life and you'll never putt any better. Because it doesn't help to correct the wrong thing. To practice the wrong thing correctly is as bad as practicing the right thing incorrectly. Neither helps one bit.

No one who ever played the game said that golf is fair; let me add that this is especially true of putting. Any one putt can involve an incredible amount of luck, either good, bad, or both at the same time. But there is no long-term luck in putting. No one makes putts because he is lucky all the time. And no one misses putts because he is always unlucky. Putting is a game of skill, probabilities, and statistics, and whether or not there is a black cloud floating over your head on the golf course, the probability is that the more putts you start on the right line at the right speed, the more that will go into the hole.

What I'm talking about here is completely intellectual and has nothing to do with your stroke per se. It is that your head is where all your learning takes place.

Your muscle memories reside in your head—in front of your habits and above your green-reading abilities (Figure 10.1.1). On one hand, accurate knowledge and understanding of what you're doing, both right wrong, will make your physical learning easier. Inaccurate understanding and groundless opinions, on the other hand, will make improving your putting more difficult, if not impossible.

Once you understand the putting game (the goal of the first nine chapters of this book), you can look inward to your common stroke faults and problems, weaknesses and strengths, abilities and inabilities, and understand what you need to change (and what not to change) to improve.

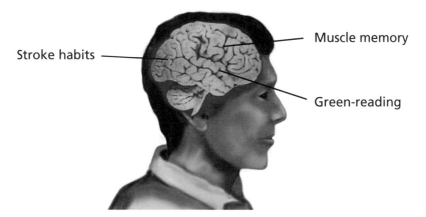

Stroke habits

Muscle memory

Green-reading

Figure 10.1.1: The "learning" part of learning to improve your putting is, above all else, in your head.

10.2 Second Comes Measurement

Since majoring in physics at Indiana University, I have believed in the scientific method. To my way of thinking, it is better to test and measure that something is true than it is to assume or think or hope it's true. That's why, even though we give every incoming student a questionnaire to fill out before beginning one of our three-day schools (we want to know their thoughts and opinions relative to their short games and putting games), we also measure everyone's putting once the school starts. We test their ability to hole putts in all of the makable lengths, and measure how well they lag putts from long distances. We measure their ability to aim their putterface and the orientation of the flow-lines of their body in the address position. We measure their stroke paths, face-angle rotation, impact patterns, and ability to read greens. We use laser beams, slow-motion and stop-action video, and specially designed skill tests to measure what they need to improve.

There's nothing worse than working hard on the wrong thing, expecting improvement from it, then ending up with nothing.

In our three-day schools, we have the time and equipment necessary to perform all these measurements accurately, on facilities specially designed to teach the short game and putting. I point this out not because I'm trying to sell schools, but because I want you to know what is available and what is the best way to learn to putt better.

There are some things we can't measure in schools and clinics, statistics only the golfer can keep track of. For example, it's particularly informative to analyze one's missed-putt pattern to see if there is a favorite way of missing. We invariably find that there is a miss preference, although golfers sometimes deny this until someone accumulates the data and shows it to them.

We quantify misses by breaking them into nine categories or zones (Figure 10.2.1), and keeping a record of them over time. Once you know if there is a pattern and, if so, which one, it becomes easier to deal with whatever is causing it. Several of the games described in the next few chapters were developed to retrain golfers' subconscious habits, resulting in the elimination of such patterns.

For example, if you learned that you tend to miss short and to the right of the hole (zone 2), the assumption might be that you strike putts on the toe of the putter. After confirming this by measurement (using Teacher Putting Impact Tape), you would practice with Teacher Clips (to improve your impact pattern) and play the game called "Safety Drawback" (to improve your feel and touch). In time, your

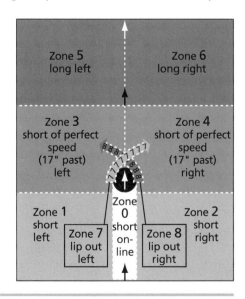

Figure 10.2.1: Measure your missed-putt pattern by recording the miss-zone for every missed putt. Plotting this data will be useful in analyzing your stroke problems and solving them.

pattern of misses short and right would disappear and you would start making more putts (more details of this problem are in section 12.3).

10.3 Third Is Analysis

The purpose of measuring and testing your putting abilities is to allow accurate analysis of your putting game, followed by a diagnosis of what you need to do to improve it *without making mistakes*. I cannot emphasize enough the importance of that phrase, "without making mistakes." The essence of good teaching is properly analyzing and correcting the student's problems without causing other problems in the process. I like to think that's why our schools help so many golfers learn to putt better.

If you are going to do this yourself (which is fine; it can be done), I caution you to be very careful: Make sure your testing and analysis are correct. Because while working hard and properly with good feedback on the right problem will almost always produce improvement, working hard on the wrong thing usually makes things worse. If you aren't 100 percent confident that you are working properly on the right building block, then stop practicing and go watch television. At least being a couch potato won't screw up your putting!

Before you conclude your analysis, you must form a strong commitment to improve, and determine how much time you have to spend on it. In figuring the time, allow for your level of discipline and faithfulness (to follow the practice regimen you prescribe). And you must decide what kind of a stroke you will commit to developing. Without a commitment to spend time on improvement, there will be no long-term success.

I make these points so you understand what you must do to improve from reading this book. And while I don't want to discourage you, I do want you to appreciate that it's far easier to improve your putting (or any part of your game) if you have a knowledgeable instructor by your side as you practice. Without a trained set of eyes watching you, it's up to you to learn what needs to change and what can be left alone (we usually find that 10 to 12 of the 15 building blocks of each student's putting are in pretty good shape). Then, once you know what to work on, you have to work carefully and accurately with feedback. This usually is the most difficult part of learning to putt better—deciding what to leave alone, what to improve, and how to improve it.

You need realistic expectations for your improvement. It usually doesn't happen overnight, but takes at least three to six months. But once you've analyzed the problem, learned how to improve, and committed to it, you can be a better putter for the long term. Just be careful and do it right. Don't get impatient and don't demand instant gratification. Don't be worried if you initially putt a little worse before you putt better; it doesn't usually happen this way, but if it does, be prepared to stick with it. It's just a sign that your subconscious compensations need some time to work themselves out after you improve (or remove) what they were compensating for.

And there's always the easy way out: Come to a Dave Pelz Scoring Game School (Figure 10.3.1). You'll still have to practice to improve, but at least you'll know you are practicing the right things in the right way.

Figure 10.3.1: I recommend you see a doctor when you're sick, a lawyer if you've done something wrong, and a putting expert if you want to improve your putting.

1) learn WHAT you need to learn

2) learn HOW to learn it

3) experience the FEEL of doing it right

Once you have a plan of where you're going and can create the mind's-eye images of how you're going to look when you get there, you're on your way. Whether you do it by yourself, with your local golf professional, or in one of our one-day clinics or three-day schools, what has to be done has to be done. Because if you don't improve your putting skills, your putting results won't improve, either.

10.4 Fourth, Find Your Prescription for Improvement

The next step is to learn how to improve—that is, how to get your putting skills from where they are to where you want them to be. Most golfers don't have a clue of what is required. They don't know how to practice properly. They don't realize that the key to learning is immediate, accurate, and reliable feedback. They don't realize that their brain can internalize fantastic amounts of information if it is presented in an organized and accurate fashion. And they don't realize how important it is to keep inaccurate information out of the process.

I estimate that only about 10 percent of the golfers I've seen practicing putting on their own actually improve. That's right, only 1 in 10. About 40 percent don't see any real improvement, while half of them get worse. Why? Again, they practice the wrong thing or the right thing the wrong way. For most golfers, this is what makes putting seem so mysterious. If you work on the wrong aspect of your stroke, it can create a new problem somewhere else, and one by one you can go through every building block of your putting, systematically destroying them all.

In many cases, putting better is not difficult. In fact, it's often easier than what you are doing now. But whatever your situation, I encourage you to finish this chapter, then carefully read all of Chapters 11, 12, and 13 *before* deciding what you're going to do for your putting game. First determine what needs to be fixed, and then learn how to fix it before you try to fix it.

10.5 Fifth: Do It!

And when I say, "Do it," I mean "Do it properly 20,000 times." Note that I didn't say do it quickly and carelessly a few times, then hope for improvement. It takes 10,000 proper repetitions to begin to form a proper habit, and 20,000 to ingrain and own it.

Ten thousand repetitions is only 100 reps a night for 100 nights. In less than four months of grooving your stroke to be in-line and square through impact, you form a habit that can last a lifetime (with a little occasional maintenance). So many golfers hit balls on the putting green for hours and hours without improving anything, honestly believing that they're working on their putting. But bad practice is worse than no practice. Grooving bad strokes ingrains bad putting habits, and ensures poor putting over the long haul.

You also must practice in the proper place. Working on your setup, alignment, aim, and stroke mechanics should be done indoors with learning aids and feedback devices. Don't practice these fundamentals outdoors on real putting greens if there is no feedback for learning about them on these greens (Figure 10.5.1). And when you're working on a particular aspect of your stroke mechanics, seeing the ball roll on an unknown and unknowable surface can be a serious distraction.

As for feel and touch, the *only* place to practice them is on putting greens, playing games and competing, getting good feedback on your distance control after every stroke. (All the games, drills, and other methods for practicing and improving your stroke mechanics, as well as touch and feel, can be found in the next few chapters.)

Schedule your putting practice time so initially you practice about 80 percent of the time indoors with feedback devices, 20 percent outdoors on the putting green (Figure 10.5.2). After about three months, go 50-50 indoors and outdoors. As your setup, aim, alignment, and stroke mechanics fall into grooved and habitual patterns, your feel, touch, and green-reading skills will require as much work as the maintenance of those mechanics.

Where to Practice

1. Stroke Mechanics—INDOORS
   a. Pick your work area (building block)
      - Aim
      - Power Source
      - Impact Pattern
      - Ritual
      - Routine
      - Face Angle
      - Path
      - Stability
      - Flow-Lines
   b. Set up feedback device(s) carefully
   c. Focus on feedback
   d. Avoid real greens and real holes (too distracting)

2. Artistic Fundamentals—OUTDOORS
   a. Pick your work area (building block)
      - Touch
      - Routine
      - Rhythm
      - Green-Reading
      - Feel
      - Ritual
   b. Measure putt distances, set up feedback guidelines
   c. Focus on speed, distance, and break (forget mechanics)

Figure 10.5.1: Before you practice, know what you are trying to change, how it will look and feel when you do it right, and have the feedback to monitor your progress.

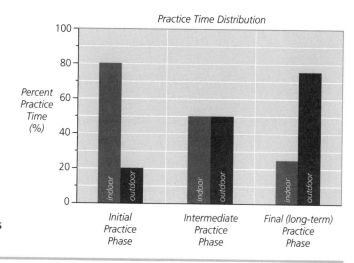

Figure 10.5.2: Practice some indoors (mechanics) and some outdoors (artistic fundamentals), always with feedback. Vary time allocations as your skill level dictates.

Remember, forming the habits of good putting is what it means to become a good putter. No one thinks his or her way through a good putting stroke, so knowing how to make a good stroke is not enough.

And before you work too long on your own, get periodic checkups with a knowledgeable professional. He or she can catch bad practice results before they become habit, as well as help maintain the interest and intensity needed for your long-term improvement.

CHAPTER 11

Establish Your Practice Framework

11.1 Set Your Ground Rules for Practice

The focus of this chapter isn't about practicing in the normal sense—that is, what most golfers think about when they think, "What should I practice?" Because (1) how you practice, (2) how you prepare before each practice session, and (3) within what framework (or foundation) you perform all of your practice, are all more important to the long-term success of your putting game than just *what* you practice. In the long term, everyone needs to practice at least several (and sometimes many) of the 15 building blocks of putting to be able to optimize their skills. What determines the success or failure of that practice (whether or not it is effective and produces good results), however, is how well you previously established your "conditions of practice," your "ground rules for practice," and the "framework within which" all of your practice was performed.

I refer to all of this as your framework for practice because it reminds me of the frame of a house in which I want you to perform your practice drills and games. It is the house of feedback, the house of successful practice, and the house of "what works later on the golf course under pressure." I hope you see my point, which is that no matter how long or how hard you practice to polish and refine the building blocks of your putting game, if you don't improve from that practice, or if what you learn doesn't fit into your putting game without messing up something else, then you have wasted your practice time and done little more than prepare yourself for frustration.

Your framework includes everything that precedes and accompanies your practice sessions (correctly setting Aimlines, using a metronome, getting the right putter fit, holding your finish, etc.). You have to get all the ingredients right, or else you won't improve. This may be more than you used to think of as practice, but I'm telling you, it's the only way to succeed.

If you're going to spend the time and effort to practice, then do it right. Many people—including students in my schools—seem to think they don't have time to practice properly, so they rush through it trying to "just get it done. " But then they find they have to make time to do it over again later, because it has to be done right. Save yourself the time and trouble and do it right from the start. You'll definitely see an improvement in your putting game.

Establish your ground rules for practice and adhere to them. Promise yourself that you'll always practice with the intent to improve, and with the feedback necessary to provide that improvement, however small. The key to adhering to such a commitment is to realize that you don't have to improve much each time you practice to become very good over the long haul. In fact, you shouldn't expect improvement to come quickly or in big leaps. Golf doesn't work that way. At best, you can expect to move a small (usually imperceptible) amount forward every time you practice. As a measure of success, be satisfied by seeing improved scores over time.

It's important to understand that practice makes permanent. So poor practice will only help you become a permanently poor golfer (and if you practice poorly, you deserve it). Only perfect practice helps move you toward perfection. My putting practice guidelines are listed in Figure 11.1.1. I hope that they will help you set yours.

These guidelines are the foundation (there's that word again!) for all my practice sessions. I follow them no matter what aspect of my putting I'm working on,

---

DP's Practice Guidelines

1. Never work on stroke mechanics outdoors on a putting green without a feedback device.
2. Spend at least 80 percent of my stroke mechanics practice indoors, with at least one feedback device.
3. Always use my personal body rhythm (natural stroke cadence) when practicing.
4. Always execute a practice *preview* stroke before stroking each ball. This allows me to practice moving into my setup as often as I practice my stroke.
5. Hold every putting stroke follow-through for at least five seconds.
6. Execute my ritual before every putt.
7. Never *ever* beat balls or practice carelessly. If I don't feel like practicing, I don't.
8. Always practice like I intend to play under pressure.
9. Keep practice balanced between indoor and outdoor (always do some of both).

Figure 11.1.1: In my commitment to improve, I always try to practice both smart and carefully.

believing that by doing so, whatever I learned or grooved during the session will stay with me when I get to the course.

Practicing this way does take more time than beating balls. However, it is infinitely more valuable and productive. And it's also more fun, because it always ends with a strong feeling of accomplishment, which is justified every time I go to the course and see good results.

11.2 Build Your Routine

To hit golf shots consistently, you must be consistent in what you do *before* you hit your shots. This is especially true in putting, where the margins of error for accuracy and precision are so very small.

The preshot routine for putting is the procedure you go through before every putt to properly prepare yourself to execute the perfect ritual and stroke. This routine of preparation starts immediately after you have decided what you are going to do (by reading the green), and prepares both your mind and body for how you are going to do it. Please note: Don't confuse the term "routine" (which refers to preparing to stroke a putt) with the term "ritual" (which, when talking about your preshot procedure, is actually part of the execution of your putting stroke, as you'll see later in this chapter).

The putting routine is different from the routine I recommend for the short game, which includes decisions relating to the lie of the ball in the grass, green conditions, hazards, and the management decisions made while weighing one shot against another. In putting, everything that precedes the preparation routine is included in your green-reading process, which I will deal with in section 13.3.

A Five-Step Routine
Assume you have walked off your putt distance, finished reading the green, and decided to play your putt dead-straight into the cup. It is now time to start your routine. In position—standing directly behind your ball on your selected Aimline—I recommend you build a routine that includes the following steps:

Step 1. While standing approximately six feet behind your ball in a fairly upright posture, with your eyes in a horizontal position, imagine your entire ball track from the ball into the hole, and as you do so, make three preliminary practice swings (Figure 11.2.1). The purpose of these swings is to get a first feel and vision of the stroke length required for this putt. Do this with your head up so your eyes are horizontal, providing perfect binocular vision of the distance. Look at the hole as you feel your swing, and try to imagine if your swing feels about the correct size to roll the perfect putt on the perfect ball track. Focus on the hole to see and feel the distance to it. Make your second swing while looking down at your stroke. Follow this with another look to the hole, again to judge and feel the distance.

Step 2. Walk to your ball along the extension of your Aimline. Try to keep your head and eyes directly above your Aimline (Figure 11.2.2), and internalize the

Figure 11.2.1: Routine Step #1: Make three preliminary practice swings to get a rough feel for distance. Imagine a ball track starting on the Aimline, rolling into the hole.

Figure 11.2.2: Routine Step #2: Walk along the extended Aimline, and internalize the Aimline into your eyes, mind, and body orientation.

direction of the Aimline in your body and your mind's eye as you walk and feel the slope of the ground under your feet.

Step 3. Set up four inches to the left of your ball, and take your putting address position, setting your body flow-lines to be aligned parallel-left of your Aimline (Figure 11.2.3).

Step 4. Make at least three, but not more than six, practice swings until you see and feel the perfect stroke that you imagine would roll an imaginary ball sitting four inches to the left of your real ball (Figure 11.2.4) along an imaginary ball track over an imaginary hole, to a resting point 17 inches behind and four inches

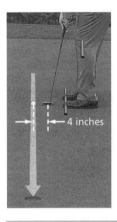

Figure 11.2.3: Routine Step #3: Set up parallel left of the Aimline, 4 inches left of your ball.

Figure 11.2.4: Routine Step #4: Make 3 to 6 practice strokes, imagining with each how an imaginary ball would track over an imaginary hole 4 inches left of real hole, and then stop 17 inches past. When you feel and see perfection, commit to it as your "preview" stroke.

to the left of the real hole. (Everything about this practice—the imaginary ball, ball track, and 17-inches-past point—should be four inches to the left of where you see the real ball track and hole, so when you move four inches over to address your putt, everything will be correct for the real putt, while still exactly the same as the way you just practiced it.)

Always make your first practice swing looking at the imaginary point 17 inches past, sensing and feeling the proper-length swing for the distance. Make the second swing while looking down at your imaginary ball, again trying to feel the perfect-size stroke. Make at least one more practice stroke while looking down, then look up after you finish the follow-through (holding it for a few seconds) and imagine your imaginary ball rolling to the perfect 17-inches-past point. If, after this third stroke, everything feels right and you believe a repeat of your third stroke will hole the real putt, commit to it as your "preview" of the best stroke you can make.

Step 5. With your decision that your last practice stroke was the perfect stroke, the one that will hole the real putt, you have created your preview stroke, the perfect stroke for making your putt. You have just seen and felt it in your mind's eye.

However, if you are not completely confident after a third practice stroke in Step 4, you are allowed one, two, or even three more practice strokes until you see and feel the perfect preview stroke. Once you feel it, commit to it and move into the address position for your real putt. Moving in is Step 5.

You're now ready to execute your putting ritual and stroke your putt. Your 5-step routine should have prepared you to make the best stroke you know how to make. The better you have seen and felt that your preview stroke was perfect, and the clearer the perfect stroke remains in your mind's eye, the more likely you are to make a good stroke when you actually putt (Figure 11.2.5).

Your Routine Can Be Time Variable

Your routine can be time variable—that is, you can make as few as three or as many as six practice swings, taking different amounts of time over each putt until you see each perfect preview stroke. How long this takes depends on your ability to concentrate under pressure. Usually, under normal playing conditions, most golfers feel ready after three practice swings (three is the minimum: one looking at the hole, one looking at the ball, one looking at the ball before looking up to the ball track). Under pressure, however, you may need some self-talk, saying to yourself, "Come on, pay attention. Will this stroke roll the imaginary ball at the perfect speed, just past the hole?"

If you have difficulty getting into your routine and feeling the right stroke, try purposefully making a stroke you know is too small so you feel what too small

My Recommended 5-Step Routine

1. Imagine your ball-track starting on Aimline
   - stand behind ball on Aimline
   - use binocular vision (eyes horizontal)
   - three preliminary practice swings (for touch)
2. Walk to your ball
   - internalize Aimline direction in mind and body
   - feel slope of ground under feet
3. Set up to imaginary ball 4 inches inside real ball
   - flow-lines parallel-left of Aimline
4. Practice swings: create and commit to "preview" stroke
   - 3 strokes minimum—6 strokes maximum
   - imagine ball rolling 17 inches past left edge of hole
   - commit to feel and vision of preview stroke
5. Move in and set up to real putt
   - eyes over Aimline (exact toe-to-ball distance)
   - one look to verify proper alignment to Aimline
   - pull "trigger" to initiate putting ritual

Figure 11.2.5: After your 5-step routine, you are ready to pull the trigger, step through your ritual, and sink the putt.

feels like. Then make a stroke that you know is too big. Now try to make one that's just right. This will get your mind's eye engaged in what you are trying to do, so you will be more successful.

Remember Your Job

Under the best circumstances, having felt the perfect-length preview stroke on your third practice swing, you must be prepared to repeat it within eight seconds. This eight-second limit ensures you will have retained at least 70 percent of the feel of your preview stroke in your mind's eye by the time you putt.

Notice I said to take at least three practice swings, or up to a total of six maximum if you need them. The purpose of your routine is to create the perfect preview stroke, one you truly believe will hole the putt. If you don't believe in your stroke, then you haven't completed your job no matter how many strokes you have taken. At this point, to avoid slow play you may have to compromise and putt with less than your best possible effort. But that's not something to be encouraged.

If you sense that you are taking too many strokes and taking too much time, then bear down. Focus, get into it, concentrate! Don't be lazy, and don't ever be so relaxed that you need more than six practice swings. That means you aren't trying hard enough to focus on your "job," not paying enough attention to what you are supposed to be doing.

Forget Stroke Mechanics

Your routine has nothing to do with your stroke mechanics. The purpose of a putting routine is to prepare you to putt with all decisions already made. You don't want to be thinking or still making decisions about your grip or how much the putt will break, or anything other than repeating your perfect preview stroke. During your routine, you must eliminate everything other than focusing on feeling and seeing the perfect-size preview stroke to roll the perfect-speed putt.

11.3 Find Your Rhythm—Measure Your Cadence

Whether you're on the golf course or just practicing, your movements should be at a rhythm compatible with your personality. So your routine and your stroke should be quick if you're naturally fast-moving, or calm and slow if your personality is laid-back. Whatever you do shouldn't take so long that it causes slow play, but it must be long enough to allow your mind's eye to focus on the job at hand. Finding your natural rhythm is especially important for your routine, because it's one of the instruments you use to turn your mind's-eye touch into your vision and feel for the putting stroke.

To find your natural rhythm, I suggest you run the personal body-rhythm test, which will help you determine the ideal speed of your routine, ritual, and stroke. You need an electronic metronome, your putter, and two pillows.

To take the test, you must know your normal walking pace. Take a stopwatch and find a flat street or field where you can walk back and forth. Walk until you fall into a smooth rhythm that feels comfortable. Once in the rhythm, start the stopwatch when your left foot hits the ground, and continue walking, counting the number of steps you take in 60 seconds. Repeat this three times, or until you're confident of your natural number of steps per minute walking pace.

Remembering that number, go back inside, and look at the chart in Figure 11.3.1. Pick the average cadence that corresponds to your steps per minute. (You'll also see the putting rhythms of a number of PGA Tour players, and how those rhythms compare to their walking speeds.) Once you've found your preliminary putting cadence, in beats per minute, set your metronome to beep at that pace.

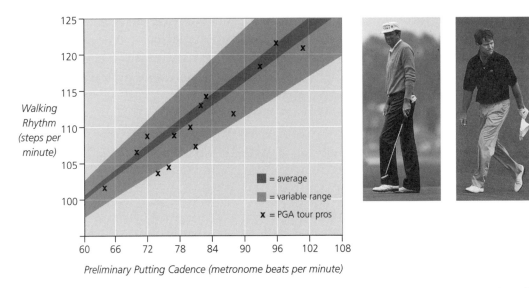

Figure 11.3.1: The faster golfers walk, the faster their putting rhythm (cadence).

The Touch-Touch Drill

Place the two pillows on the floor, 12 inches apart, and set your putter so it is addressing an imaginary ball between them. Place the metronome close by so you can hear it and adjust it conveniently. To start the test, place your putter between the two pillows (Figure 11.3.2) and begin swinging it back and forth. Work the motion into a rhythm that touches one pillow at the top of the backswing on one

Figure 11.3.2: Close your eyes, swing the putter back and forth, tick-tock, touching each pillow on a beat. Feel how much energy it takes to continue at this rhythm.

beat, the other pillow at the end of the follow-through on the next beat. Continue swinging your putter back and through, never stopping or changing rhythm, and continue to touch each pillow on consecutive beats of the metronome.

This is the "touch-touch" drill, performed at your preliminary putting rhythm. This likely isn't quite your best rhythm, so it must be refined until it fits you perfectly. Continue the drill, "touch-touch," back and forth, now with your eyes closed. Concentrate on how much energy you're using to execute this stroke at this rhythm.

Find Your Natural Rhythm

Stop and increase the cadence of the metronome five beats per minute (for example, if your preliminary setting was 80 beats per minute, set it to 85). Execute the touch-touch drill again, at the faster beat, with your eyes closed. Feel if this rhythm is easier or takes more energy than the first rhythm. (When you first run this drill, it may take several minutes to get the feel of energy required to swing your putter at each rhythm. But you'll quickly begin to recognize when a new rhythm takes more or less energy.)

If the higher cadence is easier, then adjust your metronome five beats higher and try again. But if the new cadence was more difficult, drop down by five beats per minute and it should feel easier. The goal is to find the precise cadence, to within one beat per minute, at which you swing your putter with the least amount of effort or energy. This is your natural body rhythm, the cadence at which your body moves most efficiently (using the least amount of energy).

After you find the most comfortable rhythm for the 12-inch swing, run the test again with the pillows first 18 inches, then two feet (24 inches) apart (Figure 11.3.3). If the rhythm is right, it will feel right on all putts, regardless of length. This entire test usually takes about 30 minutes, but it is time well spent, because all your putting from here on (in practice and on the course) will be at this natural body (and putting) rhythm, the rhythm at which you will putt your best, especially under pressure.

Figure 11.3.3:
Your natural body rhythm and putting stroke cadence should feel best at all stroke lengths.

Just as when you established a putting routine, finding your natural body rhythm doesn't have much to do with stroke mechanics. But the sooner you find your natural rhythm, the better, because it tells your mind that you'll always putt at this pace. It will keep you consistent as you develop the other parts of your stroke and setup. And most important, it will keep you from wasting time with any bit of stroke mechanics that won't hold up in the heat of competition.

That's why you want to determine your natural putting rhythm first. And remember it.

11.4 Create and Commit to Your Ritual

As explained back in Chapter 5, putting routine and putting ritual are two different things. The routine is creating all the information and getting comfortable with the stroke. The ritual is the "get ready, get set, go" that creates the rhythm and cadence of your backswing and follow-through. Your ritual is actually the first part of your stroke. It is a series of physical motions—made in your natural body rhythm—that immediately precede the making of the stroke. Your ritual should always be composed of the same physical motions, executed in the same sequence and at the same rhythm (therefore taking exactly the same amount of time, every time), before every putt you make, on and off the course (under the heat of competition as well as in all your practice).

The purpose of the ritual is to get your mind and body into the automatic (subconscious control) mode. Executing your ritual on the golf course under pressure the same way you've done thousands of times before on the practice green and at home on your carpet lets your subconscious know both what you're going to do and when you're going to do it. It removes the necessity for any thinking or decision-making before or during the execution of your stroke.

The ritual should take less than five seconds. Why? Because you will have just seen and felt your preview (perfect) stroke, and you lose about 30 percent of that feel within eight seconds after creating it. (And it will have taken you about three seconds to get set in your final putting address position after finalizing your preview stroke, to be ready to start your ritual.)

You Must Move Your Body

The ritual can be simple, but it cannot be mental. Your mind races when you're excited. Your heart beats faster, your brain tends to run faster, and time seems to fly when you're in the heat of competition. So you can't simply count "one, two, three, go" in your mind as your ritual. You must move your fingers, hands, arms, and/or body in a series of motions that you can see and feel. If these movements are out of rhythm, you can abort the stroke by backing off, walking away, and starting all over again.

If you can't execute your preputt ritual with good rhythm and timing, you almost certainly won't be ready to execute a good putting stroke, either. I've changed my ritual since my last book on putting, *Putt Like the Pros*, to make it last less than five seconds. While every golfer's ritual should be something he feels comfortable doing at a rhythm that fits his personality, I'll show you mine as an example.

My ritual is short and sweet, done to a count of five, at a cadence of 80 beats per minute. But rather than counting, I say the following words to myself: "down, look, look, back, through" (moving from left to right in the photographs in Figure 11.4.1). Just before starting my ritual, I lift my putter a quarter of an inch off the ground; this is my trigger, which tells both my mind and body that I'm ready to go, ready to start my ritual and strike my putt. It says that I've completed my routine, committed to my preview stroke, moved in from my preview stroke, looked at the hole once to make sure I moved in properly, and I'm ready to go (the trigger occurs after I've moved into my putting setup, just before I start my five-count ritual).

In the first photograph, you can see my putter up off the ground, which is my trigger. In the next frame, which occurs with the first count of my ritual, I tap my putter "down." Next, I "look" down my Aimline. Then I "look" back down at the ball, followed by starting the stroke (moving my putter "back" to the top of the backswing). The final step is "through," my through-stroke, which I hold at its finish until my putt stops rolling. Down, look, look, back, through. That's pretty simple. You should be aware that these two "looks" are not the same kind of looks you make when you want to see how far the hole is. The ritual looks are glances meant to move

Figure 11.4.1: My ritual proceeds with each movement completed on a beat of the metronome, at a cadence of 80 beats per minute.

my head in the cadence of my natural rhythm, to establish the rhythm for my stroke before I make it. And you should leave room in your ritual to build in one or two personal idiosyncrasies; you're likely to develop at least one. Most pros do. Nick Price, for example, sits his putter in front of his ball during his preshot ritual.

Practice the Way You Intend to Play

Always use your preputt routine, your natural putting rhythm, and your ritual during your practice sessions so you practice the way you want to make the most important putt of your life. Then, when that crucial, pressure-packed putt comes along, your stroke can be controlled by your subconscious, a natural reaction to your ritual, a simple repetition of the preview stroke you've just seen and felt.

To make your rhythm, routine, and ritual a habit, you need to have repeated them many times, over and over, the same way every time. And there's no better time or place to make these repetitions than when you're building and grooving your putting stroke mechanics. If you create your rhythm, routine, and ritual first, then use them throughout all training and practice periods, the powerful putting game you develop will be pressure-proof on the course.

Many golfers spend years developing their stroke mechanics only to putt miserably whenever they face pressure. This happens because pressure shuts down the conscious mind, forcing the subconscious to revert to whatever feels natural. If you practice and build a putting game as I've described—starting with rhythm, routine, and ritual—the stroke that your subconscious reverts to under pressure will be your natural stroke, the one you built, your best stroke.

Now you're ready to begin improving the more traditional parts of your putting game. But a last word about ritual and routine. Yours need to work for you and no one else. Don't copy mine or think anyone else's will work for you. Get on the practice putting green and think about what you'd like to do before facing the most important putts in your future. Without thinking about stroke mechanics, find a rhythm, routine, and ritual that work for you. None of the Tour professionals I work with use my ritual or routine. That may be where they start, but they modify them to fit their personalities and rhythms. You should—actually, you *must*—do the same. The rest of your putting life depends on it.

11.5 Flow-Lines

Most golfers find that the best putting setup is one in which all the flow-lines of their body are aligned parallel to their Aimline (Figure 11.5.1). Flow-lines—imaginary lines running through key parts of your body—are important because the stroke, the putterhead, and the ball move naturally in these same directions if the

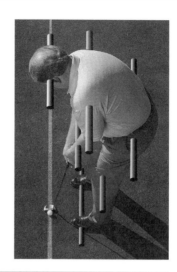

Figure 11.5.1: Your body flow-lines (illustrated with rods for clarity) dictate the natural flow motion of your putter and ball.

small muscles of the fingers, hands, wrists, and forearms are kept out of the putting motion. So set your flow-lines properly at address and you're well on the way to starting your putts in the right direction.

Shoulders Are Number One

The most important flow-line is that of the shoulders, the line running through your shoulder sockets. If your shoulder flow-line is aiming to the left, as shown in Figure 11.5.2, there's no way the putterhead can travel down your Aimline unless the muscles in your hands and arms get into the act, compensate against the natural flow direction, and push the putter and ball back toward the Aimline.

Figure 11.5.2: With the shoulder flow-line aimed left, the putter will swing naturally left, unless directed otherwise by the hand, wrist, and forearm muscles.

You can see most of your flow-lines by positioning your hands under your shoulders (relax and let gravity do the work—Figure 11.5.3) and pointing your index fingers toward each other. Assuming you've put something on the ground to indicate the Aimline, this "finger line" makes it easy to see when your hips, knees, feet, and shoulders are parallel-left of the Aimline. Once both your hands and shoulders are in this perfect position, simply swinging them back and through will create the ideal pure-in-line and square (pils) putting stroke.

The best learning aid for shoulder flow-line alignment is Elk's Key (Figure 11.5.4). "Elk" is Steve Elkington, who helped me design this device during our

Figure 11.5.3: From a relaxed position with hands under shoulders (left), you see your shoulder flow-line direction by pointing your index fingers at each other (right).

Figure 11.5.4: Elk works to get his shoulders parallel to his Aimline with Elk's Key.

struggles with getting his shoulder flow-line parallel to his Aimline. Elk's Key is set up to aim exactly on the Aimline; in your address position, you can see when your putterface is square and your eye and shoulder flow-lines are parallel to the Aimline (Figure 11.5.5). I think practicing with this device has helped Elk win more tournaments in the last three years than he had in the previous 10.

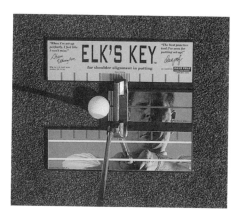 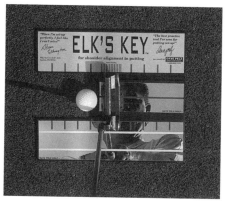

Figure 11.5.5: Proper shoulder alignment (left) vs. open shoulders (right) is easily visible as you putt with Elk's Key.

Vertical Shoulder Rotation

When you putt with a vertical pendulum (hands vertically below your shoulders), your shoulders should rotate in a vertical plane (moving up and down, not around). But many golfers (out of habit) rotate their shoulders around their spines horizontally because that's what they do in their other golf swings. If this is your problem, it's a habit you really should break.

Learning vertical shoulder rotation is easy. Get your putter and something light and about 36 inches long (a golf shaft, a wooden, metal, or plastic rod). Stand in a doorway (Figure 11.5.6) and connect the rod to your shoulders with rubber bands or hold it against your shoulders. Make sure the rod is tight to your shoulder line and that it's about one inch away from the wall on both sides when you take your putting address position. Stroke putts along an imaginary Aimline that is parallel to the doorway wall. If your shoulders try to move around horizontally, the shaft will hit the wall. Learning to make a pure, vertical swing with your hands and shoulders won't take much time. If you do this drill for five minutes a night for a couple of weeks, you'll probably never have to do it again.

Figure 11.5.6: A rod held by rubber bands to your shoulders should rotate vertically, never touching the wall, in a pure-in-line-square stroke.

Forearms Are Number Two

The second most important flow-line is that of your forearms. The usual error is to align it too far to the left (Figure 11.5.7). Many right-handed golfers set their forearms this way because it's the instinctive position for those using the conventional "right-hand-low (below)" putter grip. With their forearm flow-line pointing left, most golfers cut across their putts (it's the natural flow direction) and

Figure 11.5.7: With the right forearm in the power position (outside or over top of left forearm), forearm flow-line aligns left, causing the putter to swing left of the Aimline.

compensate by opening their putterfaces through impact. To align your forearm flow-line parallel to your Aimline, either tuck your right elbow into your body or use the left-hand-low putting grip (both shown in Figure 11.5.8).

Eyes Are Number Three

When you stand behind your ball and judge the distance of the putt (both when green-reading and making your preliminary stroke as part of your routine), keep your eye flow-line horizontal to the ground. This is called the binocular position, because both eyes are working together and feeding a properly triangulated picture of the putt distance to your brain. This is the position from which you can best estimate distance.

However, everything changes as you address your putt holding your head over your Aimline, trying to align your putter and body to it. In this case, both eyes should be on-line—that is, vertically over the Aimline—to help orient your flow-lines and putterface to it. Many golfers unknowingly set their eye flow-line so it cuts across their Aimline to the left—because they stand open to the Aimline trying to "see-the-target" better—which ironically makes it more difficult to see their proper setup position correctly (shown in Figure 11.5.9).

During setup and alignment, your head should rotate along the vertical plane above your Aimline. It's best to turn your head this way, keeping your eyes in the plane of the Aimline to help orient your shoulder and forearm flow-lines, and ultimately your putter path, to your Aimline.

Figure 11.5.8: Tucking the right elbow into the body (left), or using "lead-hand-low" putting grip (right), aligns the forearm flow-line parallel to Aimline.

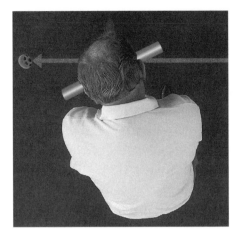
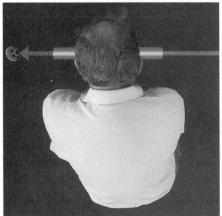

Figure 11.5.9: The better you keep your eye flow-line vertically above the Aimline (bad on left, perfect on right), the easier your shoulder and forearm flow-lines, and putter, orient themselves to the Aimline.

The Rest Are Less Important

The flow-lines of your hips, knees, and feet are important only inasmuch as they affect the flow lines of the "big three"—your shoulders, forearms, and eyes. So it is possible to stand with your stance closed or open and still maintain a properly aligned shoulder flow-line (as shown in Figure 11.5.10). However, I prefer to see my students set the flow-lines of their lower body square, starting with their toes an equal distance from their Aimline. The stance can have great influence on

Figure 11.5.10: Proper shoulder, forearm, and eye flow-line alignment is possible with closed (left) or open (right) stance. However, square stances make such alignment easier—and are recommended.

shoulder alignment, so there's a much greater chance of success keeping their shoulders and forearms in good positions if the lower body also is square to the Aimline.

A final word on flow-lines. Most golfers don't have much trouble setting them properly parallel to the Aimline on straight putts once they learn how and why to do it. Without this instruction, however, they aim their flow-lines in many different directions (Figure 11.5.11). This causes great difficulty when it comes to breaking putts, where they have no idea of where to align themselves. You can make all alignment simple by always forgetting about everything during setup except the Aimline: Concentrate on first setting up to it, then putting along it (Figure 11.5.12). This is just one more reason for going through the steps outlined in previous chapters (and the ones to follow) to help you find the perfect Aimline on every putt.

Figure 11.5.11: Setting up with flow-lines parallel to the Aimline is simple (left). A setup with the flow-lines askance tends to be inconsistent (right), especially on breaking putts.

Stance and Ball Position

The perfect putting stance, assuming everything else is normal, is to set your feet shoulder-width apart. (In section 4.10, I explain that stance width is measured from the center of your feet and the center of your shoulders: Wider than this is okay, but sometimes a little uncomfortable; narrower usually is not as stable.)

Once you're standing properly, the ball should be positioned just ahead of the bottom of the stroke arc, so it will be launched only slightly upward at impact (Figure 11.5.13). For most golfers, this puts perfect ball position about an inch

Figure 11.5.12: Choose your Aimline and commit to it. Use your preputt routine to orient your mind and body to it. Then setting up with the flow-lines parallel to your Aimline becomes automatic, even on breaking putts.

bottom of stroke arc

Figure 11.5.13: Launch putts slightly upward (out of footprints), but not enough to bounce.

and a half (almost the diameter of one ball) behind the instep of the lead foot (Figure 11.5.14), and—this is important (as you'll see in section 11.7 below)—vertically under your eye flow-line. An easy way to see and measure this position is to practice with a small mirror on a flat floor (it helps to place a thin piece of colored tape down the middle of the mirror to represent the Aimline). Once you see that your stance is perfect relative to the Aimline, and that your eyes are vertically above the Aimline, measure the distance between your toe line and the inside edge of the ball. This distance, as shown in Figure 11.5.15, is usually about the length of

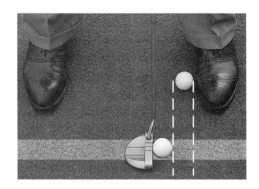

Figure 11.5.14: When the stroke arc bottom is near stance center, optimum ball position is about one ball inside lead foot instep.

Figure 11.5.15: With eye flow-line vertically above Aimline (left), the toe line will be one to two putter-lengths (right) from the ball (different for different golfers).

two putterheads, and should stay the same for all your putts on level (or nearly level) putting surfaces. When putts are significantly above your feet, you can stand slightly farther from the ball (but never more than an inch and a half, one extra ball diameter), and for balls below your feet, a little closer.

11.6 Fit Your Putter

A properly fit putter is important, but it's not the top priority in helping you putt better. It may not even be in the top 5 or 10 (it's hard to tell without seeing and measuring your putting game in person). A well-fit putter is nice, it feels good, and it may make proper setup and aim a little easier. But putting success depends to a far greater extent on your ability to properly execute the right stroke at the right time. You need to know what to do and how to do it on the greens, and no equipment can change that.

The best putters of our time—from George Archer and Dave Stockton, through Ben Crenshaw, Loren Roberts, Greg Norman, and Brad Faxon, to Lee Janzen, the late Payne Stewart, and now David Duval and Brent Geiberger—could putt well with just about any putter. This is because each one has developed great putting skills and strokes that they grooved and own. No matter what putter you hand them, whether it fit them or not, they could use their own stroke (and setup, alignment, posture, and other skills) and succeed.

In Figure 11.6.1, you see the way I use a putter that is too flat to fit me and my stroke. Rather than change my posture to fit the putter, I've done the smart thing, which is to adjust the putter to fit my stroke (in this case, standing it up on its toe). Never do the opposite, which is to adjust your posture, stance, and stroke to fit a putter someone gives you. I don't care how much you like the way the putter looks or feels, if you can only use it by changing something that will adversely affect your setup or stroke mechanics—or any of your putting-game skills—it isn't worth it. (Of course, if you really have to have it, you can take it to a qualified pro or club-fitter and perhaps have it adjusted to fit you.)

Having said that putter-fitting isn't all that important, understand that a poor fit (especially to a beginner) can be a significant deterrent to a golfer's ability to learn to putt, and, to some extent, even keep him from making good putting strokes. I see this in some of our students, occasionally even with lower-handicap players who are in love with a putter for the wrong reasons. Because when the structure of new equipment is wrong for a golfer, and he changes his posture or stroke motion to compensate for it, it's wrong. Then everything he has worked on, practiced, and grooved up to that point might as well be thrown out the window.

Figure 11.6.1: If asked to putt with a bad lie-angle (too flat) putter, I'd use my grooved set-up and stroke (no compensations) and set the putter up on its toe.

At this point, it's worth repeating what I said at the very beginning of this chapter: If you are going to practice, do it right from the start. Get fit with a good putter so you don't have to waste time getting fit and relearning later.

Two Ways to Fit

The essence of putter-fitting is to fit your equipment to your body, posture, and stroke mechanics so it allows you (and maybe even helps you) to develop and groove the best stroke you can make. It must allow you to practice putting without pain, and it must roll the ball on your desired Aimline when you make the proper moves.

Putters can be fit to golfers in two ways. One way is the "as-is" fit, which assumes the golfer will never change his stroke, will always putt the way he does at the time of the fitting. For example, if the golfer stands too far from, and open to, the line (Figure 11.6.2), the as-is-fit putter would have a very flat lie, plus head balance and shaft axis that would compensate for his propensity to strike the ball on the toe.

The other way is the "perfect fit." For this, the fitter assumes that the golfer will learn to putt from a perfect setup position, so he needs a putter of a particular length, lie, grip size, and so on to fit his body shape, size, and setup. And what happens if this golfer then changes to a strange posture? What if he bends way over at the waist, holds the putter far from his body, and crouches low to the ground? Then the perfect-fit putter wouldn't fit him anymore and he would find it awkward to use.

So what is the right way to fit putters to golfers? For the "perfect" stroke or the "as-is" stroke? It helps to know the golfer's intentions. If he's not going to come to a school, take putting lessons, or ever change his stroke, then he should be fit the

Figure 11.6.2: To fit a golfer's stroke "as-is," when he stands open and too far from the ball, the putter should be very flat (lie) and balanced to minimize energy loss due to toe mis-hits.

best way possible for the stroke he has. But personally, I prefer the perfect-fit method. Because if there is any possibility that he will work to improve his putting skills, especially his setup posture, then it's wise to fit him with a putter that will help him (or at least allow him) to make the best stroke he can. And sometimes having a perfect-fit putter might encourage him to work on improvement.

Putter-fitting is easy, painless, and can help make it easier for you to learn proper, noncompensating strokes from your most natural and comfortable body positions. If you have your putting equipment fit properly first, before you develop and groove your stroke mechanics, you won't have to relearn them later on to remove compensating moves caused by misfit equipment.

First Things First

Before you buy, bend, or cut any putter, look at the shape of the putterhead to be sure you can accurately see where it is aimed. I also recommend stroking a few putts with any new putter so you know if you like its feel of solid impact. If you can't aim a putter and you can't feel when it makes solid contact, it will require a lot more learning before you fall in love with it. And I say "learning" because you can learn to love a putter even if you hated its looks when you first picked it up. I can testify to this, as I have experienced success with some awful-looking putters that "putted themselves pretty."

So, one more time before we get into the details, you should understand the primary purposes of putter-fitting: (1) to allow you to set up properly as you learn stroke mechanics; (2) to not screw up your already established stroke mechanics (assuming they are good); and (3) to help you aim better.

How the Trevino Story Unintentionally Hurt Golfers

There was a widely circulated story about Lee Trevino going to a used-club barrel, finding a putter he liked, and using it to win the 1972 British Open, at Muirfield in Scotland. While true, the story has probably hurt more amateurs' putting than you'd ever think possible. Lee credited his win to great putting and his newly found putter. But the press didn't realize that the putter put his hands in a better position, helping him putt better because it helped his already smooth-as-silk stroke. They reported about Lee's magic putter, which sent legions of golfers scurrying to find any and every old, cheap putter they could get their hands on. A "found" putter may have worked for Lee, but for every such story I've heard over the years, I know of maybe a thousand cases of my students picking up new putters that ruined (or at least damaged) their putting. A badly fit putter can hurt you, while a perfectly fit putter will usually only *not* hurt you. A perfect putter usually won't make your stroke better, it won't make your green-reading any better, and it certainly won't knock the putts into the hole for you.

I put the odds at a thousand-to-one that a new, questionably fit putter will help you putt better. Every once in a great while, a golfer finds a putter with a head he can aim better or that sets him in a better position (like Lee's hands). But even then it usually doesn't last, because the golfer doesn't understand what happened, moves on to another bad habit, and starts putting poorly again. As for that magic putter? Well, it must have lost its magic, so back into the garage, or another barrel, it goes.

That's what putter-fitting can't do. Let's see what it can do, and what you should do about it.

Lie Angle and Shaft Length

These are the two specifications you should get fit first. Starting in a perfect setup position—eyes vertically above the Aimline, hands vertically under the shoulders, shoulder and forearm flow-lines parallel to the Aimline, posture and back-to-hip angles comfortable—there is only one lie angle and one shaft length that will position the ball exactly at the sweetspot of the putter (Figure 11.6.3), while connecting the putterhead to your hands.

By the way, the shaft can be a little long without hurting the overall balance. As long as you can move your hands down the grip, you're fine. But don't let it get so long that it gets caught in your clothing, especially in any rain gear or other weather wear. Unfortunately, that's a mistake most golfers don't realize they've made until too late.

Figure 11.6.3: The lie angle and shaft length of the perfect-fit putter positions the putterhead properly behind the ball and connects to your hands when you are in perfect set-up posture.

You Must Commit

So you have a putter with the lie angle and shaft length that fit your posture. And you like how it looks and feels at impact. Now, before you begin an improvement program, you must make a promise to yourself. You must commit to using that putter, and no other, for at least six months.

That's right. I want you to stick with this putter for at least the first six months that you start working seriously on any part of your putting, especially stroke mechanics. You're going to go through a lot of changes as your brain receives the feedback from your improving knowledge and stroke, and I don't want it confused with anything that doesn't really matter. So pick a putter, get it fit (professionally is always best), and promise to stay with it through thick and thin as you learn to putt with it.

The Long Putter

How do you know whether or not you'd putt better with a long-shafted putter (Figure 11.6.4)? Give one a try, and not for just two or three putts. Work with one for several half-hour sessions. The long putter offers several advantages over ones of standard length: There's no breakdown of the wrist joint during the stroke, and there's no rotating of the forearms, so golfers are less likely to try controlling the putterface.

I also like the long putter because it looks something like the pendulum of a grandfather clock, so it helps golfers understand the concept of the pendulum motion. It's for this reason we use long putters (in one session) in my Scoring

Figure 11.6.4: The pendulum motion of a long putter is a simple (and valid) way to putt.

Game Schools. We have every student swing a long putter as a way of seeing and feeling pure pendulum motion. We also have every student try putting with one. Having done this with many thousands of students, we've seen a very interesting result: In every school, students hole more short putts (inside six feet) with a long putter than with any other type of putter or putting method.

I never try to convert golfers to a long putter, because I believe everyone should putt with the shaft length with which they hole the most putts. But I do believe all golfers should at least give a long putter a try. It's good to feel the rhythm of the pendulum motion, and many golfers actually improve their putting with standard-length putters after spending some time putting with the long one (because they can easily feel the pendulum motion and rhythm, and experience putting without any wrist motion or breakdown, which helps their normal putting motion).

Minimize Hand Control

When you try the long putter, there is one thing you must do. Make sure you let it swing through impact without controlling its face angle. So rather than wrapping your lower hand (the right hand for right-handed golfers) completely around the shaft, giving you the opportunity to make it rotate through the stroke, take a grip that minimizes hand control. I've found the claw and fingertip grips (Figure 11.6.5) the best options for achieving this. Allowing the right forearm and hand to control the putterface and rotate through impact erases the advantages of the long putter.

The long putter has been a godsend to many golfers, giving them a chance to enjoy the game again after that enjoyment was taken away owing to problems with regulation-length putters. Of course, it wasn't the length of their putters that

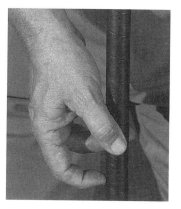

Figure 11.6.5: The fingertip (left) and claw (right) grips minimize hand and forearm control of face angle with a long putter.

caused their difficulties, it was some problem with their strokes. But once a golfer tries, tries, and tries again to improve his putting without success, it's easy to lose confidence and fall into a state called the "putting yips" (see section 14.9).

Putting with a long putter is such a dramatic change that many golfers don't carry over the habits they formed with standard-length putters. Long putters give these golfers a new start.

Are You Limited to One Putter?

I am frequently asked if I think it is smart and/or acceptable to carry more than one putter at a time. My answer is always the same: "Only if you will putt better and score lower by doing so."

In all honesty, I'd carry five putters if I thought they would help my putting and lower my scores. I think carrying 11 clubs for the power game (about 35 percent of your shots), two clubs for the short game (about 20 percent of your shots), and one club for the putting game (43 percent of your shots), is a pretty poor distribution. Shouldn't you choose the tools that will help you shoot the lowest scores?

If you putt better with a long putter on short putts, then you definitely should carry one for handling short putts (remember, short putts—under 6 feet—comprise one-half of all putts). If, at the same time, you lag your long putts closer to the hole with a short putter, then carry one of those, too. The USGA is very fair in this regard: They say you can't carry more than 14 clubs, but they don't specify which 14 they must be. So if, for some bizarre reason, you found you could make more 10- to 15-foot putts with a six-inch-long putter, then I would recommend you carry one of those, as well. I kid you not. If you want to carry two putters, more power to you. Quite a few students leave our Scoring Game Schools carrying two putters and four wedges, and play the best golf of their lives (Figure 11.6.6). But be sure to test for distance efficiency and then commit to a particular putter for putts of a particular length before you play. You don't want to be deciding on the course which putter to use.

Shaft Axis

An often overlooked component of a putter's construction is where the shaft connects to the head. It's important because it helps determine the axis around which the putterhead rotates, which can help minimize head rotation on mis-hit putts. As discussed in section 4.9, it's important to make consistent contact on, or as near as possible to, the sweetspot. (Review that section if you don't remember how impact patterns correlate with handicaps.) Golfers who tend to mis-hit toward the

Figure 11.6.6: Carrying two putters in your bag for different-length putts is perfectly okay.

toe of their putter—their impact pattern resembles the one in Figure 11.6.7—should look for a shaft that connects to the head closer to the mis-hit area, that is, farther away from the heel of the club. With this toe-impact pattern, a heel-shafted putter will twist dramatically at impact, feel bad in the golfer's hands, and send putts rolling weakly off-line to the right. Conversely, golfers whose misses are toward the heel should use a heel-shafted putter.

The important principle here is to get your mis-hits to occur near the putter sweetspot or between the sweetspot and the shaft axis of rotation of your putter. But never take this to an extreme, which would be making contact on the side of the shaft axis opposite the majority of head weight and the sweetspot. This would cause the heavy side of the head to flip over dramatically and produce a terrible putt (which can be done with "almost-center-shafted" putters). Two of the smartest golfers I know, Lee Trevino and Jack Nicklaus, have used heel-shafted putters throughout their careers. They learned from experience that their best results are with heel-shafted putters, because when they make bad strokes, they

Figure 11.6.7: Golfers with toe-impact patterns should not use heel-shafted putters.

usually miss toward the heel (between the sweetspot and the shaft axis, as recommended above).

Head Balance: Heel-Toe Weighting

There's good news and bad news regarding the balance of a putterhead. The good news is that the more a putterhead is "heel-toe" balanced—more of its weight is placed toward the ends of the head—the less it twists when mis-hit. (In scientific terms, such a putter is said to have a higher moment of inertia.) In general, this is good, and explains why heel-toe-balanced putters have sold well over the years: Putts hit away from the sweetspot roll a little closer to their intended speed and line. Of course, no putter can make putts hit away from the sweetspot roll perfectly, but the greater the heel-toe weight distribution, the more forgiving the putter is on mis-hits.

Now the bad news. The less a putter twists when mis-hit, the better it feels. That sounds good, right? Well, think about it. Using a putter that feels good even on mis-hits lets golfers get sloppy with their impact patterns, which leads to long-term degradation of putting performance. I've seen many Tour players initially putt well with a heel-toe-balanced putter, but then later begin to putt poorly and not know why. They were mis-hitting but didn't realize it because the putter masked the feel of a mis-hit. When this begins, they usually switch to a non-heel-toe-weighted putter until their stroke mechanics and results improve.

If they ask me what to do, I offer slightly different advice. I think the advantages of heel-toe-weighted putters are significant and shouldn't be given up. But I don't want the pros developing a sloppy stroke, so I suggest that they continue using a heel-toe-weighted putter on the course, and when they practice use a device called the "Teacher Clip," which trains your stroke to sweetspot contact (Figure 11.6.8). This combination helps keep impact patterns tight (more on this in section 12.3) while still being somewhat forgiving on the course.

Figure 11.6.8: Practice with a Teacher Clip on your putterface. The protruding clip prongs deflect mis-hit putts, providing feedback to train your stroke to the sweetspot. Remove the Teacher Clip for play on course.

As much as I like heel-toe weighting, I won't use a putter, no matter how for-giving, if it means sacrificing easy and accurate alignment (more about alignment in section 11.7). In the long run, good putting means consistently striking putts on the sweetspot. Do that and you won't have any problems with head balance or putter twisting. And that's why you see as many Tour pros putting with non-heel-toe-balanced putters as putting with strongly heel-toe-balanced putters. Hit putts on the sweetspot and there is no difference.

Golfers' Grips

However you choose to hold on to the putter, your grip should present the putter-face to the ball in a square position through impact, keep your forearm flow-lines in good position, and allow you to feel the flow of your stroke.

There's no doubt that the grip is important. But there is no one grip that is best for all golfers. The most common is the "parallel-palm" grip (Figure 11.6.9): Holding the grip along the lifeline of your left hand, instead of in the fingers (as in the power grip used on full-swing shots) helps the putter function as part of your arm and decreases the tendency to supply power with your hands (Figure 11.6.10). Keeping the palms parallel to the face of the putter also makes it easy to keep your forearm flow-line in good position (parallel to your Aimline).

Something else, which very few people talk about, is spreading the hands apart on the grip. The farther apart they are, the less active the wrist muscles in the stroke, which explains some of the success of the long putter. But spreading the hands also makes it difficult to coordinate the actions of the arms, so it is imprac-tical on a standard-length putter (although you might try moving your hands apart a little bit just to see what happens). Unfortunately, once you find a good

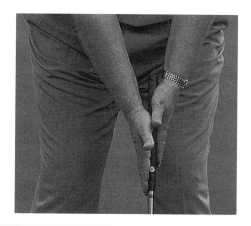

Figure 11.6.9: The "parallel-palm" grip keeps both palms parallel to the putterface, and the back of the lead hand aimed parallel to the Aimline.

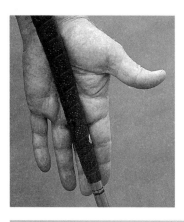

Figure 11.6.10: Gripping in the lifeline of your hand (left) instead of your fingers (right) helps to minimize hand and wrist power in the stroke.

grip, I don't know of any feedback devices that help you groove hand positions accurately other than using the flat surfaces of the putter grip itself.

There are many acceptable ways to hold a putter, such as the "reverse-overlap," "finger-down-the-shaft," "split-grip," "equal-hand," "push-hand," and "baseball" grips (Figure 11.6.11). But without seeing you putt, I can only suggest that you test and evaluate a few grips as you work to improve your stroke mechanics. Sometimes changing a grip can affect the path and face angle of your putter through impact; more on that in the next chapter.

Unusual Grips

Many players have found less conventional grips that work for them. These grips may be different, but they have proven comfortable and consistent. Take, for example, Corey Pavin's "opposed-palm" grip (Figure 11.6.12). Corey's problem used to be missing to the left. He pulled putts until he turned his left hand as far left on the putter as possible, which stopped the pulls because he couldn't turn his left forearm any farther left during his stroke. But then he started pushing putts to the right. The solution was obvious: Turn the right hand as far to the right as possible. So with his palms "opposed," he became a very fine putter, winning the 1995 U.S. Open at Shinnecock Hills putting that way.

While I said above that no one grip is best for everyone, "left-hand-low" (which really should be called "lead-hand-low") or "left-hand-low clamp" is one that I suggest every golfer try (Figure 11.6.13). Left-hand-low places the right forearm on-line with or slightly below the ideal forearm plane, taking the right arm out of the "power position" and allowing the left arm to lead or pull the stroke through. Perhaps the best recommendation I know of for the left-hand-low grip is the list of Tour professionals who are now putting, or have putted, this way.

Figure 11.6.11: Clockwise from top left: Paul Azinger—reverse-overlap; Nancy Lopez—finger-down-the-shaft; Dave Barr—baseball 10-finger; Jack Nicklaus—push hand; Andy North—equal hand; Mark Wiebe—split hand.

Figure 11.6.12: Corey Pavin's opposed-palm grip.

Occasionally uninformed golfers mistakenly refer to left-hand-low as "crosshanded" putting, but a true crossed-handed grip (which I never recommend to anyone) is shown in Figure 11.6.14. Left-hand-low doesn't work only for the pros. Only four years after taking up the game, a young man named Bob Zeigenfuss (Figure 11.6.15) made the world finals of the 1997 World Putting Championship putting left-hand-low.

Figure 11.6.13: "Left-hand-low" putting is great. Tom Kite (left), Bernhard Langer (center), and Fred Couples (right, plus inset) demonstrate their "left-hand-low" grips. Annika Sorenstam, Vijay Singh, Jim Furyk, Karrie Webb, Bob Estes, and Se Ri Pak are among the other great players who putt this way.

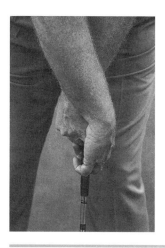

Figure 11.6.14: "Cross-handed" putting is terrible. You would have to be crazy to putt with your hands crossed.

My Man Rocky

Now, if you *really* want to talk about an unusual putting grip, you've got to meet my friend Bill Rockwell. Rocky (Figure 11.6.16) is one of the most inspirational people I've ever met. He lost his left arm and the use of his right arm in a motor-

Figure 11.6.15: Bob Zeigenfuss
putts extremely well "left-hand-low."

cycle accident a number of years ago. He watched the 1996 WPC competition on ESPN and said, "I can do that," so he bought a putter and tried putting for the first time. In July 1997, he won the putting championship at his local club, then qualified regionally for the WPC Finals. He finished 155th (in a field of 308) in the 1997 World Putting Championship, beating a number of PGA Tour professionals along the way. Ask him how he does it and Rocky answers, "Just like you do: I grab my putter and put the best stroke I can muster on every putt." I can tell you from studying his stroke that it's a good one. His "big-toe-right-foot" grip definitely keeps his putter square through impact!

Figure 11.6.16: Bill Rockwell out-putted a number of PGA Tour professionals in the World Putting Championship. Rocky's "big-toe-right-foot" grip really works!

Putter Grips

The size, shape, and orientation of the grip on your putter should be appropriate for the size of your hands, while allowing repeatable placement of your hands to encourage your best possible stroke (promoting solid contact and a square putter-face through the impact zone). Satisfying these requirements should come before worrying about the factors most golfers look for in a grip—how it looks, how it feels, and what pros use it.

Appropriate size means allowing for a comfortable hold and a feeling of control. The grip should not be so small that the fingers wrap all the way around to the opposite side and interfere with placement of the hands; nor should it be so large that it cannot be held securely.

Shape is not just a matter of personal preference. The Rules of Golf say that a grip may not aid in the placement of the fingers or hands. They also state that the shape must be symmetrical as it runs down the shaft, and that flat areas are allowed as long as they extend along the shaft axis (so there can be no twisting, undulating, or notches). Many golfers prefer a flat section along the top of the shaft, giving them a way to comfortably place their thumbs and position their palms parallel to the face. Such a grip is fine—and this is my rule, not the USGA's—as long as it allows your natural hand position to swing the putter square to the Aimline through impact. In fact, testing the Tour pros I've found that quite a few putted better when the flat side of the grip was rotated 90 degrees (toward the target side) so the flat surface is parallel to the putterface and fits against the palm of the leading hand.

No matter what grip you use, it is extremely important that it be installed squarely and correctly, not the slightest bit crooked or twisted, which would create an incorrect face angle at impact even if your hands were positioned perfectly square to the Aimline. (And if you get used to a crooked grip, realize that it's also almost impossible to replace it in the same crooked position when it wears out.)

There is no one perfect grip for every golfer, but for every golfer there is a perfect grip. It may take a little while for you to find yours, but it's time well spent.

Head Weight

The head design of the putter you select should be compatible with your ability to align it, hit it solidly, and have a good feel for distance with it. Heavier putterheads encourage golfers to swing more slowly, sometimes leaving putts short; however, heavier heads are good if your hands tend to be overactive during the stroke. Lighter putters give golfers with pendulum strokes a better feel for distance, because they can make a large swing without rolling the ball too far; but in the hands of a golfer with a handsy stroke, a lighter head can be a disaster.

If you suffer from the putting yips, try a putter with extreme weight in both the head and the shaft. While not a cure, it can help smooth out a yippy stroke, allowing you to get through impact and keep playing and having fun while working on the problem (discussed in section 14.9).

Shaft Flex

Most golfers never consider the flex of their putter shaft, but it is something that can help, or hurt, your success. Ben Crenshaw uses a very weak and flexible shaft, because he wants to feel when his putterhead is in perfect rhythm with his stroke. He also wants to feel if his rhythm is off. Most graphite putter shafts, which are both flexible and light, help do this, too.

Another great putter, Deane Beman, pioneered a completely different line of thought. Beman was a Tour player known for his great short game and putting before he became PGA Tour Commissioner. Deane wanted the stiffest, strongest shaft he could get, so the shaft wouldn't add or subtract any energy he didn't want. To determine which shaft suits you, test them on very long putts and see which provides you with the best touch and feel for distance.

Loft Angle

The loft of a putterface can be defined several ways, but only one matters to you. You need only care about its effective loft—that is, the loft angle relative to the surface of the green at the moment of impact (Figure 11.6.17). This is not necessarily the loft of the face relative to the shaft, and it certainly is not the loft of the face relative to the sole of the club. The effective loft of your putter is what determines

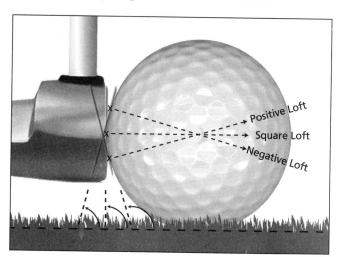

Figure 11.6.17: Effective loft angle of the putterface relative to the green surface determines where the putter contacts the ball.

where your putter makes contact—above, on, or below the ball's center of mass.

This point of contact combines with the angle of approach of the putter to determine the initial launch conditions of your putt. And yes, putts do "launch": Depending on how they are struck, they can launch down into the surface of the green, skid horizontally across the green surface, or launch upward—and do any of those with backspin, overspin, or no spin at all.

I recommend that you launch your putts ever so slightly upward, to get them on top of the grass as quickly as possible, without giving them so much loft that they bounce on the green. Because balls tend to sit down in the grass and footprints, this slight upward launch helps prevent them from having to start their roll through these potential hazards. One or two degrees of loft—relative to the surface of the green through impact—is usually enough. (If you're putting on grass with very strong grain, or on very bumpy surfaces, use a few more degrees of loft to get the ball on top of the blades more quickly.) As I mentioned earlier about ball position (section 11.5), the best results occur when impact is made with your putter traveling slightly up and away from the bottom of your stroke arc.

Offset and Onset

Figure 11.6.18 illustrates two variations in shaft/putterhead alignment. "Offset" means the face of the putter is positioned slightly behind the shaft, while "onset" is the opposite, the face slightly ahead of the shaft. Most golf shops display about an equal number of offset and in-line (shaft and face on the same line) designs; onset is much less common, but it does exist. And with a little extra looking, you'll find a few extremely offset or onset models.

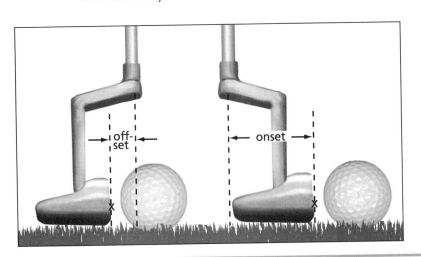

Figure 11.6.18: Distance between shaft axis and face determines offset (left) or onset (right) of a putter.

What do these designs do? Many manufacturers say that offset helps get the face square at impact and encourages crisp contact, but I know of no data that proves these claims. And I doubt their validity, since most of our students come to the schools using such putters but very few have their clubfaces square at impact.

I've run some tests with onset putters, and the results are generally positive. Most golfers seem to putt well with onset putters, saying they make it easier to see down the Aimline. Despite this, there's been no shift to onset putters or a demand for them. My staff will continue testing these designs, but until we have some con- clusive evidence, I suggest you run your own tests before buying one type or the other (or, for that matter, a straight, in-line-hosel putter).

Face Material

At the Pelz Golf Institute, we have a pet theory (not to be confused with experi- mental data or proof) that the best putter would have the softest face, because it would create the most friction. This theory is based on our knowledge that the ball follows the face-angle direction of the putter at impact more closely than it follows putter-path direction, while golfers have more control of the putter path (see Chapter 4 for details). So if softening the face would help the ball follow the putter path more closely, then softer faces would give the golfer more control.

The following example is a ridiculous exaggeration, but will let you see the basis for our theory. Imagine a putterface made of soft, sticky chewing gum. At impact, the ball would stick to the face so the player could follow-through to the hole, hold the putter over the hole, and shake it until the ball fell into the cup (Figure 11.6.19).

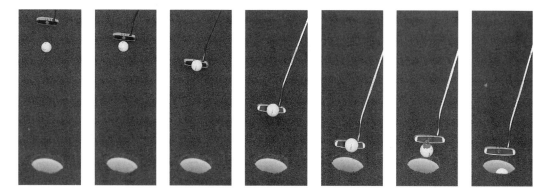

Figure 11.6.19: A chewing-gum-face putter would stick to the ball, allowing a follow-through to the hole and then a shake to hole every putt, every time.

How Times Change
About 25 years ago, when I got into the golf business full-time, one of the major golf-equipment manufacturers became tremendously successful selling heel-toe-weighted putters by promoting their specially heat-treated harder faces. In the last few years, that same manufacturer has switched to making and promoting putters with soft-material face inserts, again with great success.

Such a face eliminates the effect of face angle, allowing the ball to follow perfectly the path's direction.

Of course, such a putter would be illegal, and no one wants golfers to make every putt, regardless of their skill. But when you realize that golfers practice their stroke path while having no idea how to improve face angle through impact (and back in section 4.8, I showed how face angle has a much stronger effect than path on putting success), the thought of a softer, high-friction putting face that conforms to the Rules of Golf creates some interest.

More soft-face theory can be found in the many ads for putters that have a soft insert. These ads promote their putters' "softer feel," "better roll," and "greater control." In looking at test data to see whether or not a softer face really does make a difference in how accurately the ball follows the putter's path, I saw no measurable difference in putt direction off faces of plastic, wood, steel, and copper (within the accuracy tolerances of the test setup). But this is only one test, and we will refine our procedures and improve the accuracy. I will report the results when they become available, but until then, I'm very comfortable saying that while soft-faced putters may feel and sound better, those on the market today won't make large differences in the direction your putts roll. If these faces do have a significant benefit other than a more solid sound (which is nice), it's probably in lessening the dimple effect, as discussed in section 9.10.

The bottom line: Run your own tests of different putting materials to see if one works better for you on short putts while preserving your feel for distance on long putts. No one can do this for you, so take a little time, visit your golf professional or local golf shop, and test a bunch of different putters for yourself.

Comfort

This is an often overlooked element of putter-fitting, because many golfers don't think it's about the putter at all. Also, since the golf ball doesn't care how comfortable you are, you could argue that your comfort is unimportant. However, all other things being equal, the more comfortable you are while practicing putting, the longer you'll practice and the better your putting will become (assuming you're practicing properly). Your putter should be fit so you can be physically comfortable enough to practice sufficiently to learn to love and trust it on the course.

Another kind of comfort is how much you like the way a putter looks. You don't have to be comfortable with a putter's looks, or be comfortable standing over it, when you begin practicing with it. But it doesn't take a degree in physics to know that your comfort level will increase once you start holing more putts.

Years ago, I had dinner with Raymond Floyd, who is definitely in my top 10 list of great "career putters," especially under pressure. Ray told me that he thought his best results came with a putter that was shorter than standard length, but it hurt his back to practice with it. So despite his own evidence, he committed to and always used a longer-than-normal (38-inch) putter (Figure 11.6.20). He explained that the additional length let him stand up straighter, taking some strain off his back muscles so he could practice for hours on end. The ability to practice longer translated into more trust in his putting under pressure.

Ray's experience is a good lesson to all golfers: If you can't practice with a putter, don't even think about using it when the heat is on. So while comfort isn't everything, especially when you first try a putter, it's not something to be ignored.

Commitment

Something else you can learn from Raymond Floyd's experience is that you must commit to, practice with, and stay with a putter for an extended period of time before it can become your best friend. I don't have proof of this, but I have enough circumstantial evidence that it's something golfers should consider. The great putters stick with their putters for a reason. George Archer, Ben Crenshaw, Loren Roberts, and Bob Charles always seem to use their old, favorite putters (Figure 11.6.21). Why? Results. These old reliables fit them, let them make repeatable strokes, and let

Figure 11.6.20: One of the great pressure putters of all time, Raymond Floyd uses a longer (38-inch) putter to allow his back to withstand long periods of practice.

Figure 11.6.21:
The world's great putters stick with their favorite putting tools over the years. You should, too.

them hone their good putting habits (such as square face alignment at the moment of impact) to a fine tolerance.

The opposite example is that of Arnold Palmer, who, late in his career, took at least a dozen putters to the course with him every day. During his warm-up, if he made a few putts with one, it was in the bag for the day. No matter that the shaft and grip were different and the sweetspot was in a different place (relative to his hands) than on the putter he used the day before. I love and have great respect for Arnold Palmer as a person and a player, and it took amazing athletic gifts to do what he did (particularly with the putting stroke he had). But I wish Arnold had learned to putt with a simpler stroke, and stayed with one putter, so he could have putted even better for even longer.

Picking up a new putter every day, every week, even every month will do you more harm than good. If you think the problem is in the putter, have a competent golf professional properly fit the club to you, your body, and your stroke. Then— and this is key—commit to that club and commit to learning a better stroke with it than you ever had before. Once you learn a better stroke, keep your commitment to groove it. And, finally, once you own it, remember that you are only human, so you'll never be perfect, which means you'll have some bad putting days. But the good days will be much better than they used to be, and the bad ones won't be quite so bad. That's improvement!

11.7 Learn to Aim

If you are unhappy with your ability to align your putter, or you are just trying to choose between putters, check your alignment with every putter you consider. If by chance you find one that you can aim better than the rest, I recommend you use it. Alignment is the first fundamental of putting stroke mechanics; if you can't aim your putter and stand to your Aimline properly, you have little or no chance of making a repeatably pure stroke.

But remember, as discussed in section 4.4, aim is not just a function of eyesight. Rather, it is primarily a learned response to the way you miss. If you usually miss to the left, your subconscious will get you to aim farther to the right. If you usually miss to the right, your subconscious will aim you to the left to compensate.

I learned early in my teaching career that I could never successfully change a golfer's stroke compensation to pull putts to the left if I allowed him to keep aiming to the right. Of course, the opposite is also true.

Which raises the "chicken or the egg" question: Which comes first, missing to the left or aiming to the right? Well, I'm going to give you the "chicken or the egg" answer: I don't know. But more important, it doesn't matter, and golfers shouldn't care. Whichever came first, the other is always there. If you correct one fault but leave the other in place, the correction will soon disappear. To improve, you must always correct two things, the mistake and its compensation (correct only one thing and you'll probably putt worse).

In our schools, we have learned that the most efficient way a golfer can learn proper aim is to separate how it is learned from his stroke results. It usually takes three to six weeks of nightly practice with a feedback device. You can't do this outdoors, putting on a real green, because there is no feedback on proper aim there (whether a putt goes in or not doesn't show you where you aimed). In fact, it's possible to putt for the rest of your life on a putting green and never improve your aim.

The "LazrAimer"

The most efficient way to teach your brain what perfect putter alignment looks like (that is, when the putterface is perfectly aligned to your Aimline) is with a device called the LazrAimer (Figure 11.7.1). We use this device with every student in our three-day schools to measure their ability to aim and teach them how to improve this ability. The LazrAimer actually doubles the visible manifestation of the mistake (Figure 11.7.2), which is good because after practicing with it for a while and beginning to improve, it points out the remaining errors, no matter how small. Although three days of practice is not enough to learn to aim well, it gives students a start and makes them very aware of the problem. By the time they leave us, they know that if they don't learn to aim properly, any work they do to improve their strokes will probably be wasted.

The LazrAimer shines a low-power laser beam onto a small mirror attached to the putterface. After aiming the putter at the LazrAimer to the best of your ability, you say "on" to voice-activate the beam, which turns on for a few seconds,

Figure 11.7.1: LazrAimer (the box sitting on the floor against the wall) bounces a laser beam off the putter to teach direction of putterface aim error.

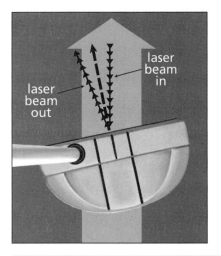

Figure 11.7.2: Laser beam reflects from the putterface mirror back to the wall, showing aim errors.

bounces off the putterface back to the wall, and shows any error in alignment.

Golfers who practice with this device dramatically improve their ability to aim, seeing results in as little as five minutes. However, by the next day, most of that improvement has disappeared. Our experience shows that it takes about three weeks for improvement to make it to the golf course. Even years after learning to aim properly, some Tour professionals work with their LazrAimers in their hotel rooms to keep their aim "spot-on."

Aim in the Putting Track

The Putting Track (Figure 11.7.3) is the poor man's LazrAimer. It can be very effective improving a golfer's ability to aim, but it takes much more time, as long as six months.

Every practice session must start with careful alignment of the Putting Track, aiming it precisely at a target that simulates the hole. With something heavy in place to prevent the target from being hit (and moved) by the putted ball, you set up parallel-left, execute your preview stroke, then step in, set up to the putt, and align your putterhead with the square-alignment lines on the track as you look at the target. Looking from your square putterface to the target gives you an accurate vision of proper aim, and over time is what teaches you proper alignment recognition. The track is neither as accurate nor as efficient as the LazrAimer at teaching alignment, but it does work over the long haul and is definitely worth a try.

Figure 11.7.3: The Putting Track provides feedback on stroke path (side rails), eye position (mirror on crossbar), and putterface alignment (stripes on rails and soda can as target).

Aim the Balance-Line

Many golfers improve their alignment by first aiming a line (or the printed words that form a line) on the golf ball in the direction that they want the putt to start (their Aimline). With the line properly aimed, they set the head of the putter perpendicular to that line as they address their putts. This isn't a new idea, but Tiger Woods (Figure 11.7.4) and Justin Leonard have been seen doing it on television so frequently that recently has become more popular. We ran a test of amateurs of all handicaps and found that a one-sixteenth-of-an-inch-wide line (preferably in red), at least one inch long, seemed to help golfers the most.

Figure 11.7.4: Tiger Woods aims a line on his ball down his Aimline.

Back in section 9.8 I showed that a ball rolls straighter along its Aimline if it is rolled on its "Balance-line" (shown in Figure 11.7.5). I've been recommending for years that golfers measure and mark their balls this way, then position them for putting with their Balance-line vertical and aligned directly along the Aimline. This means that the Balance-line can be aimed exactly along the Aimline from behind, it will help the putt roll straighter, and also serve as an alignment aid.

The Putter Face-Line
We've recently found a modification to the Balance-line, called the putter "Face-

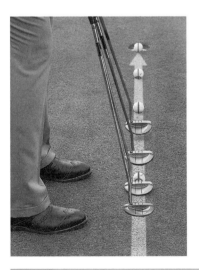

Figure 11.7.5: Using the Balance-line as an alignment aid also eliminates any off-balance ball effects, producing a pure roll.

line." The putter Face-line is a circle, centered on the Dot-Spot and perpendicular to the Balance-line, which means it will appear parallel to your putterface when the face is aimed squarely down your Aimline (assuming the Balance-line is aimed properly). The relationship of the putterface and the Face-line is shown in Figure 11.7.6; it may make proper alignment of your putter a bit easier to see.

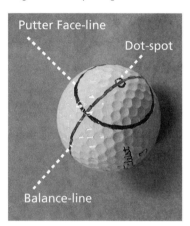

Putter Face-line
Dot-spot
Balance-line

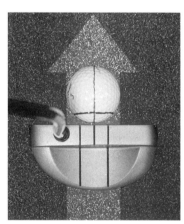

Figure 11.7.6:
When the putterface is parallel to the Face-line (which is perpendicular to the Balance-line), it should be lined up exactly square to the Aimline.

The Dot-Spot

In section 9.10, I explained the advantages of striking the spherical surface of the ball rather than the edges of the dimples. You can help assure this kind of solid contact by finding the "Dot-Spot" (the largest area of nondimpled surface) on the Balance-line. The "Dot-Spot" is usually one of the two places on every ball where the Balance-line crosses the seam: Every ball has a seam in its cover where the two halves are joined, and there's usually a little more surface area along that line than on the rest of the dimple-covered ball.

After identifying a Dot-Spot, mark the Face-line on your ball, centered on the Dot-Spot, which will make it exactly perpendicular to the Balance-line. This can get a little confusing, so we use a ball mask (as shown in Figure 11.7.7) in the following procedure for marking balls:

1. Measure the balance of your ball by spinning it in a Balance-line machine or floating it in heavy water. If you spin the ball, mark its Balance-line as it spins. If you float your ball, mark the light spot as it floats, then use a ball mask to apply the Balance-line through that spot after you dry it off.

2. Examine your ball carefully around its Balance-line and locate where the Balance-line crosses its cover seam (find the largest surface area on the Balance-line not recessed into a dimple), and mark it as the Dot-Spot (with small circle).

Figure 11.7.7: Center the Dot-Spot in the ball mask and mark Face-line with permanent-ink marker (mark four lines—rotate and mark again to complete a circle).

3. Center the ball mask on the Dot-Spot, and mark the Face-line (this takes two rotations and markings). Your ball is now ready for play.

4. After cleaning your ball on the green, always replace it with its Balance-line vertical and aimed down your Aimline. Make sure the Face-line and Dot-Spot are at the back of the ball (as seen in Figure 11.7.6).

5. Now execute your routine, align your putter behind the ball, start your ritual, and fire.

Aiming Conclusion

Since the margin of error in putting is so small, precise alignment is crucial, which means it's something you need to practice over and over. The best way to learn to aim is with a LazrAimer, periodically practicing with it to train your brain what perfect alignment looks like. The Putting Track can teach you to aim if you use it long enough (and always set it up properly). If you don't want to invest the money and time on either of these devices, at least mark your balls with their Balance-lines and Face-lines, and learn to use those lines to help you aim.

We've seen many students benefit from these improvements, and odds are that you, too, will see your putting improve as you learn to aim better. But you definitely want to test these aiming aids on the practice green before you commit to them on the golf course. It takes a little more time to line up your Balance-line with your Aimline, especially the first few times you give it a try, so practice doing it on the practice putting green to keep your play timely on the course.

Don't Forget about Your Eye Position

Finally, whenever you work on your aim/alignment, don't forget about keeping your eyes vertically over the Aimline. No matter how well you learn to aim on the LazrAimer or with your Balance and Face-lines, if you position your eyes differently for every putt, you have no chance of developing consistent alignment. Once again, don't misinterpret what I mean by "eyes above the Aimline": This does not mean exactly over the ball; one or both eyes can be behind the ball as long as they are both still vertically above the Aimline.

In the old days, to check your eye position, you could either drop a ball from beneath your eye line or have a friend stand behind you and say when a plumb line hanging from a point vertically below your eyes (usually about the tip of your nose—Figure 11.7.8) touched the Aimline. Now, however, since you know how to ensure your eye line is positioned vertically above your Aimline by measuring your toe-line-to-ball distance (see section 11.5), periodically check that distance during all your subsequent practice sessions. And remember, if you don't address the ball the same way every time, and use the same putter from the same posture every time, your subconscious can't learn to repeat, let alone submit to subconscious control, the habits of good putting.

Figure 11.7.8: Consistent alignment, no matter how you learn it, can only be maintained if you set up with your eyes vertically above your Aimline.

CHAPTER 12

Improve Your Stroke Mechanics

12.1 Refine Your Path

At last, we are ready to work on your stroke mechanics. And work on them we must, for they are what cause the ball to move. But instead of heading to the practice green as most golfers do—to putt for hours hoping something good will happen—you now know there are 15 ways (the 15 building blocks) to improve your putting, and grooving your stroke path is just one of them. Even more important, you know the stroke path you want to groove (pure-in-line), and you are committed to grooving it within a system of feedback, rhythm, flow lines, routine, and a ritual that won't let practicing this one area ruin some other aspect of your putting. You even believe that once you learn this path, you will be able to execute it under pressure on the golf course. Good, because believing in what you are doing is key to making it happen. So let's get to it.

I've already explained why the pure-in-line-square (pils) stroke (Figure 12.1.1) is the simplest and best. So grooving a perfect pils stroke would be ideal, but it should not be your goal. Because you are human, it will be impossible for you to be perfect every time. Your stroke will sometimes wobble and swing off-line. You're going to have less-than-perfect days. But that should not deter you. You can groove an *almost* perfect pils stroke, which you'll execute *almost* all of the time, and that is very good. With an almost perfect stroke, you'll almost make all of your putts, which is what the great putters do.

Put It in the Track

If you are willing to practice your stroke for a few minutes every few days in a Putting Track, your pure-in-line path will improve (Figure 12.1.2). How quickly is up to you: The faster you want to improve, the more often you practice and the more time you spend during each practice session (in that order, because frequent

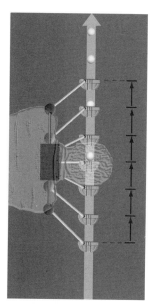

Figure 12.1.1: Hands hanging and swinging like a pendulum vertically under the shoulders, and the shoulder flow-line parallel-left of the Aimline, the pure-in-line-square putting stroke flows down the Aimline with precision.

Figure 12.1.2: The more you practice in the Putting Track, the more consistently your putter will swing in-line, and the purer the motion will feel.

short sessions are more beneficial than infrequent long sessions).

The Putting Track is the king of stroke-path feedback devices, because it defines the perfect path for your stroke and never lies about how you are doing: You'll hear and feel when you make a bad stroke, while you'll hear nothing and feel pure "noth-ingness" when you make a good one. The Track is inexpensive, easy to set up and use, and you can take it with you when you travel. It works at home, in your office, anywhere you have even a few minutes of free time (many Tour pros work with it at night in their hotel rooms). But it's crucial that you set it up properly and practice carefully. Some tracks don't have lines to show when your putter is square; others don't curve upward to follow your stroke all the way back and through. Use only ones with both, because practice without feedback is a waste of time.

Always aim the track carefully, standing behind it to ensure it is aligned precisely at your target soda can (when you sight with one eye, your putter shaft should run exactly through the middle of the track and the can, as shown in Figure 12.1.3). Use a book to keep balls from actually hitting and moving the can. (You don't need to see where the balls roll—who cares how the carpet breaks?) This drill isn't about the ball but about improving the "in-line-ness" of your stroke path, so keep your focus on making good strokes that don't make noise by touching the rails of the track at any time.

Figure 12.1.3: Never practice in the Putting Track without carefully aiming it at a target.

High-Intensity Feedback

Start with the track set up to provide one inch of total space (roughly half an inch on each side) between your putter and the side rails, and count how many of your strokes make noise by hitting the sides of the track. You want to set this space tolerance so you hit a rail on about 50 percent of your strokes, as that percentage is perfect for rapid learning from maximum feedback. You may have to adjust the rails for more or less space to achieve this level of performance (Figure 12.1.4). Practice about 10 minutes (about 50 putts) each session, multiple sessions each

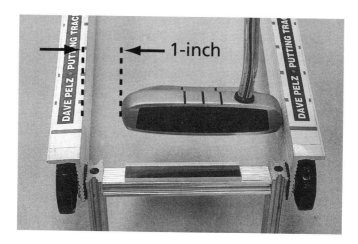

Figure 12.1.4: Set a half-inch tolerance on each side of putter in first practice session. If you bang rails more or less than 50 percent of strokes, adjust tolerance.

day if you want, until 80 percent of your strokes are quiet. Then it's time to tighten the tolerance to the half-noise, half-quiet level again.

Before you start each Putting Track session, set your metronome to your body-rhythm tempo and prepare yourself to optimize your address posture and flow-line positions as best you can. Assume your practice swing stance just outside the track (like your practice stance, four inches left of your real putts on the green), and make a preview stroke of the putt you are going to practice. Then move into your setup in the track (use tape to mark your perfect toe-to-ball distance) and execute your ritual before every putt. If you do all this, you're not only improving your stroke path, you're committing your setup, ritual, and rhythm, as well as your stroke path, to subconscious control (and habit) at the same time.

Don't be surprised if your first few practice sessions seem both physically and mentally taxing. You've probably never received so much feedback on your stroke before, and your subconscious may not be accustomed to working this hard. But this is exactly what you want, so keep it up. After a few sessions you'll begin to feel relaxed and see real improvement. That's when you're ready to add a few more feedback devices to the mix.

By adding Elk's Key (it should fit under the track without any adjustment), you optimize your shoulder flow-line learning (Figure 12.1.5). This is also a good time to start holding your follow-through position at the end of each stroke for five seconds (this habit will pay big benefits in later outdoor practice sessions).

The final addition to your Putting Track practice sessions is to work on making a pure-in-line-square, down-the-Aimline stroke on breaking putts. Don't do this right

Figure 12.1.5: After comfortable, and successful, practice in the track, add Elk's Key (shoulder flow-line), hold your follow-through finish, and, finally, move the soda can (hole) to practice breaking putts.

away, but after several sessions of good stroke-path results in the track, and when it's easy to hold your follow-through on-line for five seconds, make one small change. After aiming the track at your target can, put a small but visible piece of tape (any color, as long as you can see it) directly behind the can, then move the can six inches to the left. Now imagine you're looking at a putt with six inches of break, which requires seeing an Aimline that starts six inches outside the right edge of the cup. Don't change anything but the location of the hole in your mind's eye. Make your last look down the Aimline (at the tape, not the can), then execute a perfect in-track stroke and hold your follow-through on the Aimline (between the rails, without touching them). This is how you begin acclimating your stroke path to the Aimline for breaking putts. In the following session, move the can a few inches to the right of the tape, and practice a stroke for a left-to-right break of at least several inches. Go back to straight-down-the-line practice for straight putts in every third session.

Use the Elevated Aimline on the Green

After a few months, your path should be getting well grooved, and you will want to take some of your practice outdoors onto a green. Set up an Elevated Aimline (elastic string attached to two stakes running vertically nine inches above the actual Aimline) for a straight putt and be sure to hold your finish after each attempt so you immediately see if your path finished inside, on-line, or outside your desired path (Figure 12.1.6). Then find a 6-inch breaking putt and aim your Elevated Aimline 6-inches outside of the hole. See if you can keep your stroke under it, just like you did on your indoor breaking putt practice. But be sure you aim the Elevated Aimline properly when you practice breaking putts: You can't fool your subconscious, and you don't want to force yourself to follow through down a line that isn't right.

Another feedback device for checking your putter path is the Pathfinder (Figure 12.1.7). Several Tour caddies use these see-through plastic plates so they can

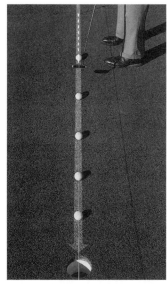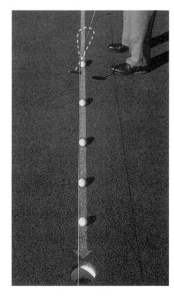

Figure 12.1.6: By holding your putter finish position, the Elevated Aimline will show you when you cut across (left), finish on-line (center), or loop inside to out (right).

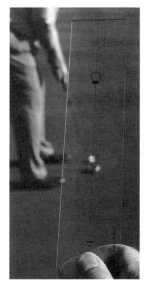

Figure 12.1.7: To use the Pathfinder, stand behind the golfer, close one eye, align the bottom circle on the ball and the top circle where he tells you he is aiming. Then watch the putter motion relative to the dashed Aimline running between the two circles.

give their players accurate practice-round feedback on their stroke paths. The Pathfinder is easy to use: After asking the player where his Aimline is pointing, the caddie places the ball in the lower circle and positions the upper circle on the Aimline (directly at the hole on a straight putt). The Pathfinder shows if the putter path moves along the Aimline or off-line.

12.2 Create Stability

For a stable stroke to be consistent (especially under pressure), it must accelerate through impact without the hands providing acceleration. It took me a few years to find a way to teach this before I realized that a smooth pendulum stroke, moving at a consistent rhythm, accelerates (and is stable) to the midpoint of its swing (that's the physics of pendulums). So when you create a perfect pendulum stroke motion at your natural body rhythm and contact the ball slightly before the halfway point of that stroke, you've naturally produced stability through impact. This means that if you centered your stroke motion ahead of the ball your follow-through will be longer than your backswing, and acceleration through impact will be assured. And as long as your follow-through is longer than your backswing and your rhythm is smooth, your putter will always be stable at impact, as shown in Figure 12.2.1. (You'll still make a slight upward strike by positioning the ball just inside the instep of your lead foot so it is ahead of the bottom of your swing arc.)

Figure 12.2.1: As long as the follow-through is longer than the backswing, the stroke is stable through impact.

Knowing that you should always putt with a stable stroke motion and actually doing it are two very different things. I want to show you how to learn to practice making stable swings so stability will become a habit and stay with you when you go to the course. To accomplish this, I first want you to learn three stable "reference" strokes (these will become your 6-inch, 12-inch, and 18-inch reference backswing strokes). Don't worry about what these strokes do, how they work, or what they are for. Just learn to make them and I'll explain them later. You need some thin strips of foam rubber that will fit across the width of your Putting Track, and some tape to attach the foam strips temporarily to the track. Don't use a ball.

Step 1. Stick two pieces of foam rubber across the side rails of the track, one each at 12 inches behind and 14 inches ahead of the ball spot (Figure 12.2.2).

Step 2. Place a dot sticker in the track, between the black diamonds on the rails, where the ball would normally be.

Step 3. With your metronome beeping at your natural body rhythm, address the dot as if it were a ball. Now execute your ritual and stroke to the beat, just as if you were putting. Make sure you touch the putter shaft to each piece of foam, back then through, on a beat.

Step 4. Hold your finish (shaft against forward foam) for five beats.

That completes one stable putting stroke (with a 12-inch backswing and a 14-inch follow-through), about what you would make for a 10-foot putt on the course. Your putter would have been stable at the point of contact with the ball and would have rolled a putt at about the optimum 17-inches-past speed for the average 10-footer. If you set up properly to the track, your shoulder flow-line was

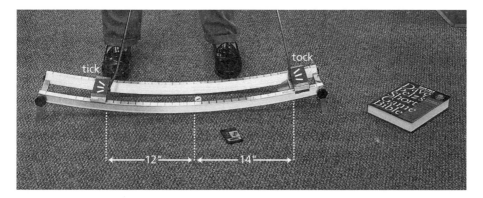

Figure 12.2.2: A reference 12-inch (backswing) stroke touches the back foam on one beat, and stops against the forward foam on the next beat.

parallel to your Aimline, your stroke was in perfect rhythm, you achieved stability without any hit or muscle power (because your stroke moved in sync with your natural rhythm), and you just saw and felt a reference 12-inch backswing putting stroke worth memorizing.

Do It Again, Sam

Now repeat this entire sequence 19 more times, the last 5 with your eyes shut. That's the entire stability drill for the 12-inch backswing stroke, and it should take less than five minutes. Do it again a few days later, except this time with the foam taped six inches behind the ball spot and seven inches ahead; this is the six-inch backswing stability drill, which rolls the ball about the perfect speed for a two-foot putt on most greens. The third reference stroke drill is for a 25-footer, and for this the foam should be placed at 18 inches behind the ball spot and 21 inches ahead.

These three stable reference strokes are typical of strokes you need on the course in every round. But by practicing with no ball, no pressure on results, and no distractions, you can focus solely on rhythm and feel. Doing these drills over a period of time (say, a few nights a week for six months) will embed the feel for stable (properly accelerating) strokes into your subconscious, and you'll begin using and feeling them on the course out of habit (an occasional repeat of these drills over the years will help keep bad habits away). Of course, you will use the 12-inch backswing stroke on longer and shorter putts, because green speeds vary and the putts may be running up- or downhill. But the rhythm and stability will be there. You'll feel them, sense them, and be able to call up these strokes from your subconscious simply by closing your eyes and searching for that feel as you are creating your preview stroke.

Everybody can benefit from the stability drills, but they are especially helpful to golfers who make good mechanical strokes yet decelerate into impact. If you're not stable (accelerating) through impact, every error you make is maximized in your results. Simply by making a tiny change from your present putting rhythm, you may be able to change your unstable stroke to a stable one. And if you do, your results will improve significantly, even dramatically, in pressure situations.

12.3 Groove Your Impact Point

If making solid contact between putter and ball is a problem, you can improve if you are willing to do some careful work. I say work because it will take about 20,000 solid practice strokes to make solid contact a habit. And I say careful because many golfers who try to change their stroke in search of more solid contact find themselves missing every putt to the right or left with their new solid stroke (because they practiced carelessly), and you don't want that.

The program we recommend has worked for almost every golfer we've given it to, without creating other problems in the process. It involves finding and marking your putter sweetspot, documenting your improvement progress, and maintaining a good stroke path while you improve your impact pattern.

If your putter has a mark on its top line, don't assume that is where you should address and strike your putts. Many manufacturers place those marks where they look good but don't do the engineering and quality control necessary to balance the putter weight so the sweetspot is really there.

Finding your putter's true sweetspot is one of the easiest chores in golf. The mistake to avoid is letting it hang vertically while you are doing it (Figure 12.3.1). You must hold the grip in your fingers so the shaft is angled to the ground the same way it is when you putt with it. This is key, because it keeps the putter properly balanced to the way you actually use it. Then tap-tap-tap across the face with a hard metal object such as a car key. When tapping away from the sweetspot, the putterhead will wobble and you'll feel the vibrations in your fingers. There will be only one spot along the horizontal axis of the putterface that will produce zero wobble and the vibrations are minimized. That is your putter's sweetspot.

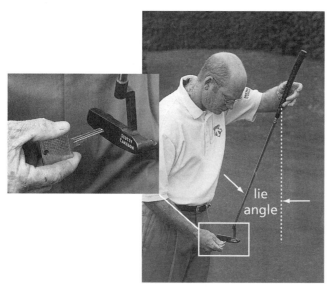

Figure 12.3.1: When you tap-tap-tap to find a putter's sweetspot, hold it at the same angle as when you putt (left); don't let it hang vertically (right).

Mark Your Putter

Once you've found the proper sweetspot, mark it along the top line of your putter with a permanent-ink marker, then tap-tap again to confirm your findings. When you are confident of the location, mark it permanently by filing in a small groove (a punch mark also will do), which you can fill with paint. This will give you a permanent identification of where to address and hit your putts.

If your putter already has a mark but you find it's in the wrong place, you can still indicate the proper sweetspot in a visually pleasing way. Again, tap-tap until you find the true sweetspot and mark it with a washable-ink pen. (Be sure to tap-tap one last time to verify that you have it marked right.) Measure the distance from the true sweetspot to the manufacturer's mark, then make a second mark the same distance from the sweetspot but in the other direction. Once you file a groove or other permanent mark on this new spot on the putter's top line, you'll have two marks with the sweetspot centered precisely between them.

Test Your Pattern First

Before you start practicing to improve the solidity of your ball contact, measure and document your skill (or lack thereof) in this area. Not only is this informative, but it will help you to see improvement and motivate you to keep working and improving later on.

Start your test by attaching a piece of Teacher Putting Tape on your putterface, being careful to position the center of the tape over the sweetspot (Figure 12.3.2). Also be sure to keep the bottom edge of the tape parallel to and just above the bottom edge of the putterface (so it won't drag on the green). Take 3 balls and hit 10 putts from each of three different distances—3 feet, 10 feet, and 30 feet (30 putts total). At each distance, putt from several different directions so this is a balanced test of uphill, right-to-left, left-to-right, and downhill putts.

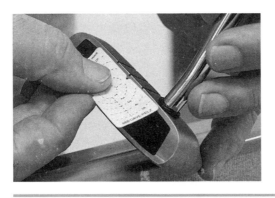

Figure 12.3.2: Carefully place Teacher Putting Tape just above the bottom edge of the putter, and centered on the sweetspot.

Remove the tape and place it in the booklet supplied with the tape, which allows you to keep an accurate record of your test results (the size and location of your impact pattern) and progress (Figure 12.3.3). Repeat this 30-putt test once a month, always placing the test tape in your booklet for a long-term record. After a number of months, you'll see the evidence of your improvement in grooving your impact pattern to your putter sweetspot and decreasing its size. But you'll improve only if you do the drills below.

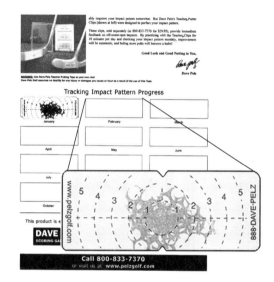

Figure 12.3.3: Keeping a long-term record of impact patterns documents your improvement (when you improve), or indicates when more work is needed (when you don't improve).

Sweetspot Practice

The best feedback device for teaching sweetspot impact is the Teacher Putting Clip (Figure 12.3.4). Teacher Clips are small, aluminum plates that stick to your putterface (using replaceable double-faced tape) with protruding prongs that bracket the sweetspot. Clips come in three tolerance sizes (standard, pro, and super-pro— shown in Figure 12.3.5), allowing less and less margin of error for missing the sweetspot before deflecting the putt severely off-line.

Start with the standard-size clip, taking care to attach it to the correct location on the face. Align Elk's Key at a target can, place a pillow or book to keep balls from hitting the can, and turn on your metronome to beep at your natural body rhythm.

1. With a ball in Elk's Key, address the putt parallel-left and four inches from the ball, as you do during your putting routine.

2. Make your preview stroke (whatever length stroke you intend to practice in this session), hold your finish as you commit to repeating that exact stroke, then

Figure 12.3.4: Teacher Putting Clips provide feedback by deflecting putts severely off-line when contact is not on or very near the sweetspot.

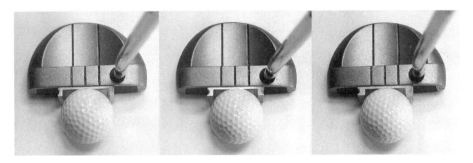

Figure 12.3.5: Standard (left), Pro (center), and Super-Pro (right) Teacher Clips progressively reduce the tolerance for mis-hits, to provide continuous challenge as impact patterns improve.

move in to your final address position for the putt (again, just the way you do on the course).

3. Look once down your Aimline to verify that you have moved in properly, start your ritual, and stroke your putt with your perfect-rhythm stroke.

4. Hold your finish for five metronome beats, and see and feel if you made solid contact with your putterface (Figure 12.3.6), or if you "pronged" the putt. If you pronged the putt, it doesn't count. Each practice session requires stroking at least 30 solid (no-prong) putts.

5. Straighten up, back away, and do it again.

Choose the Correct-Size Clip

After you've been practicing for 5 or 10 sessions (over a period of a few weeks), count the number of solid versus pronged putts in one session. For the most efficient learning, adjust to a Teacher Putting Clip tolerance so your putts are approximately half solid and half pronged. When you begin making about 80 percent

Figure 12.3.6: Make a preview stroke, step into a perfect set-up posture, execute your ritual, and hold your finish while you groove your stroke to the putter sweetspot.

solid contact, move to the next-smaller clip, which should reduce your solid contacts back to about 50 percent.

It may sound strange to hear me say this, but don't overdo this drill. One session every other day, 30 solid putts per session, is perfect. On the days between clip sessions, practice with your Putting Track to keep grooving your pure-in-line stroke path. This will prevent your subconscious from creating solid contact with the clips by making an unacceptable correction to your stroke path (and messing up your putting on the course, as alluded to earlier).

When practicing with Teacher Putting Clips (or doing any of the learning-aid drills in this book), keep a rational perspective on the point of your practice. Don't get discouraged when you prong five consecutive putts (which everyone does sometimes), and don't try to force or guide your putter to make solid contact. Always try to make good putting strokes in your natural body rhythm. You are trying to develop subconscious control of a solid-contact stroke that won't require thinking on the golf course. What you should think about is getting into a good setup with a perfect shoulder flow line position, standing a perfect distance from the ball, with perfect alignment to your Aimline (as shown by Elk's Key). Once in this starting position, don't think your way through the putting stroke, just let it swing back and through to the beat of your metronome, then hold your finish squarely down the Aimline for five counts. The rest will come with time and practice.

The Final Groove Drill

Several months down the road, when you are making 80 percent solid contact using the pro-size Teacher Putting Clip, you will have to make a choice about your next step. You can either move to the super-pro clip or begin using the pro clip inside the Putting Track (Figure 12.3.7). Both will help you groove a Tour-quality impact pattern.

Figure 12.3.7: After many, many sessions, you may be able to putt successfully with a super-pro Teacher Clip in the Track.

No matter which step you take, your ultimate goal is to become good enough to make better than 75 percent solid contact with the super-pro clip in the Putting Track, your metronome beeping, and Elk's Key getting you started perfectly every time. Once you can do that, you'll no longer have a contact problem. At that point, you'll find that your feel and touch for distance have improved dramatically, and you will be holing more putts on the course in the medium-length range. Your putting speed control will have improved significantly, and three-putting likely will be a problem of the past.

12.4 Fix Your Face Angle

If your putterface angle is not square to your Aimline at impact, you have a serious putting problem. In fact, you have at least two problems. Because face-angle errors are transferred to your putts so efficiently, if face angle were your only problem, you would probably be missing every putt. So in addition to your face-angle error, you must be making at least one compensation to counteract it (or else you really are missing every putt, in which case you're probably about to give up the game for good).

A Hard Truth About Compensations

Having more than one deficiency in your putting game isn't a life-long sentence. It just means you'll have to work on more than one correction at a time. And if your improvements don't come at the same rate, you may putt worse before you putt better. This is why I often recommend using several practice techniques (and feedback devices) simultaneously, or in tandem, one after the other. The problem and its compensation developed together, so it's best to get rid of them together.

I've seen too many well-intentioned golfers improve one aspect of their putting game, then lose that improvement when their putting results were less than they expected on the course, and give up. They reverted to their old ways or went off on a new direction looking for some other improvement (by trying a new putter, new grip, new stance, or new thought) and looking for instant gratification. You must realize, and regularly remind yourself, that you're not just removing problems, you're also trying to remove the problems caused by those problems (called compensations), so improvement may not come as easily or as quickly as you'd like it to.

If you don't understand and accept this truth, you're likely to remain very disappointed in your lack of improvement, and stuck at the same handicap for the rest of your golf career.

The Simple Tru-Putt

The easiest way to determine whether or not you are habitually making an in-swing face-angle correction during your stroke is with the Tru-Putt (Figure 12.4.1). Position your putter square to the end of the Tru-Putt and make a stroke. If your putter returns to square at impact, the way it was at address, the Tru-Putt will slide straight across the floor along the line perpendicular to your putterface (your Aimline). If, however, your stroke comes into impact with a face-angle adjustment relative to the way you aligned it at address, the Tru-Putt will tell you by rotating off the putterface and turning to one side or the other.

Because both the ends of the Tru-Putt and your putterface are flat, there's little room for error at contact. If your putter is closed at impact, Tru-Putt spins away with a clockwise rotation; the more the face is closed, the quicker the rotation. An open face produces counterclockwise rotation. My recommendation is that you practice with the Tru-Putt between three and five minutes twice a week, making your 6-, 12-, and 18-inch reference backswing strokes until you start producing straight-sliding rather than rotating Tru-Putt motions. Finish each session by stroking a few really long putts (imagine you're standing over a 70-footer) and a few very short ones (imagine 3-footers). Always leave enough room for the Tru-Putt to slide so you get good feedback on your face-angle performance. This drill

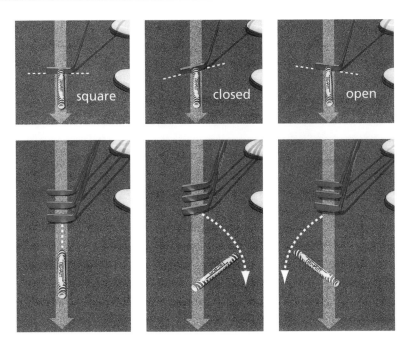

Figure 12.4.1: The Tru-Putt rotates clockwise if your putter is closed at impact (center), and counter-clockwise when hit with an open face (right). The Tru-Putt slides dead-straight down the Aimline (left) only when contacted with a square face.

is simple, easy, and inexpensive, but doesn't do anything for your aim and setup. So periodically intersperse your Tru-Putt sessions with some work with the Putting Track and/or Elk's Key to check on your stroke path, your eye and shoulder alignments, and with the LazrAimer to check your aim.

Putter Rails

Another good way to groove a noncompensating stroke with a good face angle at impact is to drill indoors with Putter Rails in the Putting Track (Figure 12.4.2). But don't do this until you're comfortable putting in the Putting Track without the rails. Start with the sides of the track spread far enough so you hit them no more than about half the time, then decrease the spacing as you improve (the spacing can be adjusted by placing the legs inside or outside the side rails, adding or subtracting washers, or by using a different-length spacer bar between the sides).

The Putter Rails attach to the putterface with double-sided tape. Stroke 50 putts per night, using all the same guidelines for careful practice mentioned in section 12.1 for improving your stroke path (metronome beeping at your body rhythm, target can aligned precisely with the Putting Track, Elk's Key positioned

Figure 12.4.2: Putter Rails add face-angle feedback to path practice when used in the Putting Track.

for shoulder flow-line monitoring, and tape indicating your repeatable toe-to-ball distance). When you first start using the Putter Rails, it will feel as if they are helping you hold your putterface square down the line. Close your eyes on every other stroke so you feel the square-face motion throughout your stroke path, all the way to the finish, and be sure to hold your finish for five beats of the metronome. The desired result of this drill is being able to swing your putter back and through the Track without the Putter Rails touching the sides at any time (Figure 12.4.3). This is the perfect no-touch, pure-in-line, and square feel you want to internalize and use on the course.

Figure 12.4.3: When you close your eyes and swing (with Rails on) through the Track without touching, you learn the feel of the pure-in-line-square stroke.

Success Breeds Success

Each time your no-touch Putter Rail success reaches 80 percent, tighten the track spacing and continue to practice this drill. By the time you reach the 80 percent success level and there's only one inch of total space between the Rails and the Track, you should be seeing a major improvement in your putting. And you can be confident that every good practice stroke you make in the Track with the Putter Rails is a stroke you can produce on the course under pressure—because, at the same time, you've also been grooving your ritual and rhythm, and committing control of your putting stroke mechanics to your subconscious.

Putter Straws

You can further work on face-angle improvement outdoors, this time on the practice putting green, with Putter Straws. It's a good idea to intersperse this outdoor Putter Straws with Elevated Aimline practice with your indoor Putter Rail practice sessions.

Putter Straws are a feedback mechanism we developed to convince golfers of the relationship between their putterface angle and their hands and forearms. With one straw on the back of my left hand and two straws on my putterface, it's easy to see this relationship when I look down and rotate my left forearm (Figure 12.4.4). Unless you let go of the grip, there will always be a consistent relationship between your left hand and forearm and your putterface. But golfers don't really understand and internalize this relationship until we make them look at what happens to the straws during a real stroke.

Watch my stroke (both the putterface and back-left-hand straws) on a straight-in, six-foot putt (Figure 12.4.5). In my pure-in-line-square stroke, my putterface stays square to the Aimline because my forearms never rotate around my body. Most golfers understand this after they see it, but they've never understood before

Figure 12.4.4: Whether my back-of-left-hand straw aims straight (left), to the left (center), or to the right (right), my putterface straws always do the same.

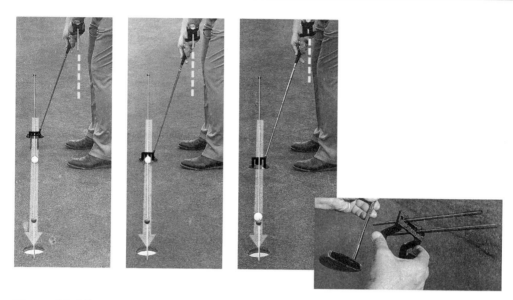

Figure 12.4.5: On straight putts, my pure-in-line-square stroke keeps my left hand parallel left, and the putterface straws straddling the Elevated Aimline.

why their putterfaces turned left after impact in their own strokes. The following drill helps them to both see and feel it:

1. Strap a straw to your forearm or back of your left hand.
2. Stick the Putter Straws gizmo on your putterface.
3. Find a dead-straight, 6- to 10-foot putt.
4. Install an Elevated Aimline from two feet behind your ball to over the hole (Figure 12.4.5).
5. Putt until you can keep the straws straddling the Elevated Aimline on your backswing and follow-through.
6. Hold each finish for five counts of your body-rhythm cadence. If you miss the Aimline with the straws, correct them to straddle the Aimline and hold them there for five counts.

Straight Putts First

Practice only straight putts until you can keep the Putter Straws aligned on the Aimline at the end of your strokes 80 percent of the time. Then try a breaking putt. Start with your Putter Straws set at the standard tolerance until you reach the 80 percent success rate; proceed through the pro level until you get to 80 percent, then change to the super-pro spacing. (The improvement process is the same as when practicing with a Track, Teacher Clips, and Putter Rails: The better you get, the tighter you make the tolerance for feedback.)

Many golfers are surprised to see that my arms and putterface stay square to the Aimline even on a breaking putt (Figure 12.4.6). But as you know by now, if you want your putt to repeatedly start rolling on the Aimline, your putterface needs to be accurately aimed there well through impact and beyond.

This drill may look a little odd on a putting green, but it gives golfers a clear understanding and feel of what causes their putterface to rotate. Remember, in almost every other golf swing, your forearms and hands rotate 180 degrees as they pass through impact. In putting, just a few degrees rotation may feel like nothing, but it's more than enough to destroy your putting results.

Figure 12.4.6: Many golfers just don't get it, but it's incredibly important. The best way to start putts on the Aimline—letting them then roll down off it and into the hole—is the pils stroke, which always stays on, and square to, the Aimline.

Truthboard

The final step in your elimination of putterface rotation should be use of the Truthboard (Figure 12.4.7), an aluminum ramp that is dead-flat so a putt can roll dead-straight on it. After you adjust the Truthboard to be precisely level (a level vial by the hole measures this), it provides a perfect surface on which to practice three-foot putts—no break to misread, no footprints, no spike marks, no poorly fixed pitch marks to affect the roll. When your putt is struck with a square face angle, the ball will roll straight up the ramp and into the hole. If your face angle is bad at impact, the ball will roll off-line and miss the hole. The Truthboard is

Figure 12.4.7: The Truthboard is always adjusted to be perfectly flat. No footprints, spike marks, no lumpy donut effects. Practice on the Truthboard removes the fear of three-foot putts.

designed to provide immediate, accurate, reliable feedback about your putter-face at impact. It reports nothing but the truth (by assuring perfect alignment at address, it ingrains a noncompensating stroke), and you can learn from that. Set up the Truthboard with the hole at full size, and level the board (adjust one leg until the level vial bubble is centered). Install toe-line tape to make sure you stand the correct distance from the ball, set your metronome to beep at your natural body-rhythm cadence, and use your preview stroke and ritual before every putt.

After making sure your putterface is square to start every stroke, roll putts firmly enough to hit the back of the hole before dropping in (they should produce a "double-click" sound, back and in). This assures optimum putting speed through the lumpy donut. Hold each finish for five metronome beats. The Truthboard drill progresses in stages as you improve your skill and ability to strike putts squarely. Drills at each level take about 15 minutes each day, and proceed as follows:

Stage 1: Putt 30 putts per session until you make all 30 in a row.

Stage 2: Putt 30 putts each session, rolling every other putt with your eyes closed, listening for the double click. Stay in Stage 2 until you hole 30 in a row.

Stage 3: After making 30 in a row, 15 with your eyes closed, add pro hole reducers (Figure 12.4.8) to make the target less than three inches wide. Putt at the pro level until you make 30 in a row, every other one with your eyes closed.

Stage 4: Add super-pro hole reducers, making the hole smaller still. When you make 30 in a row, half with your eyes closed, your three-foot stroke will be PGA Tour-quality. Once you achieve Stage 4 super-pro ability, only periodic maintenance will be required thereafter.

Figure 12.4.8: Truthboard hole width can be reduced to pro (left) and super-pro (right) tolerances for advanced stroke refinement.

Some Are Slower Than Others

Don't get discouraged if it takes you some time to improve with any of the face-angle drills discussed so far. Remember, all golfers, including you, have developed compensations for setup and aim errors, forearm rotation, loopy paths, and other mistakes. But of all the setup, aim, path, and flow-line errors I've been discussing in this and the previous chapter, face-angle error compensations take the longest to correct. And for that you can blame your subconscious, which has been controlling your face angle since you first picked up a putter. Your subconscious is accustomed to doing whatever it takes to get your putts to go toward the hole, but we're now telling it to do nothing, and as I said early on, the subconscious can be very powerful and very stubborn. So these drills can take some time to take hold.

Be patient, and let your subconscious come along at its own pace. If you use some or all of the face-angle learning devices I've mentioned in this chapter, you will quickly become accustomed to practicing with feedback. And when you see how much feedback helps, you may wonder why you were wasting your time in the past practicing on a putting green without really knowing what was wrong or how to fix it. By seeing and internalizing feedback as you practice, you are moving toward a wonderful place—being able to practice all parts of your putting game with feedback, and depending on improving from it.

A Great Practice Session

Perfect practice is an ideal, not a goal, because it is impossible to attain. But great practice is possible, even probable. You have seen several aspects of it above, as you learned how to work on the various building blocks of your putting game. Put them together and you can have a great practice session.

If you could ever use the Putting Track, Truth-board, Teacher Clips, Putter Rails, Elk's Key, and a metronome all at the same time, while simultaneously practicing your preputt routine and ritual, and holding each finish position for five counts, you would be practicing multiple aspects of your stroke mechanics. Just think how good it would feel when you made a perfect stroke under these conditions: Your ball would roll quietly, click-clicking into the center of the hole, and there would be no other sounds or feel from the Track, Rails, or Teacher Clips. You actually would feel the lack of any feedback, sensing only the knowledge that you had made a perfect stroke. And that's exactly the way it will feel on the course when you do it perfectly there.

> **Practice Smart**
> Once again, I want to mention that the learning aids mentioned in this book are not the only ones available. But they are the ones we use successfully in our schools. When you're evaluating any training device, the most important consideration is how much feedback it will provide as you practice. Let me stress again that practice without feedback is a waste of time. So if you don't use the learning aids mentioned here, that's fine. But please use other ones, so you can learn what you need to learn when you practice.

12.5 Retrain Your Power Source

I've got some good news and some bad news. Let's deal with the bad news first: Even after discussing all of the practice drills and learning aids above, I still haven't talked about your power source and how to improve that part of your putting game. The good news is that if you've been working on the drills and exercises already mentioned in this and the preceding chapter, you've already been learning how to work on it.

All the drills that deal with rhythm and the metronome involve work on your source of putting power. Because in the pure-in-line-square pendulum putting motion, rhythm and timing replace muscle power and hitting. That's not just good news, that's *really* good news.

Retrain Your Muscles to Be Quiet

By working on putting in your natural body rhythm, you also are working on *not* putting with the muscles of your hands, fingers, and wrists. You may be wondering, "How can I feel *not* doing something?" I assure you, it will come. You not only can, but you will learn the clean, pure feel of the dead-hands stroke.

What follows are a number of drills to help you recognize these perfect feelings.

Head Motion

Your head should not move during your putting stroke. If it does, particularly if it moves in the opposite direction that your putter moves, work on the "hair drill."

Stand facing a wall with the toe of your putter about half an inch from the baseboard and your hair just touching the wall (but don't rest your head against the wall). Execute your ritual and a putting stroke, hitting a ball if you like, but it's not necessary. If your head moves during the stroke, you'll feel your hair brushing the wall (Figure 12.5.1). Spend a few minutes a day for several weeks putting this way and you'll learn the feeling of not moving your head during the stroke. (If you don't have enough hair to provide good feedback, wear a soft hat.)

You also can get head-motion feedback outdoors by making putting strokes while watching your shadow. Find a reference object that won't move (like the hole in Figure 12.5.2) and stand so your shadow falls next to it. Then you'll be able to see any head movement during your stroke.

Figure 12.5.1: If you feel your hair brushing against the wall, you know your head moved.

Body Motion

I discussed body motion in Chapters 3 and 4, mentioning that I often see poor putters turning and sliding their bodies during the stroke. Body motion is harmful because (in addition to adding unwanted power) it influences the putter's face angle. Your upper body, shoulders, arms, hands, and putter are all taking a free ride on your lower body, so when your hips rotate, everything above them rotates, too. In Figure 12.5.3, you can see what happens when I lock my arms and putter to

Figure 12.5.2: The shadow test will show if your head moves during your stroke.

Figure 12.5.3: Without moving my shoulders, arms, hands, or wrists, my putter both swings and rotates (face angle) when my hips rotate around my spine axis.

my chest, then rotate my hips around the axis of my spine: My arms and hands didn't do anything, yet the putter moved and rotated.

The subconscious very often is aware of body movement, so it compensates, slowing the hands and arms so the ball won't roll too far. That might be an acceptable compensation, except that body motion is neither repeatable nor consistent, so the subconscious doesn't know what to expect from one putt to the next.

A common result is the unexpectedly weak putt that either doesn't make it to the hole or breaks dramatically to the low side. If you have this problem or suspect that your hips rotate or slide as you putt, practice putting with your hips against a doorjamb (Figure 12.5.4). Just as with the hair drill above, it won't take you long to learn how it feels to not move your hips.

Figure 12.5.4: Putt with hips pressed against a doorjamb to learn the feel of putting with no lower-body motion.

Stand in Cement

Here's a way to solve all of your lower-body motion problems, but it will work only if you have a good imagination and react to visualization. Stand over a putt and imagine that your lower body—from feet to hips—is inside a barrel filled with cement. Then imagine that the cement has hardened solid as a rock. If this image is vivid enough, you won't be able to move your lower body (Figure 12.5.5) when you putt. Try this on a practice green and I'll bet you leave the first putt short. (I accomplish the same effect in our schools by holding the student's body still.) Keeping the lower body still robs golfers of power they never knew they were giving to their putts, so they leave them short until they learn to putt without the extra motion.

Balance Board

If your hips slide forward or away from the hole during the stroke, try making putting strokes while standing on a balance board (Figure 12.5.6), keeping it bal-

Figure 12.5.5: Putting while standing in a barrel of hardened cement will keep your lower body still.

Figure 12.5.6:
Putting on a balance board is fun. It overstresses your balance muscles and improves your lower-body stability on the greens.

anced so neither end hits the floor. I recommend this device because it's fun and it gets the golfer to focus on his or her body motion and balance.

The balance board doesn't teach a motionless lower body, but it strengthens the muscles that influence balance. Stepping off the board after just five minutes' work, the balance muscles in your legs will be quivering and tired but your lower body will feel solid as you stand on the ground. If you use the balance board over a period of time (3 times a week for 12 weeks), your lower-body stability on the putting green will be greatly enhanced.

You can make your own balance board by attaching a wooden rod to a wooden platform about 12 inches deep and 18 inches long. But don't center the rod: Most good putters keep 55 to 60 percent of their weight on their forward foot, so attach the rod about 55 percent of the way to one end. Then stand on it with the small side toward your target as you stroke your putts (it takes more weight on the shorter side of the rod to keep in balance).

Eliminate Wrist Collapse

Changing wrist angles through impact (usually referred to as wrist breakdown or collapse) causes face rotation and putts to start left of the intended line (for right-handed golfers). This happens as power is being supplied to the ball by the wrist muscles, and happens most severely if the right forearm is overpowering the left arm at the same time (which it often does). As I've already said numerous times, powering putts with the wrist muscles will get you into trouble when adrenaline kicks in under pressure. Still, many golfers continue to control roll distance this way.

It is possible to make a slight hinge of the wrists—as demonstrated by one of the best putters on the PGA Tour, D. A. Weibring, in Figure 12.5.7—without affecting either the power (no adrenaline) or roll direction (as long as the hinge and the putterface stay down-the-line). But anything more than that becomes a

Figure 12.5.7: D.A. Weibring employs a slight down-the-line wrist hinge. D.A. keeps his putterface square, and as long as he doesn't transmit power through his wrists, his putting is great.

"power hinge" (Figure 12.5.8), certain to hit putts left of the target under pressure. Here are two ways to counter it.

Pendulum Filler

You can stop your wrist angles from breaking down with the Putt Triangle, a device that keeps your pendulum putting triangle intact, inhibiting any change in the relative positions of your left or right arms and hands (Figure 12.5.9).

Wearing such a device (there are many aids that serve this purpose) during any of the drills discussed in this chapter will allow you to feel the motion of a solid pendulum stroke. After a few sessions, you will begin to forget you have the Putt Triangle between your arms, because when you keep your putting triangle constant, you generate no feedback from this device. A sure way to accomplish this is

Figure 12.5.8: Powering putts with the wrist muscles is an invitation to putting disaster under pressure.

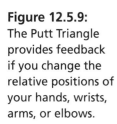

Figure 12.5.9: The Putt Triangle provides feedback if you change the relative positions of your hands, wrists, arms, or elbows.

to combine this practice with sessions featuring the Track and the Truthboard, being sure to make your strokes to the cadence and rhythm of your metronome.

Left-Hand-Low Grip (or Lead-Hand-Low)

The best way right-handed golfers can stop their right-hand wrist from supplying unwanted power to the stroke—as they usually do when they break down the left wrist—is to use the left-hand-low-clamp grip popularized by Bernhard Langer (Figure 12.5.10). After switching to this grip early in his career, he has played in 17 Masters tournaments (winning twice), was the world's leading money winner (1993), played on nine European Ryder Cup teams, and brought his world-wide victory total to more than 60. His left wrist never broke down once during all the strokes it took to accomplish these feats, so don't think this isn't a great way to putt.

Place your lead (left for right-handed golfers) hand below the trailing hand on your grip. This moves the trailing hand from a position of power to one of sub-mission during the stroke, meaning it won't control either the power or direction of your putt if it tries to add any adrenaline-aided power. This position also elim-inates the tendency for the trailing hand (usually the more powerful of the two) to force the wrist of the lead hand to break down and pull putts.

Vertical Rotation

Before we move on to the more "artistic" aspects of putting in the next chapter, let's discuss how your shoulders should move in the putting stroke. I'm not saying you should putt with your shoulders (although you could do worse), because

Figure 12.5.10: Bernhard Langer became one of the world's best players putting left-hand-low (note the in-line-square putterface at the end of the stroke).

when I do say that, golfers tend to move their heads in the opposite direction from their putters. Apparently they assume their heads are sitting on their shoulders, which they are not; your head sits on your spine. However, when golfers are told to rock their shoulders, they often rock their heads the other way (as seen earlier in the shadow motions shown in Figure 12.5.2).

But your shoulders will move when you swing your arms in a proper pendulum motion, and if your hands are vertically below your shoulders during this time, your shoulders should move in a vertical plane. To see and feel this motion, stand in the middle of a doorway with a long broom handle or something similar held across your shoulders (use two strong rubber bands to hold the rod against your shoulders, as shown in Figure 12.5.11). Without aiming at a target hole, swing your putterhead parallel to the wall. If you rotate your shoulders at all horizontally, the broom handle will bang into the doorjamb and immediately stop the motion. Just a few minutes of feeling proper vertical rotation motion, which does not touch the broomstick to the doorjamb, and you will get the right idea.

Figure 12.5.11: Swing back and through without touching the rod to the doorjamb, to feel pure vertical shoulder motion.

CHAPTER 13

Develop Your Artistic Senses
(Feel, Touch, Green-Reading)

13.1 Touch and Feel Are Different

I am frequently asked to explain the differences between touch and feel in golf. Many golfers use the two terms interchangeably without thinking about it (as I used to do). Now that I understand a little more about how much is going on in a golfer's mind and body, however, I think we need separate terms to describe these distinct attributes. Very simply (and you can read Chapter 5 again for more details), I liken touch on the greens to knowing *what* to do, and feel to knowing *how* to do it (as detailed in Figure 13.1.1).

With these distinctions, it becomes possible to focus on and measure your touch and feel abilities, and see if one, or both, needs improvement and work. I'll discuss how to improve touch first and then feel (as well as how to improve your green-reading) later in this chapter.

Touch	Feel
Touch is knowing WHAT IS REQUIRED for this putt:	Feel is knowing HOW TO SUPPLY what is needed for the putt:
• What is the length of the putt? • What is the speed of the green's surface? • What is the roll: uphill, downhill, flat, or some combination? • What size swing (what power) is required?	• How does this practice swing look for this putt? • How does this swing feel? • How far will this swing roll the ball if I use it? • How perfect is this preview stroke?

Figure 13.1.1: The difference between Touch and Feel.

13.2 Sharpen Your Touch

Good touch is knowing somewhere in your mind's eye what is needed to roll a good putt. It's knowing what the putt will require—how far, how much up- or downhill—and what it will look like as it rolls toward the hole. And it's knowing what the stroke that will produce that roll looks like before any of these things happen. Here's an example that might help clarify what touch is.

When I work with Tour pros on their putting, at some time in our sessions I want to make sure they understand what I mean by touch. So I ask them to evaluate my stroke for a 10-foot putt.

First they watch me make a stroke that is obviously not long enough. They say, "No, that's no good. That will never get the ball to the hole."

Then I make too big a swing and ask, "How about this?" and they say, "No, that's way too much."

Finally, I make a reasonable-sized swing (all three swings are shown in Figure 13.2.1) and they like it.

Then I tell them that they are using their touch to make these evaluations. Knowledge from within their mind's eye told them, just by looking at my swings, that my first stroke wasn't enough, my second was too much, and my third was about right for this particular 10-footer. On their part, this required knowing not only how long the putt was, but also how much power it required and how much power my stroke was likely to deliver. If their knowledge of all these was good, they have good touch. If it was perfect knowledge, they have perfect touch for that putt. But in either case, even if they knew perfectly well what was needed, they may or may not have the proper feel to produce that perfect stroke.

That's touch, knowing how long the putt is, knowing how much power it will require to roll a ball there, and knowing what stroke would provide such a roll. Now let's work on improving yours.

Figure 13.2.1: For a 10-foot putt: My first stroke (left) is too short; my second stroke (center) is too long; my third stroke (right) is about the right size.

Seeing (Recognizing) Distance

To have good putting touch, you first must know how long your putts are. When I began playing the game, no one worried about how long a putt was or, for that matter, the distances of shots coming into greens. No one had yet thought of using a yardage book on the golf course, and no one walked off distances from sprinkler heads. (Of course, they weren't marked with distances.) Veteran players said knowing the actual yardage would hurt your game because it removed feel. They said they could *see* the distance. However, things have changed with the times.

Today, there isn't one player on the PGA or LPGA Tour who doesn't use yardage books (as well as pin sheets) to know the absolutely precise distances of the game. It has been proven that it's better for your game to *know* your distances than it is to *see and guess* them.

This also holds true for the length of your putts, although few realize this (yet!). While you can be fairly accurate (to within a few feet) just by looking at and guessing the length of a putt, your subconscious needs much more accurate information than that if it is going to consistently roll your putts to within a few inches of 17 inches past the hole. And there are times when your eyes can deceive you, times when things appear to be different from reality.

Optical illusions do exist, and on occasion putts appear to be longer or shorter than they are. These "tricks" are caused by the way light bounces off the grass, the shape of a green or hillside, a green's surroundings, even the position of someone else's ball on the putting surface.

Learn a Metric

You need to learn to recognize your putt distances accurately, and more important, how to incorporate that knowledge into your touch before stroking a putt. It doesn't matter if you learn to recognize your putt distances in feet, steps, yards, or aardvarks (which are generally about four feet long). Any measuring system (what scientists call a "metric") that lets you accurately judge and differentiate lengths consistently, from one putt to another, from practice green to golf course, and from one year to the next, will do.

I use a system that seems easy to me, and obviously to others, as it is very common. I measure putt-lengths in feet, based on how many of my normal walking steps it takes to get from my ball to the hole. I played football years ago, where I learned, with the help of the 10-yard marks on the field, how to take 10 steps in exactly 10 yards (30 feet). So "one step = three feet" has been my distance reference ever since. To measure my putt length, I walk between ball and hole, count my steps, multiply by three, and subtract or add whatever inches or feet remain at the end.

If you don't already walk this way, it's simple to learn. Measure your putter and learn where 36 inches falls (plus or minus) relative to its length. Find a level part of a practice green and mark off 10 yards with balls, using as a reference the 36 inches on your putter. Finally, measure how it feels to take three-foot steps by walking back and forth along your yard markers (Figure 13.2.2).

Figure 13.2.2: To use my metric (1 step = 3 feet), measure your putter for a 36-inch mark. Then place balls every 3 feet on a fairway or practice green. Walk back and forth until you learn to make 3-foot steps.

Know, Don't Guess

You can know, not guess, the length of your putts by walking them off. If you don't think this precision is important to your putting touch, think about this. On your next 40-foot uphill putt, as you stand behind your ball making your preliminary touch stroke for distance, do you want to think that it's "about" 37 feet uphill, because that's what it looks like, or know that it's exactly 40 feet uphill? That may not seem like much, but being off by three feet takes you outside the six-foot circle around the hole that you want to find with long putts. And that can be the difference between a tap-in second putt and a knee-knocking four- or six-footer for a save.

For the benefit of your long-term touch development, walk off both practice putts and real putts on the course. Remember, distance recognition is incredibly important to your touch, and if you're going to hone your stroke recognition (touch) to a fine degree, you've got to know exactly how far it is that you're supposed to roll the ball.

Triangle Drill

This is my favorite touch-development drill. Pick three holes. Walk from the first hole to the second, count your steps, and determine the distance. Walk from the second hole to the third and repeat your distance measurement. Then walk from the third hole back to the first, completing the triangle.

You now know the three distances of 12 different putts, as shown in Figure 13.2.3. First putt around the triangle in a clockwise direction, from the outside of each hole. Then putt around again in the clockwise direction, but this time from the inside of each hole. After these six putts, play the triangle counterclockwise from both inside and outside of the triangle. You've tried 12 different putts, four of each distance. By walking (and remembering) only three distances, you can test your touch to sense the subtle differences required for each of the four putting situations (back and forth, inside and outside the triangle) to each hole.

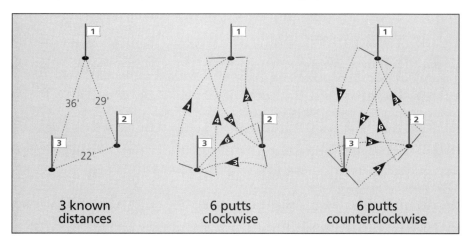

3 known
distances

6 putts
clockwise

6 putts
counterclockwise

Figure 13.2.3: Triangle Drill: By walking off and remembering 3 distances, you can practice your touch on 12 different putts.

Edge-of-Green Drill

Putting to the far edge of the practice green is a good drill for a course you don't know. It will both acquaint you with the speed of the greens and warm up your stroke mechanics. Take three balls and walk off the distance from one edge of the green to another. Putt that distance back to where you started from (Figure 13.2.4),

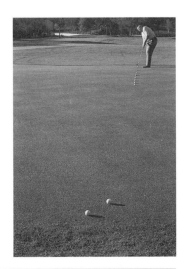

Figure 13.2.4: Edge of Green Drill: Lag 3 balls back and forth between edges of the green. Try to stop all the putts as close as possible to the edge without touching it.

trying to roll each putt exactly to the edge of the green without touching it. As you walk to your three balls, notice if you were putting with or against the grain. Then putt the balls back in the opposite direction, over the same distance to the edge of the green, to see if you can detect any differences caused by the grain. Doing this several times won't take long and will adjust your touch for the unfamiliar greens.

Draw-Back

"Draw-Back" is the best game of all for developing and refining touch for putts longer than 35 feet. Because the odds of making long putts are so poor, the real skill in lag putting is rolling your putts consistently close to the hole, taking the pressure off your short putting and eliminating any chance of three-putting. And Draw-Back is designed to develop exactly that skill. (The rules are listed in Figure 13.2.5.)

The reward in Draw-Back comes in lagging your first putt close enough to the hole so that after drawing it back 34 inches, the next putt is significantly less than six feet, so the probability of making it is great. You can play Draw-Back by yourself, but you will learn far more quickly if you play nine-hole games in competition with good lag putters and with something at stake. (I don't want to encourage gambling for money you might not have, but you need to care about winning each hole and each game if you are to see maximum improvement.)

Never play Draw-Back on putts of less than 35 feet. If you do, the training to your subconscious is to lag those close rather than trying to maximize your make-percentage by rolling them 17 inches past the hole.

Safety-Drawback

"Safety-Drawback" (rules in Figure 13.2.5) is a drill that you can play as a game designed to sharpen your touch on putts of less than 35 feet. The purpose is to exercise the ability of your mind's eye to recognize the stroke needed to produce the perfect putting speed and distance to optimize your chances of holing putts in this range. To develop your touch on these "makable" putts, you want to play Safety-

Rules of the Game

Drawback (DB):

1. Play for putts of 35 feet or greater.
2. Prior to each putt (except first), ball must be drawn back straight away from hole 34 inches, from spot previous putt stopped (use putter length—usually 35 inches—to measure 34-inch drawback distance).

Safety-Drawback (SDB):

1. Play for putts of 15 to 35 feet.
2. First putts coming to rest in "Safe-Zone" are exempt from drawback and can be putted out from where they stopped.
3. First putts which stop outside "Safe-Zone" must be drawn back 34 inches straight away from hole before putting again.
4. All putts after second putt must be drawn back 34 inches before putting.

Double-Safety-Drawback (DSDB):

1. Play for putts between 10 and 30 feet.
2. Rules similar to SDB, except when first putt stops in "Safe-Zone," it must be drawn back 34 inches prior to putting.
3. If first putt misses "Safe-Zone," and on all putts after second putts, balls must be drawn back double (68 inches) prior to putting.

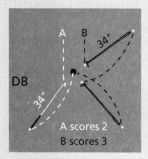
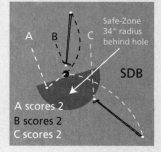
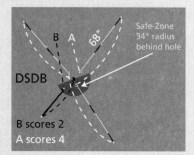

Figure 13.2.5: Rules of the Game. (Maximum score each hole = 4, except no maximum on last hole.)

Drawback to many different holes. You are penalized when you don't roll the ball the proper speed, rewarded when you do. It's the judging of your speed and distance result after each putt (whether it stops in the Safe-Zone or not) that teaches your mind's eye the proper touch for the future. And because of the penalty for finishing either short or more than 34 inches past, you instinctively learn the touch required to roll putts 17 inches past the hole more frequently. This is the touch you want to carry over into all your putting for makable-range putts up to 35 feet.

Double-Safety-Drawback

This is the ultimate pressure drill for practicing touch on putts between 10 and 30 feet (again, the rules are in Figure 13.2.5), because the penalty for rolling first putts the wrong speed is so severe.

This game also emphasizes the skill of holing 6- to 10-footers, putts you often face whenever you play. It's best to play Double-Safety-Drawback to a new hole every time: This makes your mind's eye focus on a new putt, a new distance, and the touch for a new stroke each time.

Finally, remember that it is of the utmost importance that you use your routine and ritual during all of these games to maximize on-course benefits later.

Chiputting

Every golfer should run the "Chiputt Test" to determine the distance at which the chiputt becomes a better choice than putting. The chiputt is a stroke made with a putter but utilizing a chipping grip, stance, posture, swing, and follow-through (Figure 13.2.6).

Several years ago, I ran a series of tests that showed the longer a putt is, the more likely it is to be left short. There are two reasons for this: (1) Bending over in the normal putting posture restricts the power of the putting stroke; and (2) bending over makes it difficult to get a good perspective for distance (Figure 13.2.7). Together, these two factors mean amateurs have a hard time giving their putts enough power to roll 80, 90, or 100 feet. (This problem is made worse since most golfers seldom practice putts this long.)

So when you have a long putt that you will likely leave short, don't putt it, but stand tall and chiputt it. You already know how to chiputt: Just chip the ball using your putter. The only question is, at what distance will you chiputt better than you putt? To find out, run the Chiputt test:

Walk off distances from 50 to 100 feet and mark them with tees in increments of 10 feet. At 50 feet, putt three balls, then chiputt three. See which technique rolls

Figure 13.2.6: Chiputting is using a chipping stance, posture, grip, and swing with a putter. Ball position is at stance center.

Figure 13.2.7: Posture for Chiputting is upright, as it is in chipping (left), not bent over as in putting (right). An upright posture helps distance perspective.

your balls closer to the hole on average. Move to 60 feet and do the same—three putts and three chiputts. Again, evaluate the results for closest average distance to the pin. Repeat from each remaining distance.

At some point, chiputting will become easier and produce better results (say, on 70-footers and longer) than putting. This becomes your chiputt distance for the day. Repeat the test on several different days, finding the average distance from which you consistently chiputt better than you putt. Thereafter, use the chiputt technique on the course for all level putts greater than this length.

If 70 feet is your switch-over distance on level putts, you probably will find the switch distance for uphill putts at about 55 feet, and on downhill putts it will be 80 or 90 feet. Try chiputting in all these situations to get a feel for it.

You also should find that your touch for chiputting will be close to your touch for chipping from off the greens. And you can refine your chiputting touch the same way you do for lag putting, with repeated practice sessions and competitions where the rewards go to stopping the ball near the hole.

Phony-Hole Drill

The "Phony-Hole Drill" is one of my favorites for working on touch, especially when the putting green is crowded. It utilizes a device I carry in my bag at all times, the Phony-Hole, a thin, flexible circle of black rubber, just smaller than the diameter of a real hole. The Phony-Hole almost looks like a real hole when it lies on the surface of a green, is thin enough to let putts roll smoothly over it, and comes in handy when the practice green is full of golfers and there is no open hole available. By throwing down a Phony-Hole (Figure 13.2.8), you create your own target to putt to, get away from the majority of the lumpy-donut effects, and work on speed control by seeing if the putts you "make" (those that roll over the Phony-Hole) stop near 17 inches behind the hole.

To practice the Phony-Hole Drill, mark a spot near the edge of the green with a tee, then walk off the putt length you want to practice. Drop the Phony-Hole and walk the same distance to the other side. Mark this spot with another tee and you are ready to putt.

Figure 13.2.8: Using a "Phony-Hole" eliminates most lumpy-donut effects, and lets you evaluate speed (for 17 inches past) after every putt.

The rules for the Phony-Hole Drill are the same as for one of our primary feel-development drills, the 20-foot drill (for details, see pages 315 and 316). The one difference is that when practicing touch with the Phony-Hole, change your putt distance every time you drill.

Putting to the Phony-Hole is also good for a quick warm-up before a round. Putt three balls from opposite directions at least twice before every round you play, rehearsing your routine and ritual, and holding your finish to watch your putts until they stop (about 17 inches behind the Phony-Hole). You will be surprised at how quickly your touch for distance improves.

Putting over Level Changes

The best way to adjust for putting over a level change on a green—say, from one tier to another—is to not adjust your touch at all. Instead, imagine a hole behind or in front of the real hole on a level green (ignore the level change). If you are changing levels uphill, imagine the imaginary hole is farther away; if your putt changes levels downhill, imagine the imaginary hole is closer to you. Learn to estimate how much these level changes affect your normal roll distances, and then learn to see your imaginary hole at that adjusted distance. It's much easier to imagine another hole than it is to adjust your touch for distance, which you've worked so hard to develop (to that perfect touch of rolling the ball 17 inches past on putts inside of 35 feet, exactly to the hole on longer putts).

Train yourself to see imaginary holes (at adjusted distances) by using the Phony-Hole on two-tier practice greens. Lay the Phony-Hole in front of (or behind) the real cup and imagine you are putting on a level surface to it when you take your practice stroke looks to determine your preview stroke. It will take only a few minutes of practice to learn how far behind or ahead of the real hole the Phony-Hole should be placed to get good results.

13.3 Refine Your Feel

Now that you have good touch, you need good feel to be able to transform what your touch tells you is needed into a stroke that feels right and that you believe will provide the perfect roll (speed and distance) required.

Remember, touch is knowing "what" to do, while feel is knowing "how" to do it. So when you practice feel, you must assume you already know what is needed (the size of the required stroke), and you're trying to create the how (feel) to do it. Although this assumption isn't always the case on the course (sometimes your touch gives you its best estimate of what is needed but you doubt its accuracy), you must trust your touch when you practice feel on the putting green. This means feel practice should be very repetitive, internalizing the process of producing a given stroke and roll after you know the power and distance needed for that putt.

To practice feel, you must practice using your mind's-eye memories and prior training to visualize how the stroke should look and feel to create optimum distance and speed. Knowing this relationship *is* your feel in putting. You then can recognize a job well done by the good feeling you get as you swing through impact and reach the end of your follow-through. You'll know even before looking up to see where the ball has gone: If you feel, "Ahhh, yes, that's as good as I can stroke it; I made an exact repeat of my preview stroke, and that's the exact stroke I wanted to put on the ball," then you know you did a good job feeling the putt.

However, if you look up and see the ball going nowhere near the hole—that your stroke rolled it way too fast and past the hole—you know your touch failed you. This is a condition you don't want in your practice of feel. And that is why you should always practice putting to the same hole over and over again (so your touch of knowing what is needed becomes obviously accurate) when you are working on feel.

There are times when you may have the opposite experience. You'll strike your putt and before looking up you know that you don't like it. You know in your mind's eye that the ball is not going where you planned it to go. The reason will be one (or a combination) of the following:

1. You did a poor job of feeling your practice swings and never produced a good preview stroke.
2. You misread the putt, and your subconscious knew it.
3. Your touch for distance or power was bad and your subconscious knew it.
4. You blew the stroke execution.

The first three reasons are curable, or preventable, if you follow the teachings in this book for improving your touch, feel, and ability to read greens. But I'm afraid you're stuck with the bad stroke-execution problem, because sometimes, even when we know what to do and how to do it, we act human and just plain blow it. If you can't handle blowing one from time to time, then you'd better give up golf and go play tennis, or roll over and die, because there's no other way to totally escape the human foibles of the putting game.

Feel Practice

You develop and refine your feel for a putt during your preparation routine. When you make a practice stroke, you evaluate the physical sensation and vision of the stroke against your mind's-eye image of what you think you'll need to feel and see during the real stroke. So practicing feel must include (1) performing your routine and ritual, (2) executing your stroke, (3) seeing your results, and (4) comparing what actually happened with what was supposed to happen (Figure 13.3.1).

The best feel practice scenario is to putt three ball cycles over and over again from the same spot. Walk off the exact distance and read the break (see section 13.4 below). Then go through your five-step routine and ritual (Chapter 11), and stroke the first ball. If your results are perfect, you feel good after impact and follow-through, and you look up and the ball is going into the hole at the right speed. Then do it again and again, to groove and ingrain what you just did. Remember: Before each putt, perform your routine, making at least one practice stroke you like for your preview stroke, move in, do your ritual, and putt.

If the results of your first putt are less than perfect, back away and figure out why. If the problem was playing the wrong amount of break or sensing the wrong touch, start all over again with your preparation routine (Figure 13.3.2). When you are practicing feel, you must know exactly *what* you are trying to do before you try to do it. Then refine the process until you can do it precisely and correctly.

To get as much feel training as possible, keep repeating these 3-ball cycles again and again for the same putt. You should be able to refine your feel to a fine degree after a few cycles.

Figure 13.3.1: Feel Practice: One must always create a good preview stroke (which you believe is your best— shown on the left), before you make your real stroke (right). Comparing results with expectations refines your feel for similar future putts.

Figure 13.3.2: During preliminary strokes (for touch) in the first step of your routine, look at your putt for distance. The rest of your routine should be spent creating the feel of what you believe will be the perfect preview stroke for the perfect ball track.

Always remember to perform your complete preputt routine on each first putt of each cycle, then back away from your position by four inches and make at least one preview stroke before hitting each of the following second and third putts. This assures you will get as much practice moving into your putts as executing them (from the wrong setup, even a perfectly stroked putt will miss every time).

20-Foot Drill

The purpose of the 20-foot drill is to train your subconscious to feel and perform the best it possibly can on the speed and distance of 20-footers. You need to practice the 20-foot length because my putting data shows that it is a frequent length for first putts. The drill consists of putting groups of three 20-footers from two opposite directions until you can roll 10 in a row at the proper speed.

We define proper speed as that which allows the ball to pass the back edge of the hole and stop within a 34-inch radius behind the hole (Figure 13.3.3). We call this area the "Safe-Zone," and you will hear it referred to many times in my putting drills. The rules of this drill are as follows:

1. Start at the hole and walk 20 feet (seven three-foot strides minus one foot), and mark the spot with a tee.

2. Mark a spot 20 feet away in the opposite direction from the hole.

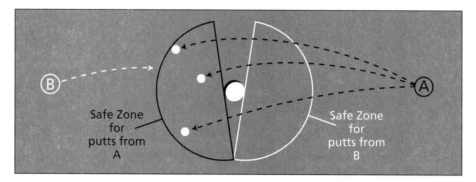

Figure 13.3.3: The Safe-Zone is a 34-inch-radius semicircle behind the hole (perpendicular to incoming putt direction).

3. Stroke three putts (making a preview stroke before each one), watching to see if each stops in the Safe-Zone. If any putt does not stop in the Safe-Zone (putts that fall into the hole count as in), you must start all over with putt #1.

4. When all three putts pass the Safe-Zone test, go to the opposite side of the hole and putt three more times. Again, if all three stop in the Safe-Zone, reverse sides of the hole and continue, three putts from each side. If any putt misses, start over with putt #1 from the side of the miss.

To finish this drill, you must roll 10 putts in a row that stop in the Safe-Zone, and the 10th must be putted from the opposite side of the hole than the ninth. Remember, all putts that fall into the hole count as good (as if they've stopped in the Safe-Zone).

This drill is great for developing feel because it makes you putt the same two putts over and over after you know what is needed and your touch is no longer in question. Also, as you near the last few putts, the pressure mounts to not miss, which is a good test of how well you focus and concentrate on your feel under pressure.

Put Gloves on and Close Your Eyes
One way golfers can improve their ability to visualize the feel in their mind's eye is to putt wearing ski gloves on both hands (Figure 13.3.4). Thick, padded gloves remove all kinesthetic messages of feel from the shaft and putterhead to the hands. So all they have to determine the size of their stroke (and preview stroke) is their mind's-eye vision.

When you first try practice putting in ski gloves, you'll be surprised to find that most of your feel actually is in your mind, and you'll probably putt better than you expected. That's when you realize the physical feel in your hands is "icing on

Figure 13.3.4: Feel Drill: Putting in ski gloves minimizes the kinesthetic side of feel and helps refine one's mind's-eye feel for putts.

the cake" in putting. It also may be when you finally understand why you don't want to supply putting power with your hands and wrists: This kind of power overwhelms the small kinesthetic messages of feel that are there, and removes your chance of benefiting from that "icing."

A way to heighten your feel for the physical (kinesthetic) sensations of putting is to make practice strokes with your eyes closed. Begin your usual routine, keeping your eyes open for your first practice stroke, looking at the hole, and seeing the distance. Then close both eyes, ending all visual input to your brain. Make a practice stroke and feel what you expect the results of that putt would be. Do this several times, until you're comfortable with the feel of your stroke, then open your eyes, step in, perform your ritual, and stroke your putt. Creating a preview stroke with your eyes closed is the opposite of putting with gloves on, as it forces you to feel through your hands, where the sensations are weak. It will also convince you that putting with "dead-hands" (no power supplied by hands) allows you to achieve maximum sensitivity and feel from your hands in the putting stroke.

Too-High Drill

"Too High" is a game we use to help our students learn (1) what it feels like to play too much break, and (2) how to float putts in from the high side when you want to be sure to avoid a three-putt. You can play Too High by yourself or in competition with any number of players. Find a hole on a pronounced slope and mark the ball-hole line through the center of the hole, extending in both directions, along the line you intend to putt from (Figure 13.3.5). You can putt from anywhere along or beyond this line with one rule: The ball that stops closest to the hole without going into the hole or below the line wins.

Figure 13.3.5: Too-High Drill: On a fast downhill slider, I play nine feet of break, trying to stop putts above the ball-hole line as close to the hole as possible.

Several winners are shown in Figure 13.3.6, but any ball that falls in the hole while playing Too High cannot win. (If the ball falls in, it wasn't too high, was it?) But holing out doesn't necessarily mean you lose if all the other balls also roll in or below the line.

You'll be surprised how difficult this game can be. On fast greens or severe slopes, leaving putts above the hole can be a real challenge. But getting the feel for making happen what you want to happen will serve you well on the course.

To maximize the feel benefits of Too-High, roll the same putts, to the same

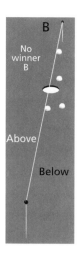

Figure 13.3.6: Too-High Drill: The closest ball to hole that doesn't touch the ball-hole line or go in, wins.

hole, again and again. Try to stop your putts ever closer to going in, without going in, while always staying above the ball-hole line. Holding a competition is the best, but practicing by yourself is also good since it helps you focus and concentrate on feeling how to produce the floating-in-from-too-high putts.

Safety-Drawback

If you want to work more on feel than touch, play Safety-Drawback (see details in section 13.2) to the same two or three holes over and over, refining your feel for those distances to the maximum degree possible. After a few cycles around the same three holes, you'll know exactly what is required for each putt (you've seen them roll, and your touch for what is needed is confirmed), so you can concentrate purely on your feel, on feeling the perfect preview stroke for each putt.

Two-Hole Drill

Here is a good way to practice your feel while also refining your rhythm. We call it the "Two-Hole Drill" because you putt back and forth between two holes in line with each other to the beat of a metronome set at your natural body rhythm.

Find two holes on the putting green that you can monopolize without offending anyone. Get behind the closer hole, imagine parallel Aimlines that work for both of them, and place two balls close together on those lines, 2½ feet from the closer hole (Figure 13.3.7). Turn on your metronome and putt the first ball (the

Figure 13.3.7: Two-Hole Drill: Find two holes that have parallel Aimlines. Set up two balls on those Aimlines, 2½ feet from one of the holes.

short putt), using your routine and ritual to the beat of the metronome. Immediately look at the second hole, make the best preview stroke you can, step into your address position, execute your ritual, and stroke the second ball to the second hole (Figure 13.3.8). Again, make this stroke to your body-rhythm cadence.

At first, it's not important that you hole the second putt or even come very close. What you want to do is begin to feel comfortable making a long swing in the same rhythm as your short swing. Only by keeping your rhythm constant for putts of all lengths can you develop optimum feel for speed and distance based on the size of your swings. By putting back and forth, you end up feeling and making the perfect stroke for both putts at the same rhythm, which is great practice for all of your on-course putting.

Figure 13.3.8: Two-Hole Drill: Roll both putts with strokes at the rhythm of your body-rhythm cadence.

Short-Putt Drills

Short putts—of less than about five feet—are the most common shots in golf. Most golfers have a short putt on most holes, and almost half of the 43 percent of the game that is putting is short putting. If you can't make your short putts, the game won't be much fun and you won't score well.

What do you think causes most short-putt misses? Even though the distance is small, many of these putts are missed because they are rolled at a speed that is either too slow or too fast.

Almost every golfer I know could improve simply by remembering this one rule: All putts are speed putts. The title of Chapter 8 is "Speed Is More Important Than Line": As I explained there, if your putts don't roll at or near the right speed, it doesn't matter where you aim or what your stroke mechanics are like—you won't make many.

What follows are my five favorite short-putt drills, which will help you learn the proper feel to make these putts, while rolling them at the right speed.

Drill 1: Closed-Eyes Drill The purpose of this drill is to learn the feel of the three-foot-putt stroke, which supplies optimum power to roll putts consistently through the lumpy donut without producing lip-outs. Drop three balls three feet from the hole and putt them in. Then move 90 degrees around the hole and do it again, and again, and again, until you've circled the hole and made 12 in a row. If you miss any putt, start over until you hole all 12 consecutively.

Next choose one of the four positions you putted from before, and starting there, roll three putts in from three feet, but this time with your eyes closed. If you miss one with your eyes closed, putt three more with your eyes open, to reestablish your feel, then repeat three with your eyes closed again. If you miss one again, repeat the cycle of six putts until you make them all. (A note for when you miss: It's always good to notice if your misses roll 17 inches past the back edge of the cup to ensure you are rolling your putts at or at least near the optimum putting speed.)

Drill 2: Getting-Longer Drill To start, place four balls three feet from a hole, one at each of the 3:00, 6:00, 9:00, and 12:00 o'clock positions, and putt them in. Every time you make all four putts, move a foot farther away and putt them all again. Each time you putt this drill, try to improve on your previous record for how far away from the hole you can get without missing. Always begin at three feet and move progressively outward, and always use your rhythm, routine, and ritual on each putt. As always, notice how far past the hole your misses roll. By doing so, the Getting-Longer Drill will quickly teach you that dying putts to the hole is as bad as jamming them too hard and causing lip-outs. Again, the goal is to groove a feel for the optimum speed for holing putts.

Drill 3: Pure-Push Drill A pure-push putting stroke is not legal (it doesn't conform to USGA rules because it has no backswing), but it is a good way to practice. My friend Peter Jacobsen showed this to me, and it helped take his short-putting to the next level. The Pure-Push Drill is designed to help you learn the feel of keeping your putterface square to the Aimline on your follow-through. The drill is the same as the Closed-Eyes Drill above, except you don't make a backswing in your stroke; just push the ball toward the hole (Figure 13.3.9) directly from the address position of your putter. Make 12 push-putts in a row with your eyes open, then push in three in a row with your eyes closed. After doing this drill a few times, you will begin to notice the similarity in feel between your finishes in the Pure-Push Drill and your other short-putt drills, with your putterface staying square to your Aimline.

Figure 13.3.9: The Pure-Push Drill: From your address position, push the ball down your Aimline into the hole. Do *not* take any backswing whatsoever.

Drill 4: Back-of-Hole Drill Many golfers baby their short putts, afraid to roll them firmly to the hole because they worry about not making the putt coming back if they miss. But a short putt is particularly susceptible to the green imperfections you can't see—footprints, the lumpy donut, etc.—because in addition to having to roll fairly slowly (it's close to the hole) through the lumpy donut, it's probably also sitting in a footprint that wants to knock it off-line even before it gets started. If you find it hard to roll your short putt firmly, you need to work on this simple drill for 15 minutes once a week until you see improvement.

The drill is performed by putting three-footers from the four different quadrants around a hole as firmly as possible without the balls popping out of the hole. Make a game of it, trying to bounce the ball off the back edge of the hole up into the air without producing lip-outs or flying over the cup (Figure 13.3.10), and don't worry about your misses. Of course, I don't recommend stroking the ball this hard on the course, but if you consistently roll your short putts weakly to the cup, you need to experience the other side of the mountain during practice, so you can settle in the middle on the course.

Drill 5: 17-Inches-Past Drill Rolling putts 17 inches past the hole makes sense to most golfers until they face a short putt. Then they are surprised when I tell them that the 17-inches-past speed is good for putts of all lengths, even the very short

Figure 13.3.10: Back-of-Hole Drill: Don't worry about misses—keep rolling putts firmly into the back of the cup. See how high you can make putts bounce off the back edge of the cup without flying over the hole.

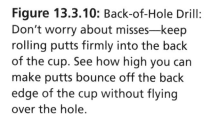

ones. The hole doesn't know or care where the putt is coming from; it just cares whether or not the ball hits the hole, and if so, at what speed.

To establish and maintain your feel for the perfect speed on short putts, practice this drill from time to time (10 minutes about once a month will do—it doesn't take long). This drill is to be done by yourself on the green, using the Phony-Hole and a dime placed 17 inches behind it. Take three balls and putt them from different distances, trying to roll all of them over the cup. Hold your finish (until each putt stops) and watch carefully how close each ball finishes to the dime. If you don't have a good feel for how far 17 inches is, half the length of your putter is close enough.

You'll probably be surprised how easy this drill is. That's good. It is intended to convince your subconscious that if it will just let you roll your short putts the proper speed, you won't have any trouble making them.

Lag-Putt Drill

The three-putt is one of the most irritating and needless mistakes in golf. Unfortunately, it is also one of the most common. Avoiding the three-putt is simple: Just lag your first putt into a six-foot circle around the hole; that will leave you a shorter-than-three-foot putt, which you can handle.

"Sure," you say, "it's simple if you can roll your putts within three feet of the cup, but that's what I can't do!" If that's what you're thinking, it's time you change the way you look at long (lag) putts. Look at me in Figure 13.3.11, holding the flagstick in a six-foot-diameter hole. I'm sure you'd bet that you could make every putt on every green if the holes were that big. When you see a real hole this big, it looks *enormous*!

But avoiding three-putting is as simple as putting into a six-foot hole. So if it's so simple, why do you still three-putt? Not because it's so difficult, but because

Figure 13.3.11: This photograph doesn't do this 6-foot-diameter hole justice. In real life it looks enormous!

you don't properly practice lag putting enough, and you don't have good feel or touch for your long putts.

To get the feel for lagging long putts close, try our "Lag-Putt Drill," which establishes three reference-distance putts—40, 50, and 60 feet—that you practice again and again. Every time you do this drill, putt from different angles and slopes, but always from 40, 50, and 60 feet to a hole. You'll find that once you begin to build confidence from these three distances (this will likely take repeating the drill on 10 different occasions), other long distances will become easier, too.

Start by walking off your three distances and marking them with tees. Putt three balls from 40 feet, followed by three from 60, and three from 50. Do this cycle twice more, then end with three putts from 50 feet that stop within your huge six-foot imaginary hole around the real hole (which means all three remaining putts are shorter than three feet). You haven't completed the drill until you get the last three in a row to finish in the six-foot circle.

As you continue to practice this drill, those last three good lags will become easier and easier, and you'll come to be dissatisfied on the course with lag putts that leave you second putts longer than three or four feet.

Compete

Given proper feedback conditions, competition is the best environment for learning. So compete against the best putters you can find at every opportunity when you practice your putting. All of the drills above can become games if the goal becomes winning. For example, in Too High or the Lag Putt Drill, the winning (closest to hole) putt (playing with any number of others) counts one point and the first golfer to win six points wins the game.

But any old competition is not good enough. For example, don't play "aces" (which golfers instinctively equate to ramming putts well past the hole when they miss) or "closest-to-the-hole" games on putts of less than 35 feet in length (which teach stopping the ball at the hole, 17 inches short of where you want your touch and feel to be focused). Choose games that improve your weaknesses and avoid those that tend to be more destructive than helpful. Remember, the most aggressive (and smartest) putters are those who roll makable putts (shorter than 35-footers) at the optimum speed to stop 17 inches past the hole if they miss. And the smartest and best lag putters stop the ball dead around the hole. These are the results you want to develop as instinctive in your touch and feel.

13.4 Develop Your Green-Reading Ability

Golfers, we have a problem. We don't read greens well, we don't play enough break in our putts, we compensate for this subconsciously in our setups and stroke manipulations, and because of these misreads and compensations, we miss more putts than we have to miss. We could make more putts if we could get rid of the whole mess, start all over, learn to read greens properly, then use one pure, non-compensating stroke for all of our putts.

I keep saying "we" because when I tested 1,500 golfers, they *all* had this problem. And I had it, too.

The question is, do you? There is a simple way to find out, by measuring whether you tend to miss regularly above or below the hole.

Measure, Then Admit

Look at the diagram in Figure 13.4.1, showing zone A, which is above the hole, and zone B, which is below the hole. You know from earlier data that most golfers miss about 85 percent of their putts below the hole because they don't play enough break. Prove if this does, or does not, apply to you by keeping track of your missed putts over your next five rounds. Mark your scorecard as shown in Figure 13.4.2, total the As and Bs at the end of each round, then add all five rounds of data. If your misses are split evenly between zones A and B, you are reading greens well. If, however, significantly more (60 percent or more) of your misses were in one zone or the other, your green-reading needs to improve.

Learn to Analyze Your Misses

On the putting green, after every practice putt, learn to be aware of whether you missed your putt above (A) or below (B). Six months after reading this book (and

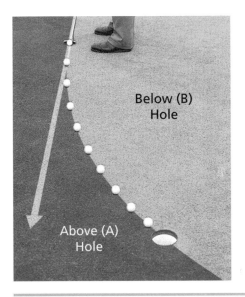

Below (B) Hole

Above (A) Hole

Figure 13.4.1: Learn to notice how your putts miss the hole; Above = A, Below = B.

Figure 13.4.2: On your scorecard, mark an A or B for every missed putt (don't mark anything for makes).

every six months thereafter for the rest of your golf career), analyze your miss frequency for A versus B putts for at least five rounds. This awareness should become part of your game, so you don't let your old "underread-and-compensate" habit return once you get rid of it.

Don't fight the truth. If this is a problem you have, admit it and get rid of it.

It's like any other problem in life: If you don't admit that you have it, you deny yourself the opportunity to eliminate it and the benefits of that elimination (in this case, making more putts). Dealing honestly with reality is the first step to making it easier to see the true break as you stand over your putts examining the greens.

Two Green-Reading Problems

First, let me clearly define the situation most golfers are in, so there can be no misunderstanding. Based on my test data, three circumstances are true:

1. Golfers don't see the true break (they continually underestimate what break is really there when they read putts).

2. Golfers don't realize that they miss most (80 to 95 percent) of their putts low.

3. Unless something changes, golfers will never play more break (even if someone tells them they need to), because subconscious compensations cause them to miss putts high when they do, and to play more break and then miss high makes no sense (unless you truly understand the entire green-reading phenomenon).

As you can imagine, poor green-reading is not something that can be fixed easily. As the three circumstances above now exist, they self-perpetuate errors and compensations. (Hey, it's taken more than 400 years to even recognize that there *is* a problem!) And here's the important fact to remember: Green-reading isn't one problem, it's two problems:

1. Golfers underread how much putts really break.

2. Golfers subconsciously form habits to correct for their underreading, compensating with their aim and in-stroke putting mechanics to play more break than they read.

You can read all the detail in Chapter 7, but the net effect of the two problems is that the compensations don't quite make up for the full amount of underread. So most golfers today miss about 85 percent of their putts below the hole, without realizing either that such a high percentage miss to the low side or why any one putt misses (they usually blame some mechanical error, such as pulling the putt, pushing the putt, or not hitting it solidly). Then yours truly comes along and points out the mistake they are making. And what happens? Some of them try to correct the situation by solving problem 1, so they play more break, miss high, get confused, and ultimately putt no better, and possibly even worse. Or they work on problem 2, try putting accurately (without compensations) on the line they've read, miss everything low, and ultimately putt worse. The result is that in neither case do golfers learn to read the true break or start putting better. They don't understand how to solve the problems, and can't stand the negative results when they try to.

There is only one way to solve this green-reading problem, and that is to correct both problems at the same time.

The Pelz Proposal for a Solution

I will devote the remainder of this chapter to showing you first how to see how much putts truly break—that is, how to read greens (predict how much putts will truly break). Then I will show you how to groove a noncompensating stroke that will start your putts on your Aimline without subconscious compensations. This noncompensating stroke will be the one stroke that works for all your putts from here on out. It will make your putting game simpler and more effective than ever before.

Recognize Green Speed and Slope

Before you can predict how much a putt will break, you must recognize the slope of the green, and how fast the ball will roll on it. Back in Chapter 7, I told you that the more a green slopes, the more a putt will break. And the faster the green (the lower its surface friction), the slower you must roll a putt, and again, the more it will break. So it stands to reason that the better you recognize slopes and green speeds, the better you will recognize how much putts will break.

First I'll deal with green speed (Figure 13.4.3). If you can become proficient at knowing how fast greens are, you can imagine how fast the ball is going to roll. Without this, there is no way to predict how much it is going to break. There are three ways to learn green speeds: (1) measure them exactly; (2) measure them approximately; and (3) observe other golfers' results over time.

1. The best way to learn green speeds is to have the course superintendent report the measured speed to the golf shop every morning (accurate to 0.1 foot). Then make it a habit to ask about the greens before you play. Each round, knowing the day's green speed (8.7 today) will make you aware of how different speeds affect roll, and over time you will become an expert (as the Tour pros have done).

2. The next best way is to use your three reference strokes (the 6-, 12-, and 18-

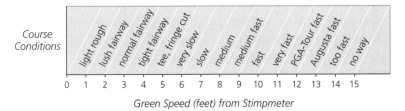

Figure 13.4.3: Generic course conditions vs. Stimp readings.

inch backswing strokes discussed in section 12.2) on the practice green before you play each round. Make it a habit to roll three balls on a flat part of the putting green, one with each reference stroke. Then roll them in the opposite direction to average out any slope or grain effects. Over time you'll learn what to expect, while each day you'll get a visual judgment of how the greens are rolling. The accuracy of this method depends on the consistency of your reference strokes; therefore, this method will never be as accurate as learning the green-speed scale from the superintendent.

3. As usual, the easiest way to do something provides the least satisfying results. You can try to get a feel for green speed by watching other golfers putt, noticing how much speed their putts seem to have as they roll, versus the way the greens look. This is better than being oblivious to green speed, but there's no point of reference and at best it gives you only an approximation of the speed you'll be dealing with on any given day.

How About Slopes?

Have you ever trained yourself to see slopes in greens? Can you see, detect, or differentiate between one slope and another? Unfortunately, for most golfers, the answer to both of these questions is no. It's not that seeing a slope is difficult, it's just that most golfers have never looked at slopes with any point of reference (again, no feedback) that would allow them to learn which is what.

The learning process to recognize slopes is almost identical to learning green speeds. There are three ways: (1) measure them; (2) learn to recognize them relative to a reference system; and (3) pay attention when you are on the course and hope for the best.

1. Few golfers (myself and several Tour pros I work with) care enough about green-reading to expend the effort to accurately measure slopes on real greens (using precision instruments not commercially available). However, there is no better way to learn to recognize slopes. Measure the slope of a green near the hole, look at it as you read your putt's break, then putt on it. Your brain will do the rest. After measuring a number of slopes and putting on them, you'll begin to recognize their severity without having to measure.

2. The next best way to learn to see slopes is to be consistently exposed to a few reference slopes, while knowing their values, one relative to another. I can help here in two ways, first by showing you what a 4-slope green surface looks like (Figure 13.4.4). The Tilt-Green on the right is set at a 4-slope, compared with the 0-slope (dead-flat) green on the left. The difference between zero and 4-slope is pretty obvious, but when you see these greens being set at different slopes every day (as we at the Pelz Golf Institute do), even the 1, 2, and 3 slopes in between become recognizable. The key is seeing them often enough to learn what they look like. It's not difficult, it just takes exposure.

An even better way to learn to recognize slopes is by practicing on the Sport Court brand of artificial putting greens, made for backyard putting (Figure 13.4.5). After testing to find the best-rolling artificial surface available, I went to Sport Court and offered to endorse their product on the condition that they install Dave Pelz Signature Greens with precision 1-, 2-, and 4-slope areas at all of my teaching facilities. You need to be serious about your putting (or into family involvement and training) to install a putting green in your backyard, because they are a bit expensive. But I highly recommend these surfaces because they putt consistently true, are virtually maintenance-free, and I know of no better way to learn to see slopes than by constantly looking at and putting on them in your own backyard. After learning how these known slopes break on your own green, you'll soon begin to recognize these same slopes and breaks on golf courses.

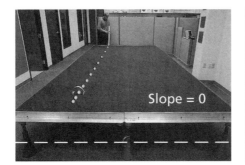
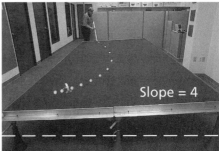

Figure 13.4.4: A 4-slope green (right) is very obvious compared to a flat green (slope = 0, left).

Figure 13.4.5: In my backyard I have a Sport Court "Dave Pelz Signature Green" with known reference slopes. When I see these same slopes on the golf course, I feel "at home" with the putts.

3. Finally, just as with learning green speed, you can try to watch and learn as you go, noticing how the putts of other golfers break on different slopes as you play. While this won't ever make you an expert at slope recognition, it's better to develop some awareness of the severity of the slope you are about to read and putt on than to not think about it at all before you putt.

Seeing True Break

In theory, once you know visible break is about a third of true break, it should be easy to see a putt's true break. However, I don't want to mislead you about the difficulty of seeing even the visible break when you first start looking.

To see what I mean, study the two ball tracks for the 15-foot breaking putt (shown in Figure 13.4.6). Both are the same putt, viewed from opposite directions. The outgoing track on the right is what you see as you watch from behind the ball (the golfer's view) as your putt rolls away from you toward the hole. The track on the left is the incoming view, as you would see it if you were standing behind the hole.

Which do you think provides the worse perspective for evaluating visible break? Of course, as the perversity of nature demands, the worse view is the golfer's view, from behind the ball, because it shows the less obvious vision of the visible break (it appears smaller from this view).

You need to practice seeing visible break. Every time you see a putt curving to the hole, try to focus and lock your vision onto its ball track. Make a mental note of where the ball reached its apex, when it got to its highest point away from the ball-hole line (the straight line between the ball and the hole). That distance is the visible break (Figure 13.4.7).

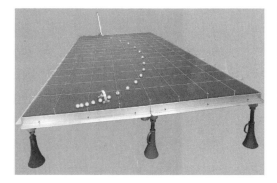

Figure 13.4.6: The amount a putt breaks is more obvious from the incoming view (left), but golfers see the outgoing (downline) view (right).

Now take that visible break, imagine moving it out to the distance of the hole, multiply it by three, and you'll have the true-break point and Aimline for the putt (or at least something very near to it), as shown in Figure 13.4.8. The more you look at putts this way, with a sharp focus and awareness of visible break, and what that means in terms of how much true break the putt showed, the easier it will become to see them both. Watch not only your own putts, but also everyone else's in your group (and not just on the course, but when you are competing and doing putting drills on the practice green, too). The more breaks you "see" this way, the more accurately you will be able to imagine them (read greeens) in the future.

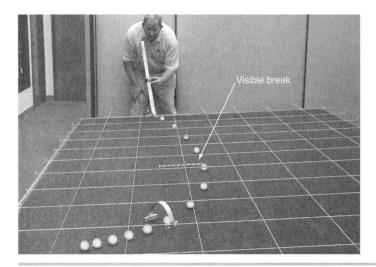

Figure 13.4.7: Visible break can be easily seen: It's the distance the apex of the ball track departs from the ball-hole line.

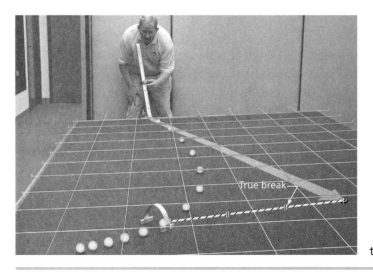

Figure 13.4.8: In your mind's eye, move the visible break (13.4.7, above) out to the hole—multiply it by three—and you'll see the true-break point and Aimline.

Putting Facts

A quick reminder about some of the facts of putting so you won't have to look back to Chapter 7:

1. Perfect putts should always start on the Aimline, which runs from where the ball sits on the green to the true-break point.
2. Any putt that starts rolling on the Aimline will always roll below it, on the visible-break ball track, because of gravity pulling it downhill.
3. The visible break of a putt (the farthest the ball ever rolls above the ball-hole line) is usually about one-third the size of its true break.
4. If you aim at, and start your putts rolling on, a line aimed at the apex of the ball track you expect to see (if you "apex" putt), gravity will pull every one of them down below that apex and you will miss them below the hole.

Roll Putts with a True Roller

Another good way to see how much putts break is to roll balls with a True Roller (Figure 13.4.9). It's the best device I've seen for providing true and accurate feedback on what the green is doing to putts. The True Roller never lies to you or tries to coddle your ego the way your subconscious does. It won't pull or push putts for you, so when you don't aim it to play enough break, you miss the putt low and learn from the immediate feedback.

A gentle fingertip release allows you to accurately control the speed of each

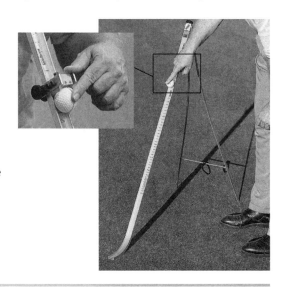

Figure 13.4.9: The True Roller starts balls rolling on the Aimline you choose, at the speed you select. If you don't play enough break at that speed, you miss the putt low every time. The True Roller provides immediate, accurate, and reliable feedback.

putt, so by the second or third try you are rolling the ball at near the optimum putting speed. Once you have the right speed, finding the right Aimline to allow for the correct amount of true break comes quickly.

Because the True Roller is the best tool for learning to read greens I know of, I wish every golfer could try putting with one. We expose every student in our three-day Scoring Game Schools to how it works, and, of course, some of our Tour pro students practice with it a lot. You wouldn't believe how good some of them have gotten with the True Roller. But that just proves that once you know how to read greens, putting with the True Roller becomes as simple as starting the ball on the right line at the right speed.

I'm not recommending for you to buy one (they're expensive and cumbersome), but believe me when I say that rolling and watching putts for just a few minutes from the True Roller will convince you that the true break in putts is much greater than what you used to think it was.

Reading Greens Better

Once you become proficient at green-speed and slope recognition, and you know what to look for to see the visible break in putts, you are ready to begin developing your ability to predict how much putts will truly break. Making these predictions for where to aim so your ball tracks will find the hole is the skill of green-reading. And that means it's at the heart of becoming a good putter. Of course, your future green-reading will improve by knowing and remembering what your putts did on similar greens in the past, particularly when you have reference knowledge that helps to compare how similar the conditions were. This is why I try so hard to convince you to work on getting better at seeing green speed, slope, and true break. But by "seeing" better, I don't mean improving your vision so it is sharper than 20/20.

There is more to seeing than meets the eyeball. While getting new glasses or contact lenses can change the way light is focused in your eyes, you also can change the way your brain understands and interprets that light. For example, instead of seeing a large metal box in your kitchen with round circles on the top, you want to be seeing an electric range with heating coils used to cook food (and which would burn your hands if touched). Likewise in putting: If you understand more and better interpret the meaning of what your eyeballs take in from the greens, the more and better you can see the true break in putting.

For example, if instead of seeing a green that slopes to the right, you could see a 2-slope green that will make your nine-foot putt break six inches to the right, that would be good. If instead of seeing a pretty fast green, you could see a 10-speed green just like the one you putted on last week when you ran the ball eight feet past the hole, that would be very helpful. And if instead of seeing a putt that looked as if it broke two inches into the cup, you'd see a visual break of two inches, which you know means you need to start the ball six inches above the hole (because it will truly break six inches), you would be much more likely to make the putt. In all of these cases, you would be seeing more and seeing better.

This isn't as complex or confusing as it sounds. Green-reading isn't physics: Anyone can learn to do it. You've already been looking at and seeing all these things every time you putt. But you've been interpreting them incorrectly and making your subconscious deal with trying to make things right. The truth is, the better you read (see the break in) greens, and the less your subconscious has to compensate, the better you will putt. If you take the trouble to improve how you "see" greens and break, as I've outlined above, you will begin to read greens better.

And now comes the companion step: If you also learn how to putt without unnecessary compensations, you'll be on your way to great putting.

Eliminate In-Stroke Compensations

Golfers don't understand what line their putts start on, because they are looking down as they putt. They don't see their ball's starting direction, then when they do look up, they assume their ball is rolling on the line they aimed at and started it on. However, due to their in-stroke compensations and gravity (which always pulls putts downhill), neither assumption is correct. If you are ever to solve the problem of these unwanted compensations in your setup and your stroke (which you probably have on all breaking putts), you must learn to practice without them.

> **Be Careful What You Teach Yourself**
>
> The golfer who reads a putt to break three inches, pulls it up the slope nine inches above the hole (without knowing he pulled it), and holes it, condemns himself to a future of poor putting when he says, "See, I made it. I knew it broke three inches, and it did. My read must have been perfect. My stroke may not always be great, but the one thing I can really do well is read greens."

How do you establish a "no-compensations-allowed" condition of practice? It's simple. You've already read how to practice indoors using the Putting Track, Putter Rails, Straws, and the Truthboard. All of these devices help you learn to orient your stroke to your Aimline and show if you make any compensations. The next step is to take the same approach outdoors on the putting green. Orient your stroke to start all your putts on an Elevated Aimline, and don't allow any compensations to take hold.

You do this by practicing breaking putts with your Elevated Aimline marked and guarded on the high side. How to set up this condition is shown in Figure 13.4.10.

1. Read your putt, which in this example you read to break six inches right to left (in Figure 13.4.10, the first figure on the left represents part of my five-step green-reading process, to be detailed later in this section).

2. Mark the spot from which you will practice this putt, because you will practice it repeatedly (and you must putt repeatedly from exactly the same spot each time).

3. Position one end of your Elevated Aimline six inches to the right of the hole (at the true break point where you read the putt to break from).

4. Stretch the Elevated Aimline exactly over the middle of (and 9 inches above) your ball, leaving enough room behind the ball to make a backswing.

5. Place a second ball directly under the Elevated Aimline, 17 inches in front of the ball to be putted. Place a blocking plate with a quarter-inch clearance from the second ball on the uphill side of the Aimline. Remove the second ball, and you are ready to putt.

The Elevated Aimline stakes are connected by elastic thread, which is suspended nine inches above the Aimline of your putt. The blocking plate (a book, soda

Figure 13.4.10: To practice breaking putts (photographs from left to right): 1) read putt; 2) mark your ball spot; 3) place Elevated Aimline stake where you read true-break point; 4) install Elevated Aimline precisely over ball by placing second stake two feet behind ball; 5) locate blocking plate ¼ inch above second ball, which is 17 inches ahead of ball spot under Elevated Aimline.

can, or almost anything else) is positioned just above your starting line (Aimline) to prevent your subconscious from pulling or pushing your putts uphill.

If you set up to putt as in the example above, your first few putts probably will hit the blocking plate as shown in Figure 13.4.11. (I've seen thousands of golfers do this, so don't think you're the only one.) The subconscious of most golfers reverts to habit and pushes the first few putts a little uphill into the blocking plate (shown on the left). Then, when you finally get your first putt to roll past the blocking plate without hitting it (shown on right), the ball will probably miss the hole on the low side of the cup if your speed was anywhere near the optimum (17 inches past the cup). The low miss happens because the Aimline most golfers choose initially is too low and doesn't allow for enough break once their normal compensation uphill is blocked.

If this happens to you, reset the Elevated Aimline higher, move the blocking plate to again guard the high side of the new Aimline, and putt again. Repeat this re-aiming, re-setting, and putting until you can make the putt by starting it along your Aimline, rolling at the optimum speed.

Yes, this is more trouble than your usual putting practice. But it is also the best way to learn to make breaking putts. I recommend you use Elevated Aimlines and blocking plates on all your breaking-putt practice for at least three to six months, all the while concentrating solely on making the ball start on the right line at the right speed (because that's what good putting is all about). Once you get the Elevated Aimline set for the true break, keep your blocking plate sitting just a quarter

Figure 13.4.11: Your old habit of in-stroke compensating to roll putts more uphill than you aim will make you hit the blocking plate initially (left). Then when you miss the plate, if your Aimline didn't play for enough break, you'll miss the hole on the low side (right).

of an inch above a ball on that line, guarding against any subconscious compensations. After practicing this way for a while, your subconscious will begin to learn that the best way to hole breaking putts will be with no compensations to your pure-in-line-square stroke, starting putts on the true-break Aimline.

Read Greens Better, Make More Putts

If you practice this way (without compensations), while simultaneously learning to read greens better, you are well on your way to becoming a great putter. This system works because you learn a noncompensating in-line stroke *and* learn to read greens better at the same time. This system works because when you do both correctly, you are rewarded by making more putts. This is in contrast to what has happened over the years to golfers who worked hard to learn simple, noncompensating strokes, then found they didn't work (they missed too many putts) when they took them to the golf course and continued to underread the break in their putts. Of course they didn't realize that their poor green-reading was the cause of the problem.

By being open-minded, understanding about subconscious compensations, and learning how to putt on greens without them, you open the door for your conscious mind to feel free to read the proper (true) break. When you do both (read true break and use noncompensating strokes), you make putts. With accurate (true break) Aimlines, when you make better strokes—with no compensations and solid impact, a square face angle through impact, and better touch—your putts go into the hole. As you continue to practice making noncompensating strokes, and the better you read the true break of your putts, the more putts you will roll into the center of the hole.

This situation allows you to commit to that simple, noncompensating stroke I talked so much about earlier in the book—the pure-in-line-square stroke: the best, easiest, and most reliable way to putt. It will work for you now because when you read the true break in putts, you no longer need bad setup positions and in-stroke compensations to have a chance to make them.

The key, then, is to learn to read greens more accurately, to see the true amount of break your putts will take, and at the same time improve your putting stroke mechanics to allow you to make noncompensating strokes on the greens. Throw in developing better touch and feel and all this starts to get really exciting.

My Five-Step Green-Reading Procedure

I have one more concept essential for improving your ability to read greens. It's basis is that the more consistent and repeatable you are at performing tasks, the more boring, simple, and habitual they become—the key word here being "habitual." The more of a habit you can make green-reading, the less effort and concentration you have to expend doing it. Therefore, since we all have only so much capacity and energy to perform, the less you extend yourself in the rudiments of reading greens, the more you have left to focus on the difficult part, the visualization of how much putts will actually break. After studying this for a few years, I have come to believe a five-step process for reading greens is about the best you can do in the time available on the golf course. I recommend you learn to do it quickly, the same every time, without leaving anything out (Figure 13.4.12).

1. Determine the pure downhill direction around (within six feet of) the hole.

2. Stand behind the hole on the extended ball-hole line and verify in your mind's eye that you believe the downhill direction seen in step 1.

3. Walk around and stand behind the ball on the ball-hole line and reverify your chosen downhill direction.

4. Move downhill (usually only a side step) until you can begin to imagine a perfect ball track rolling into the hole. Visualize the amount of visible break on that ball track.

5. Visually move this visible break distance out to the hole, multiply it by three, and move downhill until you are on the true-break Aimline and you can

Figure 13.4.12: Make green-reading a habit by moving into these five positions, in the same sequence, for every putt.

"see" the true-break ball track at the perfect "optimum-17-inches-past" speed in your mind's eye.

This establishes your Aimline for the putt. Now you are ready to begin your preshot routine.

Here's a little more detail on each of these steps:

In step 1, always be sure to stay more than six feet from the hole to avoid creating any fresh footprints that you might have to putt through later. Try to position your body directly below (on the downhill side of) the hole: This is easy when the green slopes perceptibly, more difficult on nearly level greens. In that case, try to imagine the direction water flowing out of the hole would move (Figure 13.4.13). Water always flows downhill.

In step 2, move directly behind the hole on the ball-hole line and imagine what would happen to a ball rolled from the True Roller aimed straight at the hole. If your mind's eye sees such a putt missing below the hole, that verifies your subconscious belief in the downhill direction determined in step 1. This second step should take no longer than 3 or 4 seconds.

In step 3, walk below the ball-hole line (never above, where your putt might hit your fresh footprints) to a spot behind the ball, and stand on the extension of the ball-hole line. Again, imagine rolling a ball straight at the hole from the True Roller, and let your mind's eye reconfirm that such a putt would miss below the hole. If you still believe the ball will break in the same direction, you should be comfortable about the direction of the break, and it will have taken you no more

Figure 13.4.13: Do this on your practice green (fill hole with water, then watch overfill run off downhill). This makes it easier to "imagine" the same thing happening in step #1 of your green-reading (see Figure 13.4.12).

than 25 to 30 seconds. Now you must determine how much this putt breaks (the true break).

In step 4, as you move your body slightly down the slope (staying the same distance from the hole), imagine a new ball track from each new eye position as you go. You must always move downhill from the ball-hole line so you can look at the possible starting lines (Aimlines) of your putt, which will always be uphill (or at least less downhill). Once you see the most believable ball track, try to visualize and measure the visible break along it.

In step 5, imagine you move a narrow rule (the length necessary to measure the visible break) out to beside the hole, then multiply it by three. This will give you the true break point and the direction of your putt's perfect Aimline. Move downhill until you are standing and looking exactly on that extended Aimline, and look to see if you believe your putt will roll into the hole if it starts on that exact line. If you believe it, then commit to that line and start your routine. If you don't like that Aimline, change positions until you find one you believe, then commit to it and go. It's your turn to putt, and you should be ready to get ready (to do your routine) to hole it.

At the end of this green-reading process (which should take no longer than 45 to 60 seconds—some of which can be done before it's your turn to putt), you are ready to initiate your preputt routine (section 11.2), create your preview stroke, execute your ritual, and hole your putt. If you practice the drills, make some of the changes suggested in this book, and begin missing more than 50 percent of your putts on the high side, then good for you. Keep practicing this way for a few months. You've probably been missing 85 percent of your putts low for years, so a few months of missing high won't hurt that much, especially if it will help you make more noncompensating pils strokes in the future. Stay with it, and be willing to take one step backward so you can take several forward in the future.

Polish Your Attitude

Now here comes what is, for many, the hard part. You've got to keep believing, keep the faith, and trust in what you have been learning. The power of positive thinking is a wonderful thing in life and in golf. As I said earlier, positive thinking won't make you a good putter, but it definitely can help you do the things that will allow you to become a good putter. And a bad attitude is the same as giving up.

If you have a bad stroke and don't know where to aim, no amount of positive thinking is going to make your putts go into the hole. However, a positive attitude is essential to keep you on track and in good mental balance for always making the best stroke you can make, in every situation. It can keep you willing and capable of practicing and learning to get better, now and for as long as you play the game.

When you miss six eight-footers in a row (and you will), you'll no doubt get discouraged. Most golfers do, and it's hard to blame them. They say to themselves, "I might as well change my stroke, because this one is not working. I can't do worse than miss them all."

But that's not true. You *can* do worse: You can miss them all for the rest of your golf career. If you keep changing strokes, never learning what is right or wrong about one, and never fixing and committing to the one stroke that could make you a better putter, you can drive yourself crazy with bad putting. So don't do it. Don't give up and start all over just because you miss a few putts; don't throw away the good work you've done. Be patient and keep the faith. Lady luck can't find your side if you don't have one.

Even on your bad days—and you're going to have them—you need to keep the faith in your new stroke and your ability to hole putts. Because all you have to do is hole the next few and your average isn't any worse than anyone else's (or what you were doing with your old stroke). But very soon, when your improved putting abilities start taking hold, and your feel, green-reading, pure-in-line-square stroke, and confidence all start paying dividends, you will start to putt better. Really better. Measurably better. Lower scores better. But only if you keep on grooving and improving and polishing those building blocks of your putting game. I've discovered a telltale sign of a Tour pro in putting trouble. I ask, "How's your stroke?" and he (or she) answers, "Which one?"

Great putters don't give up and change strokes every time they miss a few putts. Great putters almost make every putt, even though they (like the rest of us) miss a lot more than they make. But all great putters have a stroke that they are committed to perfecting, and they spend their careers working on it to make it better. I can't think of a better example of this than Loren Roberts, the "Boss of the Moss" on the PGA Tour (Figure 13.4.14). If you've seen him putt once, you've seen him putt every time, because that's his stroke (it's a great one) and will continue to be for as long as he plays.

Build Confidence

Success breeds success. That does not mean that if you make 6 billion one-foot putts in a row, your confidence will soar and you'll become a great putter. To build true confidence in putting, you need to learn the feel of a great stroke, practice making lots of putts with that stroke, then *experience* making lots of putts on the

Figure 13.4.14: Loren Roberts has a great stroke (see how square his putterface remains—long after impact) that never seems to change.

golf course with that stroke. Then, and only then, after you've made hundreds of them over at least a few months, does it become easy to believe that you are going to make the ones that follow.

So what does it take to be a great putter? You have to build a great putting stroke. And you also must understand the putting game, as well as develop great feel, great touch, and great green-reading abilities. You have to learn to read the true break in putts, and then learn to set up and use a noncompensating pils stroke along that Aimline . . . both *at the same time*. For most golfers, improving the 15 building blocks of putting comes one step at a time. But believe me, with smart practice they do come. And when they come together, you are on track to being a truly great putter.

CHAPTER 14
Face Your Special Problems

14.1 Nobody's Perfect

This chapter is a special little place for some special little problems I've encountered over the years. It includes problems I've seen, observations I've made, and several experiences I've had as a teacher. These problems aren't the fundamentals of putting but the nagging little annoyances every golfer seems to have and isn't sure how to handle. Well, if you haven't heard this before, let me be the first to tell you: The secret to golf, as to life, is how you handle your problems.

Every golfer has problems. Even the best of them, the most talented, the greatest ball-strikers the game has ever known, have problems with their putting. For example, Tom Purtzer and Hal Sutton are two of the best ball-strikers I've ever seen (Figure 14.1.1). Gifted athletes, yet both often aim their flow-lines way to the left, and both have struggled with their putting because of it. Or look at Craig

Figure 14.1.1: Even PGA Tour pros have problems with their putting.

Stadler, a wonderful player now, as he has been for many years (Figure 14.1.2). But he sometimes moves his upper body so much during his stroke that he almost can't find the ball, let alone the hole, when he putts. Some golfers make way fewer than the average number of 10- to 20-footers, while others struggle with short putts. Some can't make left-to-right-breaking putts, and many golfers can't get the ball to consistently reach the hole. However, it's interesting that few great golfers have trouble lagging their putts close to the hole. I'd say that's because lag putting isn't all that difficult (as I discussed in Chapter 13).

Figure 14.1.2: Craig Stadler has at times moved his head and broken his wrists to the extreme. His putting has suffered from it, too.

Tom Watson, Greg Norman, David Duval, and Tiger Woods may be the best players since Jack Nicklaus, but they all have room for improvement in their putting games: Watson has had trouble making the short ones consistently; Norman sometimes loses his tempo, becomes too deliberate, and his conversion of 6- to 12-footers suffers as a result; Duval occasionally rushes and pushes too many putts; and Tiger keeps trying to keep putts from breaking, and blows too many short ones past the hole, causing too many lip-outs. Watch the pros and you'll see that all of them are constantly working on their putting. But they have a lot more to lose than they have to gain when they work on any part of their game, so they must be especially careful to pick the right part (building block) of their putting game to work on. Then they must improve in a way that benefits their putting game and allows their improved putting game to fit into their whole game without causing any other problems elsewhere.

My point is that while every golfer has putting problems, every one of these problems is fixable. Poor golfers can putt better, average golfers can learn to putt great, and great putters can putt great even more consistently. (And yes, poor putters can learn to putt great, but it comes in stages: First they must putt better, then good, then really good, then almost great, and finally great.) Look at the change Hal Sutton has made in the position of his left wrist through impact (Figure 14.1.3). For a while, Hal was breaking down badly and his putting was miserable for a few years. But he worked through it and was one of the stalwarts for the U.S. team in their 1999 Ryder Cup victory, after having a great year in '99, while putting like a magician.

Figure 14.1.3: Hal Sutton spent several years putting poorly, but turned it around and has putted really well the last few years.

So whether your problems are in the fundamental building blocks of your putting game or in the nagging little details to be discussed in this chapter, you must believe you can solve these problems and become a good putter. And you can.

14.2 Too Many Three-Putts

I mentioned in Chapter 13 the bad effects of three-putting and how it can be reduced. I'll repeat what I said then: Golfers three-putt so frequently, they would save more strokes by eliminating three-putts than they would by learning to make more first putts.

Look at the illustration of two lag-putt patterns in (Figure 14.2.1) for 60-foot putts. The pattern on the left is typical for golfers in the 20- to 25-handicap range, while the pattern on the right represents a typical lag-putt pattern for 5- to 10-handicap players. The pattern size for the lower-handicap players is about half

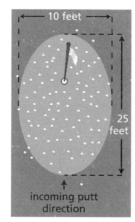 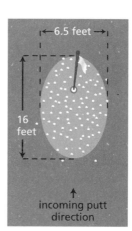

Figure 14.2.1: Improving your ability to lag putts a little will decrease your number of three-putts a lot.

that of the higher-handicapper's pattern. This improvement, while only by a factor of two, drastically reduces the frequency of three-putting for these players.

How great is this improvement? It's between three and five shots per round. And there is an additional benefit, too. If you can decrease the size of your lag-putt pattern by a factor of two, you'll make *four times* as many of those putts. Decrease the pattern size by a factor of three and you'll hole *nine times* more putts. (The probability of lag putts finding the hole is proportional to the ratio of the hole radius to the radius of your lag-putt pattern, squared.) Although this won't change your score as much as eliminating your three-putts (because the probability of making these long putts is small to begin with), it's always nice to hole a long one now and then.

As I have asked you to do several times in this book, it's time again to measure something about your game. The question is: Do you have a three-putting problem? Do you three-putt on average more than once per round? If you do, that qualifies as a problem. Keep track of your three-putts on your scorecard at the same time you mark your above (A) and below (B) putting misses. Count up your total number of three-putts over 10 rounds, add them all together, divide by 10, and come up with your average number of three-putts per round. Compare this number with one three-putt every four rounds of golf, which is what the touring professionals average.

You don't have to three-putt often. I've worked with PGA Tour players who (when putting well) three-putt only five to 10 times all year, while playing 72 holes almost every week on some of the most difficult courses and greens in the world. How do you think they do it? They practice hard, hit their putts consistently solidly on the sweetspot, and convert their short putts. If they can do it, you can, too.

The lag-putt drills in section 13.2 can take care of your three-putt problems, specifically (1) Stepping Off Distances (page 304); (2) the Triangle Drill (page 306); (3) Edge-of-Green Drill (page 306); (4) Playing Draw-Back for putts over 35 feet (page 307); (5) Chiputting (page 309); and (6) Playing the Phony-Hole Drill over level changes (page 311). If you spend enough practice time playing or executing these drills, I assure you this will at least minimize, and maybe even eliminate, your three-putt problem.

14.3 Putting from Off the Green

This is a problem for many golfers because they don't have a rule to follow. My basic rule for whether or not to putt from the fringe is: Putt if there is no reason not to.

This *is not* a question about distance from the edge of the green or distance to the pin. It *is* a question of good lies and smooth rolls. For example, if you are playing Augusta National in The Masters or Pinehurst No. 2 in the U.S. Open, you can depend on your ball rolling smoothly through the approaches and fringes around the greens. Courses like these have the best maintenance crews, who take loving care of the green sites, so you can putt from many positions around the greens and be sure of good results.

On most courses, the first three feet of fringe is usually safe for putting. After that, it becomes questionable. If your lie is good and the fairway between your ball and the green is smooth, the chiputt technique works well from off the green (putters usually have two or three degrees of loft, so they perform almost like the old chipping irons from good lies in the fairway or fringe). When there's a steep bank in the way, I recommend putting if at all possible; chipping or pitching into banks, where incoming impact and bounce angles should be considered, is far more difficult.

However, never putt from a bad lie. If your ball is in high grass or any position where blades of grass will get between your putterface and the ball at impact, don't use your putter (Figure 14.3.1). If your ball is sitting down in a depression, bare spot, or pocket of any kind, don't use your putter. If the grass is high anywhere between your ball and where you want it to roll—and you have the option of pitching (flying) it over the grass—don't putt it. Assume that if your ball can get hung up rolling through such tall grass, it probably will. (Consider that Pelz's Corollary to Murphy's Law.)

When there's grass behind the ball, the bellied wedge is a much smarter shot than a putt. The head of a wedge is heavy and bottom-weighted, so if you swing it with your putting stroke and contact the center of the ball with the leading edge of the face, the ball will roll like a putt at about the speed you expect. This shot works because the wedge doesn't have to go through the grass before hitting the ball, while a putter (Figure 14.3.2) must travel down through grass, trapping blades of grass between ball and face, where grass cushioning can seriously affect the roll.

If your ball is sitting down in tall grass, even if it's close to the edge of the green, the putter is the *last* club you want to use. Among the clubs that will work better are a 5-wood (small head, rounded bottom, good loft), a 3- or 5-iron, even a wedge played well back in your stance. All these shots are shown in my *Short Game Bible*, and all will work better from deep grass than putting.

Finally, an important point to remember. For most golfers, *how* you swing is more important than *what* you swing on shots like these. When Phil Mickelson and Payne Stewart played their off-the-green shots in the 1999 U.S. Open at Pinehurst No. 2 with "back-in-their-stance" wedges—while most of the field played these same shots with 3-woods and putters—the differences were in the players, not the clubs. You could have given Payne and Phil woods and putters and they still would have

Figure 14.3.1: With grass behind your ball, but smooth rolling in front of it, use your sand or lob wedge—not your putter.

Figure 14.3.2: When there's grass behind the ball, use your putting stroke and hold your wedge off the ground to contact the ball in its center (left). Swinging your putter (right) is no good.

been playing in the last group on Sunday, because they had become really good at these shots. They have practiced them over the years, with many different clubs, and they knew how to hit these shots. You must practice these shots with your putter (or whatever club) to find out when it will and when it won't work for you. Simply choosing the right club won't solve this problem if you don't know how to hit it.

14.4 Putting on Slopes

Do you have difficulty stopping your uphill or downhill putts near the cup? Many golfers do, and I think one reason is that how long a putt looks can be very deceiving on sloped surfaces. Just as I showed in Chapter 4 that a putterface swinging pure-in-line and square along the Aimline can appear to be rotating depending on where your eyes (or a camera lens) are located, it is also true that the length of a sloping putt can appear to be different when viewed from different positions.

Look at the three 10-foot putts illustrated in Figure 14.4.1. While all three distances are the same from the balls to the holes, they appear to be different when viewed by a golfer standing vertically over his ball in the address position. The discrepancies occur because in each case the eyes of the player are a different distance from the hole (even though the balls are not). The funny thing is that on uphill

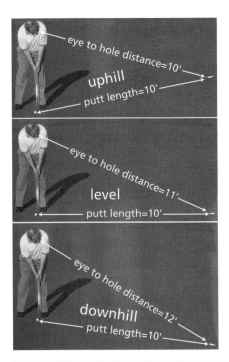

Figure 14.4.1: The perversity of nature dictates that putts needing more than normal energy to roll uphill look shorter than they really are (top). Putts needing less than normal energy rolling downhill appear longer (bottom). Both effects are relative to your calibration distances on level ground (center).

putts, which need to be given more energy, the distance always appears shorter than it really is, while on downhill putts, which should be rolled more carefully and with less energy, the distance appears longer.

I've already recommended that you can improve your touch by stepping off the distance of your putts. It's even more important to do this when putting on sloped surfaces or where there are significant uphill or downhill areas between your ball and the hole. Just be sure—and this is important—that you walk in both directions on a sloping green and average your number of steps, because you'll take different-length steps when walking uphill versus downhill.

Even with all these little "problems," I'm not saying you need to think about any numbers. Just walk past the hole to your putt, count your steps, calculate a putt distance (which goes into your brain), then forget about it. It's better to know how long your putts are than to guess their length, but don't let your concentration get diverted from your putting. Give your subconscious brain the facts, then let it deal with them while you focus on reading the true break and creating good touch, feel, and a perfect preview stroke.

Avoid the Common Mistake

You also can help your putting by becoming aware of the most likely mistakes golfers make, and avoiding them, when you encounter various situations. For example, when putting uphill, the most common error is leaving it short. By being aware of this you can make sure your preview stroke will get your putt to the hole. Also, realizing that you're unlikely to roll a putt significantly past the hole on uphill putts can be comforting.

You already know how much more sensitive downhill putts are than uphill putts regarding distance control (see section 2.6). Also realizing that most downhill errors come from rolling too far past the hole will let you focus your preview stroke on floating the ball in softly from above the cup.

Downhill putts become extra troublesome if they are also sidehill. This is what we call the downhill slider, the most dangerous putt in golf. The trouble comes because most golfers underread the break, which forces their subconscious to try to keep the putt from breaking its normal amount, which it does by rolling the ball faster. As a result, it rolls way past the hole into three-putt-land. Again, being aware of this common mistake lets you be extra careful and try to float the ball in gently from the high side.

If you play on courses with fast, sloping greens that give you trouble (like too many three-putts), go practice some lag drills on those slopes. Rather than complaining about your putting and blaming it on some natural talent deficiency you claim to have, practice to remove the problems. I can assure you that Tour pros spend extra practice time on their lag-putting drills when they get to courses with fast, sloping greens.

14.5 Killer Downhillers

Do you have trouble with severe downhill putts? Do you feel that no matter what you do, the ball is going to roll past the cup, possibly way past? I know two ways to take speed out of putts, particularly on really fast downhillers.

The more common way to soften impact is to strike the ball out on the toe of the putter, well away from the sweetspot. This technique will affect your putts in two ways. First, your putts will roll with less than the normal amount of speed, which is what you want. Second, and what you don't want, is they will start slightly off-line because the putterface rotates open at impact (Figure 14.5.1). So while it's good that they won't roll too far past the hole, you seldom make these putts.

A better way to remove power is to grip down the shaft of your putter to make it effectively shorter. For any given motion of your hands, the shorter the shaft, the less power is transmitted to the ball. Then still stroke the putts solidly on the sweetspot. This combination not only reduces the speed of your putts, it also starts them on-line, retaining your chance of holing the putt if you have read the green correctly.

Use this grip-down technique on "killer downhillers," when you fear losing the

Figure 14.5.1: Striking a putt on the toe minimizes power transfer to the ball, and starts it slightly off-line to the right (left). Striking the putt on the sweetspot with a shorter-shaft putter minimizes power and keeps the ball on-line (right).

putt past the hole even if you stroke it as gently as you can. A good example of how to use this technique is illustrated by two-time U.S. Open champion Lee Janzen (Figure 14.5.2). On the left, Lee is holding his putter at normal length, which you should do as you make your practice swings and preview stroke. When he steps into his final address position, ready to start his ritual and putt (shown on the right), he grips down on his putter (the softer he wants to impact the putt, the farther he grips down). This gives him the best stroke his touch and feel can create through his preview stroke, plus the added benefit of using a slightly shorter putter to take that last little bit of power out of a really scary putt.

How much speed will a toe strike or gripping down take out? Only you can answer that, and only by practicing on the actual slopes and greens you play. Again, don't use either of these techniques for normal downhill putts. You want to hit those solidly, as close to the sweetspot as you can, using your normal, well-developed putting touch to control your putt's speed.

Figure 14.5.2: On scary-fast or killer-downhiller putts, grip down on your putter shaft after your preview stroke.

14.6 Cheat on Breaking Putts

I advocate "cheating" on short putts (less than eight feet) when they are on side slopes and have more than four inches of true break. By cheating I mean using physics to prevent one of the difficulties of the game from giving you trouble.

The difficulty of the game I refer to is that all golfers are human, and occasionally mis-hit putts. When this happens on short breaking putts, there is always a preferred side of the putterface (the uphill side of the putter from the sweetspot), where it is okay for you to mis-hit a little bit and still hole the putt. Contact the ball on the downhill side, however, and your putt has no chance at all.

To help you understand this, first let me show you what normally happens on right-to-left-breaking putts, assuming you putt left-handed, as shown in the three examples of Figure 14.6.1:

1. For a mis-hit on the heel (uphill side of putter) as shown on the left, this putt starts farther uphill (to the right) than the intended Aimline. However, because it was mis-hit and didn't get the expected energy to roll at the optimum speed, it breaks more than expected to the left and rolls down into the cup.

2. For a hit solidly on the sweetspot, the ball will roll perfectly into the center of the cup (center figure).

3. For a hit on the toe (downhill side of putter) shown on the right, the putt has no chance of going in. It starts slightly downhill from the intended Aimline (because the putterface opens at impact), then breaks more downhill than expected (because less energy was transferred). It finishes well below the hole every time.

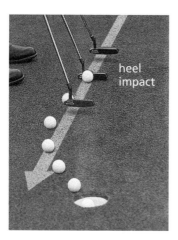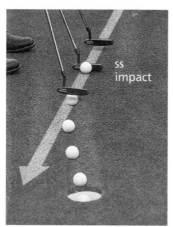

Figure 14.6.1: One of three possible impacts occurs on every putt: 1) heel; 2) sweetspot; or 3) toe. All three are shown here, with their common results for left-handed putters or a right-to-left breaking putt.

This mis-hit phenomenon goes in the opposite direction for left-to-right putts for lefties as shown in Figure 14.6.2:

1. For a mis-hit on the toe (uphill side of the putter) the two effects of the mis-hit go in opposite directions and tend to cancel each other out. The putt starts uphill too high, but then breaks too much because it is rolling more slowly than planned, and will still find the hole (as shown on the left).

2. For a hit on the sweetspot (it is always best to hit your putts solidly), as shown in the center image, the putt will roll perfectly into the hole.

3. For a mis-hit on the heel, the putt has no chance of going in. Both effects of the mis-hit—the putterface closing at impact so the putt starts slightly downhill to the right, and the weak roll allowing the ball to break too much to the right—react in the same downhill direction, so the putt is odds-on to miss to the right, below the hole (as shown on the right).

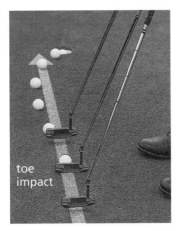  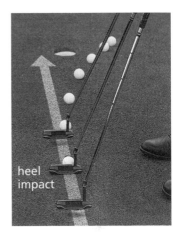

Figure 14.6.2: The three different impact locations (toe, sweetspot, heel) produce the opposite results on a left-to-right breaking putt.

Make sure you understand what I'm saying here. Most golfers address these tough little putts normally, then hit some solid, some off the heel, and some off the toe, always missing the ones they hit on the downhill side of the sweetspot. My advice is to cheat by an eighth of an inch toward the uphill side of the sweetspot at address, then make your normal stroke, trying to hit it there. If you do, you're fine; if you mis-hit slightly in either direction you're still fine because a small miss farther toward the uphill side of the putterface will still go in (you missed the sweetspot by perhaps a quarter-inch, which you can get away with on short putts). If your stroke missed in the downhill direction, you cheated away from it, so you'll actually hit the sweetspot, and the putt will go into the center of the hole. Accomplish cheating by first addressing your putt normally, then move slightly closer to your ball when you want to cheat toward the heel, slightly farther away when you want to cheat toward the toe. And when I say move "slightly," I mean only an eighth of an inch. (This is important. Don't overdo this, as the energy transferred to your putt will start to drop off drastically if you move too far, causing impact too far away from the sweetspot.) Figure 14.6.3 shows how much I recommend to cheat in your address position of putterface to ball.

Please note: I wrote this section for lefties to make sure you right-handers were paying attention. If you are right-handed, or putt right-handed, reverse the heel and toe references in Figures 14.6.1 and 14.6.2 above (if this bothers you, it may help you appreciate more what left-handed golfers face their entire lives, constantly being told to "reverse for left-handers").

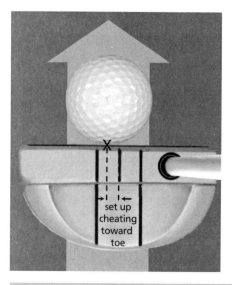

Figure 14.6.3: To cheat, move your putter (and yourself) downhill from the ball by an eighth of an inch. By addressing the ball on the uphill side of your putter, this assures you will never mis-hit to the downhill side of the sweetspot.

Pelz's Law of Slight Mis-hits

For putts shorter than eight feet, which break more than four inches, assuming you read the break and aim properly:

All putts mis-hit on the *uphill* side of the putter sweetspot should still go in. They will start too far uphill, break more than expected because of the mis-hit, and with any luck at all, will float down into the hole.

No putts mis-hit on the *downhill* side of the putter sweetspot will ever go in. They will start downhill, then break more than expected downhill, and never have a chance of finding the hole.

If you mis-hit these putts on the downhill side of your putter sweetspot, you deserve to miss the putts!

Don't ever try to "cheat" this way—toward the heel or toe—on putts longer than 10 feet, because mis-hitting reduces the energy too much for putts of that length, and they'll all finish short. Always hit longer putts as solidly as you can, even if they have a substantial amount of break, so they at least have a chance of getting to (and going in) the hole.

14.7 You Lost It

You've missed six putts in a row from inside five feet and four of them were four-footers. You're normally good at putts of that length. Plus, you felt good over all of them and thought you stroked them well.

Then it happens again the next day. And again the following week. You used to be a good putter, but suddenly you seem to have lost it completely. What happened? Why is this happening (Figure 14.7.1)?

Figure 14.7.1: Why me? What happened? Do I deserve this?

If you recently installed a new grip on your putter or started using a new "magic wand," it could be that the grip is twisted even the tiniest little bit from what you were used to. I've seen this happen countless times over the years. The new grip looks right and feels right; the new putter should be perfect. But the back of your lead hand has a relationship with your putterface (see Chapter 12 for details), and the more you practice and groove your stroke mechanics, the more repeatable that relationship becomes. A difference of just one degree from the way the flat of your grip was previously aligned to your putterface will cause the ball to miss on a dead-straight putt from six feet, even if you make a perfect stroke with your hands in the perfect position through impact, and use a perfectly balanced ball.

So if you have suddenly gone from good to bad on short putts (you'll never notice it on long putts because you don't make them often enough to tell the difference in a one- or two-degree starting-line error), check your new grip or the grip on that new putter. It's always possible that your old grip wasn't straight and the new one is, so you'll have to start a new relationship with it.

14.8 Your Preferred Break

If you have a preferred break direction (right-to-left or left-to-right) on makable putts in the 10- to 20-foot range—and many golfers do—there is a reason. It's probably because you have a bias in your ability to aim your putter. (If you have a preferred break on short putts, it could be due to such an aim bias, explained below, or to the effects detailed in section 14.6 above, caused by hitting your putts consistently toward the heel or toe of your putter. If you think it's the latter, re-read Chapter 12 and learn to groove your impact pattern on the sweetspot.)

If your tendency is to aim farther than you intend to the right (what I call a "right aim-error"), it effectively increases the amount of break you're playing on a right-to-left-breaking putt. That may actually help you because, as you now know, most golfers underread the true break. That little extra aim-error may be enough to get you closer (after compensations) to playing 100 percent of the true break.

But imagine what happens in the opposite direction, a right aim-error on a left-to-right breaking putt. When the break under-read and the aim-bias go the same way, it makes things worse. Sometimes a lot worse.

So if you love right-to-left-breaking putts and hate left-to-right breakers, you may have a right-bias in your aim. That is, you probably aim a little farther right than where you think you're aiming on all putts. And if you love left-to-right breakers best, you may be aiming a little to the left of where you intend.

Here's a true-life example, an experience I had with Lee Janzen in the summer of 1998. Lee had come to my Scoring Game School several years earlier and done very well. To my mind, he is one of the world's great putters. We had worked together several times since, but he wanted to come in for some work one week before the 1998 U.S. Open, and he had a problem. He couldn't make a left-to-right breaking putt of any length "to save his life" (his words, not mine). As evidence, he told me what had happened recently on Tour. One day he shot 62, followed the next by a 78. He said he hit the ball about the same (terrifically well) both rounds, but when he shot 62, all the putts broke right-to-left. The next day, all his putts broke left-to-right. He said his left-to-right putting was so bad, he had started trying to play his approach shots to the sides of greens that would leave him right-to-left putts.

Lee's problem turned out to be a very slight right aim-bias. He eliminated it in one week of hard work with Elevated Aimlines (Figure 14.8.1) and putted like a god the next week to win the U.S. Open at The Olympic Club in San Francisco. Again, it was a small error in his putting that was creating a very large consequence. Lee wasn't missing his left-to-right putts by much, but he was missing them all. While I don't know what caused Lee's aim to go off in this case, it doesn't take much to cause this kind of a problem. I've seen this problem a number of times with good players. (Our school students and most amateurs have much worse aim than this because they use aim to compensate for their stroke errors. See Chapter 11 on learning to aim so this doesn't happen to you.)

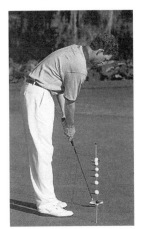

Figure 14.8.1: Lee Janzen works on his aim under the Elevated Aimline.

"Facing" Putts

Here's another circumstance that can cause problems with breaking putts and lead you to favor one direction of break over the other.

Several years ago, PGA Tour pro Tom Sieckmann showed me an interesting problem he had on what we now call "facing" putts. On big-breaking right-to-left putts, when Tom looked up from his address position, he looked down the Aimline (which is good). Because Tom is right-handed, on these big breakers the hole was slightly behind him, out of view, and he was never tempted to look at it during the last moments of his preputt ritual. He looked down his Aimline the way he was supposed to, and never cheated a peek at the hole.

But the situation was very different on left-to-right putts. When Tom looked up on these, the hole seemed to be right there, facing him, and he couldn't help but look at it. Even though he knew that during his preputt ritual he needed to be focused and looking down his Aimline preparing to start his putt rolling there, he found himself peeking out to the right at the hole.

Are you a right-handed golfer having difficulty with left-to-right putts? This could be your problem, too. If you look to the hole, you might be tempted subconsciously to start your putt in that direction because your training has been to putt where you look (supposedly down the Aimline), which would prove to be disaster in this case.

Just like the "Killer-Downhiller" situation discussed above, being aware of the problem should help you concentrate on doing the right things to avoid it. Anything that distracts you from focusing on and starting your putts along your Aimline at the proper speed will degrade your putting and must be avoided. So remember, orient your stroke to your Aimline during indoor drills, and keep your focus during your ritual on the Elevated Aimline during outdoor practice. Once you form a habit of starting all putts on your Aimline, "facing-putts" will no longer be a problem for you.

14.9 Yipping the Short Putts

Short putts always have been, and always will be, missed on occasion. When the ball is within six feet of the hole, it's probably sitting in a footprint. And because it's so close, you know it has to be rolled slowly to the hole. Then there's the lumpy donut to roll through. This combination of difficulties is why so many short putts are missed.

And not just by amateurs. Fine professionals like Doug Sanders (1970 British Open), Scott Hoch (1989 Masters), and Ed Sneed (1979 Masters) have missed very short putts that cost them the chance to win a major championship (Figure 14.9.1).

Misses happen. Blowing a short putt does not mean you have a problem with short putts. More important, it does not mean that you have the "yips."

However, if you consistently miss short putts because you flinch or yip during your stroke, you have a problem. And if you know you're going to miss even before you putt, then you do, indeed, have the yips.

Some of the game's greatest players have developed the yips. Ben Hogan and Sam Snead had the yips (Figure 14.9.2). LPGA Hall of Famer Beth Daniel had the yips. I've seen Tom Watson yip short putts consistently over several years. And I watched Jack Nicklaus struggling over short putts for a short period of his career.

Despite what people think and say, the yips are not caused by a player's age. Bernhard Langer had the yips at age 19 before he became one of the world's great players. Susceptibility to yips seems to correlate with three personal characteris-

Figure 14.9.1: It doesn't take much of a footprint, wind, dimple effect, or mis-hit to miss a short putt on a fast green.

Figure 14.9.2: Three of the game's greatest players developed the yips. Ben Hogan stopped playing the game because of them. Sam Snead conquered them by changing techniques. Beth Daniel beat them by fixing her stroke, then practicing until the new stroke became habit.

tics—intelligence, caring, and a devotion to practice. Plus, they must be combined with a putting stroke deficiency. Without a stroke problem, golfers don't get the yips.

The yips are nothing to be ashamed of. In fact, the three necessary characteristics—intelligence, caring, and lots of hard work and practice—are all what I would consider prerequisites for greatness. While you don't have to be intelligent to be a good putter, I think you do have to be intelligent to be a good putter for a long period of time. All humans have good and bad performance periods, and to get past the bad times you must be smart enough to know what and why you do things, and how to fix things when they go wrong. You also need to know what not to fix (or change).

Johnny Miller was one of the best ball-strikers I ever saw, but he drove himself from competitive golf because of the putting yips. Arnold Palmer struggled to be competitive for the last 15 years of his career—during which time he hit the ball tremendously well—but suffered with the yips on and off. These two players, plus Hogan, and many others, have as much talent as a player could ever want. They are all smart, and they all care about and practice their games. But they didn't beat the yips. Not because the yips can't be beaten, but because they didn't know how to beat them. The key to solving the yips, as with many other problems, is to first understand you have them and then learn how to fix them.

I see golfers cure their putting yips every year. Of course, it takes time, effort, and patience, but they can be conquered. As evidence I give you Beth Daniel, who won nine tournaments worldwide (Figure 14.9.3) only one year after coming to me with a serious case of the yips (which had caused her to miss 10 cuts in a row, and many two-footers). Beth conquered the yips as many golfers have—by persistent hard work to improve her stroke, in a system that allowed her to putt in a consistent and rhythmic ritual.

Here are my recommendations for conquering the yips:

Figure 14.9.3: Two of the all-time greats, Beth Daniel and Davis Love III.

1. Don't putt to a hole while you rebuild your stroke. This removes the hole from judging your stroke (so you don't worry about the ball not going in, and can focus on the quality of your putting motion).

2. Examine your stroke and find your weaknesses (the stroke deficiency that caused the missed putts, that over a period of time caused your yips).

3. Design a practice regimen with feedback that can fix your stroke-mechanics problems.

4. Schedule your practice regimen, which must include use of the Truthboard while putting with your eyes closed. Plan to follow this practice schedule for at least six months.

5. Make 20,000 good strokes to form a habit of your new stroke, which is stronger than the memory of your old stroke (keep your hand muscles out of your new stroke). Build your new stroke around a routine and ritual you can trust for the rest of your career.

6. Take your stroke to the course and do practice drills with pressure "closers"— gambling games or self-imposed rules ("I won't leave until I hole 10 straight three-footers").

7. Test your stroke on the course, and keep the faith. Different golfers require different amounts of time and practice to recover from the yips. They required different amounts of time to develop the yips, and they will take different amounts of time to work their way out of them, usually nine months to a year.

8. Before retraining your putting stroke, reread Chapter 3 of this book and choose a different grip and a different putter (e.g., left-hand-low grip, a long putter) from whatever you had been using. Use this new grip or putting technique on the course throughout the rebuilding period of your stroke (this will avoid your trying to use your rebuilt stroke before it is ready). This new style isn't meant to be permanent (although you may learn to love it), just something to get you by until you prove to yourself that your rebuilt stroke can be trusted on the course.

9. After you've put in all the work, putt however you putt best, and enjoy this great game. After curing your yips, always practice smart, with good feedback thereafter. Never again let a bad stroke habit sneak into your mechanics and "fester," producing bad results for an extended period of time (get help finding the problem as soon as you sense trouble).

CHAPTER 15
Wrap-Up

15.1 Overview Concepts

The single most important concept in putting is that it is part of a great game. Never forget that golf is a game to be played and enjoyed for its beauty, the thrill of competition, and the many and varied joys to be encountered while in the process of trying to post the best score you can on any given day.

Yes, it is just a game, but a very special game, one of the best ways to spend and enjoy your time. It's very true, as people often say, that golf can be a microcosm of life itself, with struggles and heartaches, trials and tribulations, victories and defeats, as well as fun and jubilation with family, friends, and total strangers alike. It is the lifetime sport you can play for as long as you can move your body, and you can enjoy it at any level of proficiency. It is a game impossible to master, yet simple and basic enough for even the most mundane of us to enjoy trying.

Putting is but one of six games that make up golf (Figure 15.1.1). Yet it constitutes golf's most frequent shots (almost half), and is an endeavor utilizing a skill set unlike any other in the game. The golfer's swing, stance, posture, grip, knowledge, and attitude are tested differently in putting than in any of golf's other games, and golfers who don't putt well don't score well.

Figure 15.1.1: The six games of golf (left) fit together (center) to create a sport that flies like the wind, stops in a heartbeat, and rolls like a ball (right).

Golf is beautiful outdoor corridors, carpets, trees, holes defined by sand and water, sunshine, birds, rain, wind, companions, calling us to play "Come see what score you can post today." Within golf, putting is sloping and undulating greens, growing grass, and a moving hole, which, from a new and unique position every day, dares us to go for it, yet hides behind an almost invisible veil of footprints and gentle breezes.

Putting Concepts

With putting, as in many endeavors, the better you understand how to do it, the easier it becomes to do.

Putting:

1. Is a game that tests one's skill for rolling a round ball into a circular hole with a flat-faced stick. The proficiency of a golfer's putting skill can be traced to his or her understanding of the rules of the game, and the subsequent development of 15 independent skill sets (building blocks), each of which can be exquisite or shoddy. The combination of these skills can produce putting performances with great, or a total lack of, precision.

2. As science (Figure 15.1.2) includes seven building blocks, mechanical in nature, measurable, quantifiable, constituting what is generally known as putting stroke mechanics.

3. As art (Figure 15.1.3) consists of eight building blocks residing in the mind's eye. These skills are controlled by the mind, internal to the body, not measurable, not quantifiable, and constitute what is often considered the mysterious God-given (or not given) talent of putting.

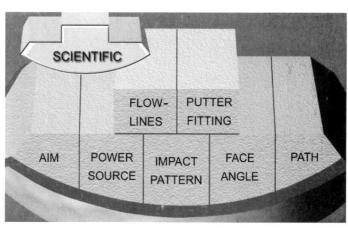

Figure 15.1.2: Seven of putting's 15 building blocks (stroke mechanics) are scientific in nature.

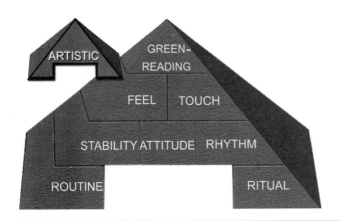

Figure 15.1.3: Eight of putting's 15 building blocks (artistic) are in the mind's eye of the golfer.

4. Is a combination of physical and mental skills, which can be improved, developed, enhanced, degraded, or ruined (depending on the presence of learning and feedback, or the lack thereof).

5. Is easy to do, difficult to *learn* to do.

6. Involves no net luck, yet a significant amount of luck is involved in every putt.

7. Obeys the rules of physics, greens, and nature, plus the initial conditions established between your putter and ball at impact.

15.2 The Putting Game

Rules of the Game

Do you read the instructions on how to open a package before you open it? How to operate a new VCR before you turn it on? Where to put the batteries to dispose of them properly? Most of us don't, and most of us putt without knowing the rules of the putting game. Knowing the rules is good, and sometimes helps (Figure 15.2.1).

Putting Science

Putting can be (although for most golfers is not) a simple mechanical motion, controlled by your mind through a series of simple mental considerations. But you don't have to be a genius to understand *everything* about putting.

The physical act of putting is an exercise in physics. Balls being struck by swinging pendulums, rolling across uneven and imperfect surfaces, falling into or missing holes in greens, is not rocket science (and I have studied both putting and rocket science, so I should know). But it is simple science, and obeys simple scientific rules (friction, gravity, square putterfaces, and in-line stroke paths).

Pelz's Rules of the Putting Game

1. Wind can affect the roll of putts; don't worry about it.
2. Cheating on short breaking putts is both legal and wise.
3. It's more important where you putt from than how you putt.
4. Not all well-struck putts go in.
5. There is some luck, good or bad, in most putts.
6. There is zero net luck in putting.
7. Simpler is better.
8. The natural in-line-square stroke is easier to execute than the natural screen-door stroke.
9. Downhill putts are more dangerous than uphill putts.
10. Straight downhill putts are easier to make than straight uphill putts.
11. Speed is four times more important than line.
12. Face angle is more important than putter path.
13. Dead hands for power means sensitive hands for feel and touch.
14. Everyone should putt at their own personal body-rhythm tempo.
15. Attitude affects learning ability.
16. Plumb bobs don't work for putting.
17. More putts lip in from above than below.
18. Line is intuitive, speed must be learned.
19. 17-inches-past is the optimum speed.
20. Three-putts are a waste of time, score, and enjoyment.
21. True break is three times visible break.
22. The smaller your impact pattern, the lower your scores.
23. A good routine and ritual are essential.
24. Balls rolling on their Balance-line roll truer.
25. True break is invisible.
26. Contact on a ball's spherical surface eliminates dimple effects.
27. Aim is the first fundamental of putting.
28. The worse you aim, the worse you putt.
29. Practice makes permanent.
30. Adrenaline degrades results in muscle-controlled strokes.
31. A pendulum swings at the same rhythm no matter how long its swing.
32. The lumpy donut is alive and well, waiting for your next "too-slowly" rolling putt.
33. The true-break Aimline is a very precious commodity.
34. Getting a rotating putter square at impact is like trying to be on time. You can never do it exactly.
35. If you're undecided, play more break.
36. Nothing putts like a well-balanced, on-line ball, at the right speed.
37. Good putters have more fun.
38. Long strokes for long putts, short strokes for short ones.
39. If it feels good and natural when you first try it, it's probably wrong.
40. Leaving half of your makable putts short is like giving 5 extra shots to your opponent.
41. If you haven't seen and felt the stroke, you're not ready to putt.
42. If you don't believe you'll make it, you won't.
43. Putting is the great equalizer: If you can putt, it's a great game.
44. The only reason to rotate your putter through impact is to give your opponents a better chance to win.
45. Touch is knowing what to do; feel is knowing how to do it.
46. Overspin? Forget about it!
47. Speed control is the essence of good putting.

Figure 15.2.1: Pelz's Rules of the Putting Game.

To execute your putting stroke mechanics:

1. Simpler is better. It has been proven that for any given skill or talent factor, simpler is easier and better to learn to execute with precision and accuracy.
   a. A pendulum motion is the simplest and easiest motion to putt with, both mechanically and rhythmically.
   b. Of three possible motions, the two nonvertical pendulums cause putterface rotation and path curvature around the body.
   c. A vertical pendulum formed by the hands hanging below the shoulders provides a pure-in-line putter path motion, and keeps the putterface square to the line through impact.
2. The pure-in-line-square (pils) stroke has been shown to be natural (requiring no manipulations) and the simplest motion to putt with (Figure 15.2.2).

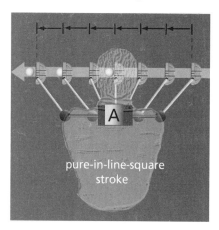
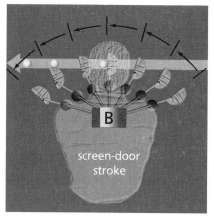

Figure 15.2.2: The pils stroke (left) is simpler, easier, better, more consistent, and just as natural as the screen-door stroke (right).

   a. A pure-in-line putter path is superior to a curving path for making a putt roll on-line.
   b. A square-to-the-line putterface angle is superior to a rotating face for making a putt roll on-line.
   c. The screen-door putting stroke, while also a natural motion (non-vertical pendulum), is almost never square and almost never on-line.
      i. Its curved path is not good for producing solid impact down a straight line.
      ii. Its rotating face angle makes producing a straight-line roll difficult.

   iii. Timing the impact of a curving and rotating putterface becomes
   critical (the early or late, but never on-time, syndrome)

3. Face rotation is a disadvantage in putting. The pils stroke beats the
   screen-door stroke in every department: simplicity, repeatability, reliabil-
   ity, being in-line, and being square.

4. An address setup position with parallel flow-lines makes in-line putting
   down your Aimline easy and absolutely natural (Figure 15.2.3).

Figure 15.2.3: When your body flow-lines are all
aligned parallel to your Aimline your putter will
naturally flow in a pure-in-line-square stroke
motion—if you don't do something to screw it up.

5. A pendulum motion requires short swings for short putts, long swings
   for long putts. By using a pendulum motion with no "hit" power, the
   adrenaline effects from hand and wrist muscles are eliminated.

6. By moving everything together, the triangle and putter make a pure pendulum motion.

7. Shorter backswings and slightly longer follow-throughs keep pendulum
   strokes stable through impact.

One of the nice things about looking at putting from a scientific point of view
(which is what I spend much of my time doing) is that the more you study and
understand it, the simpler it seems to be.

The Art of Putting
The mental side of putting is a set of simple processes (but so many of them that

golfers often assume it to be complex). Taken one at a time, they're not only simple, but anyone can both understand them and do them well.

The mind's eye carries the artistic side of putting. To prepare to putt, and control putting mentally, you must:

1. Understand what is required:
   a. The rules of the game.
   b. A system or procedure to follow:
      i. Green-reading process.
      ii. Routine for creating a preview stroke.
      iii. Ritual to use for creating rhythm and timing.
2. Have knowledge of and recognize the speed and slope of the green, wind, and other factors that might come into play.
3. Have reference values from past experience available in the mind's eye for comparison with current values (for slope, wind, green speed, and other variables).
4. Be able to evaluate and "see" a visible break. This is a simple, but critical, requirement of your preparation.
5. Have the imagination to move from visible break to a true-break point and create an Aimline from which an optimum-speed ball track finishes in the hole (Figure 15.2.4).

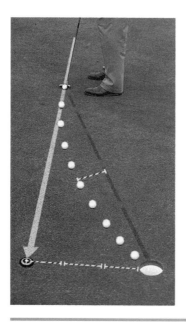

Figure 15.2.4: Once you see visible break, imagine true break and an Aimline. Then move around, adjusting the Aimline until your mind's eye tells you the ball track starting on that Aimline is the one. Commit to it and there is only one thing left to determine, the feel of your preview stroke to produce that ball track.

6. Be capable of using your feel and memory (mind's eye and kinesthetic awareness) to create a preview stroke that you truly believe in.

7. Concentrate as you move into a final address position and pull the trigger to start the ritual in less than five seconds.

8. Focus on repeating the size and rhythm of your preview stroke.

9. Execute from habit by staying in rhythm with the cadence of your natural body rhythm.

10. Analyze your putt results as good or bad feel, good or bad touch, good or bad green-read, and good or bad stroke execution (mechanics).

11. Learn from your mistakes for the future.

You can learn to recognize the slopes and speeds of green surfaces at a glance with proper training. The force of gravity is a constant no matter where in the world you are. Reality exists, and every putt has an "optimum" ball-track, speed, Aimline, and true break. Best of all, once the mysteries and myths about putting have been removed, learning to correlate the combination of slope, green speed, and putt speed is an understandable and learnable skill. It is as learnable to you as it is to any Tour professional, but only if you have the proper training and feedback.

And I assure you, the better you learn the skills of putting and the more accurately you "see" the true break and ball-tracks of your putts, the more putts you will make.

Putting's 15 Building Blocks

Listed below are the 15 skill sets involved in putting, any one of which, if done poorly, can ruin your results. No golfer makes only one mistake in putting, or else he would miss every putt. Most golfers putt with a few stroke and technique flaws, then pile compensation after compensation on top of those flaws as they practice to try to improve. After a while, they have so many compensations in their setups and strokes that they can't make a good simple stroke to save their lives.

If you can sift through the information in this book and fix the few or several things wrong with your putting game, you can putt more simply and better than ever before. Even if you follow *all* the recommendations made in this book (admittedly more than several), your putting will be much simpler than what you've been doing.

You can evaluate each of your building blocks and change them, shape them, groove and polish them until they fit seamlessly into your putting game. This must be done while allowing your putting game to fit smoothly into your golf game, without any adverse effects on the other five "games" (and yes, habits formed in one game can slip into the others).

To improve your putting game, make sure your:

1. Aim is proper. Aim is the first fundamental of putting. If you aim incorrectly, you can never learn the pure-in-line-square stroke without compensations, because it will miss every time (and your subconscious will never allow that).

2. Power source does not use the small muscles of your hands and wrists. Using those muscles to determine where your putts roll makes you susceptible to the effects of adrenaline, thereby condemning you to poor putting under pressure (Figure 15.2.5).

Figure 15.2.5: The dead-hands stroke of PGA Tour and Senior PGA Tour putting phenom George Archer.

3. Path is pure-in-line on your Aimline. No other motion even comes close to offering you the repeatability and accuracy of this vertical pendulum stroke.

4. Face angle is square to your Aimline through impact. By maintaining a square face on your pure-in-line stroke, you have the best of all putting motions.

5. Impact pattern is small and centered on your putter sweetspot. This gives you maximum room for error with minimum side effects.

6. Flow-lines are aligned parallel to your Aimline—most important, your shoulder, forearm, and eye flow-lines. From this position, nature is with you in getting your putter head and ball to "flow" down the Aimline (Figure 15.2.6).

7. Putter fits your body posture, positions, and putting stroke. A perfectly fit putter won't make your putts for you, but a badly fit putter can hurt your ability to make good strokes.

Figure 15.2.6: Steve Elkington working on his flow-lines.

8. Routine prepares you to putt properly before every putt. If you don't believe your preview stroke will hole the putt (or lag it dead to the hole on putts over 35 feet), you are not ready to putt.

9. Ritual is in perfect rhythm with your natural body-rhythm cadence. After you see the perfect preview stroke, move in and pull the trigger on your ritual so impact occurs in less than eight seconds.

10. Touch tells you about the power needed for your putts. Step off putt-lengths to enhance your accuracy both in practice and on the course. Make your last look for touch using binocular vision (from behind your ball during your preliminary touch stroke), and visualize the size of the stroke required.

11. Feel is the focus of your mind's eye during your practice swings, to develop and perfect your preview stroke. Look for the "aahhh, that will be perfect" feeling after your preview stroke.

12. Green-reading is based on reality. Once you learn to read the true break in putts, you can use a pure-in-line-square, noncompensating stroke to make them. (You won't believe how easy this makes putting compared to what you've been doing, with different subconscious compensations on every putt, Figure 15.2.7.)

13. Stability is a habit in your stroke. This is probably the simplest fix of all: Just position your stroke so your follow-through is slightly longer than your backswing. It's a no-brainer if you practice it a few times.

14. Rhythm is your natural body rhythm. Remember, pendulums swing in a constant cadence, and your stroke should always be at your natural cadence (rhythm) for all putts, no matter how long they are: short swings at your rhythm for short putts, long strokes at the same rhythm for long putts.

Figure 15.2.7: Once you know how to read greens, good putting comes from simply practicing enough to start your putts on the Aimline at about the right speed.

15. Attitude is upbeat, positive, determined, and aggressive. You never met a putt you couldn't make, and you never will. This won't make your putts for you, but it will allow you to do the things you need to do, to prepare yourself to be a great putter.

15.3 The Learning Environment

If you're going to learn to putt better, you've got to:

1. Learn the rules of the game (as detailed in Figure 15.2.1, page 367).

2. Learn what you need to change in your putting game—and what not to change.

3. Learn how you can change and improve the building blocks that need work.

4. Make the changes, and learn to do things in a new, different, and better way.

5. Finally, after learning how, you've got to groove it, doing it properly 20,000 times to make it a habit

You'll notice I've used the term "learn" a number of times. Learning is what improving is all about. Many golfers want to change and improve their putting, but they don't realize that to change successfully and reliably, they need to *learn* how and what to change. It's either that or hope for long-term good luck, which isn't likely to happen too often.

Don't think learning is difficult. Learning how to aim is entirely instinctive once the golfer receives proper feedback (and he or she stops aiming based on where putts are missed). Learning how to make a pure-in-line-square stroke isn't difficult. Nor is learning to keep the putterface from rotating open and closed. Becoming aware of how putts break isn't difficult. Something many people never realize (and not just in golf, but in school, at work, in life) is that learning often doesn't involve much thinking. If you are exposed to the right information (feedback), you can't help but learn. It's automatic—your subconscious does it for you.

Speaking of the subconscious, realize that it is a very powerful force that can be used to help you improve or, if you don't use it correctly, will keep you from improving. The subconscious will take over if given half a chance, so you want the "habits" that it reverts to (under pressure, when you're nervous, when you're scared) to be good ones. And the way to get good habits into your subconscious is to understand what they are and then practice them—properly.

Indoor Learning

Putting stroke mechanics are best learned indoors (away from the practice putting green) with immediate, accurate, and reliable feedback from appropriate learning-aid devices (for details, see Chapters 11, 12, and 13). Elimination of the hole and where the ball is going to roll is a major benefit to such practice. By eliminating the distraction of making or missing putts, you can focus on what you are trying to learn, get feedback on how you're doing, and learn faster and more efficiently (Figure 15.3.1).

This is very different from practice for the full swing, where hitting balls at a driving range can provide benefits intuitively (when you make a good driver swing, you see a good drive; when you make a good 8-iron swing, you see a good 8-iron shot; when you make bad swings, you see bad shots). A driving range is a relatively good learning environment for the full swing. However, practicing putting is nothing like that. Most golfers miss putts when they're "practicing" on a putting green, and have no idea why. The reason is, they're not getting reliable, helpful feedback, and more practice doesn't help the situation.

Outdoor Learning

Touch, feel, and green-reading must be learned outdoors, on putting greens (real or artificial). Again, good feedback is beneficial, and you must get into the habit of

Figure 15.3.1: Practice with immediate, accurate, reliable feedback makes learning and improving both instinctive and easy.

evaluating the proper aspect of your results to provide it (Chapters 12 and 13 detail the drills and games to play).

It has been both interesting and informative to watch and experience how the staff at the Pelz Golf Institute learns what to expect balls to do on sloping greens. The more we test, measure, and identify slopes, the easier it becomes for us to recognize them in our mind's eye the next time we see them (before we even measure them). The more we measure and quantify green speeds, the better we get at estimating how fast they are, and how much putts will break on them, before we actually roll any putts (Figure 15.3.2).

Spending time in this environment has not only improved my green-reading skills, it has convinced me that all golfers can learn to read greens more accurately given a little time, feedback, and reference information. While my staff is constantly refining and learning about how golfers play the game, we also see our concepts constantly being proven in our schools. As they work more and more with the tilt-greens, True Rollers, and other feedback devices, they have begun to see and feel in their subconscious minds that reference slopes, speed evaluations, and focusing on visible break really does take hold and work. Even some of our nongolfing personnel have learned to read greens pretty well.

The learning environment is the key: Once you have learned how to learn about putting, the "learning-ness" of your practice environment becomes the key to your putting improvement.

Figure 15.3.2: After many tests, we came to expect this putt to break between 75 and 80 inches . . . and it does, right into the hole.

15.4 Practice Makes Permanent

The more you practice putting, the better you will putt, right? Wrong!

The more you practice putting poorly, the more consistently poorly you will putt. And, I say, the more you deserve it.

My rules of putting practice are listed below. If you don't believe them, you are in for a lot of trouble in trying to improve.

Only perfect practice can lead you toward putting perfection. And while you'll never get there, I see no reason why you shouldn't keep trying for it. Be smart enough to practice exactly the way you want to putt under pressure, and always include the glue (your routine, your ritual, and your rhythm) for transferring your practice to the course.

My Rules of Putting Practice

1. Practice does not make perfect.
2. Practice makes permanent.
3. Bad practice makes permanently bad putters.
4. Poor practice makes permanently poor putters.
5. Perfect practice makes improvement.
6. Continued perfect practice makes good putters.
7. Long-term continued perfect practice makes great putters.

You must be careful. Even the balls and putting greens can fool you, lying to you too often on your putt results. Your aim, setup, and stroke mechanics must be learned, then refined *away* from the greens and the hole with feedback. Fortunately, everyone, regardless of age, can learn to putt better, and even better ways to learn will be with us in the not-too-distant future.

I'm not interested in selling learning aids, but I am interested in your learning, so I continue to mention them. My point is, and I repeat again, if you care enough about improving that you're going to practice, you might as well benefit from that practice. And the key to productive practice is the right kind of feedback, the kind you get from practicing with the right kind of feedback devices (Figure 15.4.1).

Figure 15.4.1: Use the learning aids we use, or other ones (I don't care who makes them, only that they work). But please, if you're going to practice, do it with good feedback!

Don't use devices that force or control your body to move in a certain way or do it for you. Use feedback devices that *allow* you to control your movements (you need to learn how to do it right, without interference or help from outside agencies), then tell you when you do it right or wrong. The ultimate test of any feedback device: Does it give you the same feeling when you do it right in practice that you'll get when you do it right on the golf course?

15.5 Watch Your Progress

Keep track of a few things in your putting game as well as your putting improvement:

1. If you see statistical improvement over time, it keeps your spirits up for more good practice (and avoids depression from a few bad days).

2. Statistics can help you see problems developing early, which can keep you from grooving really bad habits.

3. Make on-course measurements of Above vs. Below (A vs. B) for all your missed putts. Notice how your percentage of putts missed below the hole changes with time (it should get better as your green-reading ability improves).

4. To compare your putting with Tour professionals, record and plot your conversion percentage for putts at varying distances (percentage holed vs. length of putt), and compare your data to that of the pros (Figure 1.4.1, page 7).

5. Keep track of your three-putt percentage (and your most common three-putt distances if you really want to see where to practice).

Seeing improvement is addictive. It can spur you on to better and better putting, and no one has yet found the limit on improvement. Fewer putts mean lower scores, which means more enjoyment.

Young Is Good, Old Is Better

It does my heart good to see young golfers putt well, and I always encourage parents to send their children to one of my schools while they are young so they learn what they need to learn to become, and remain, good putters for life. But don't take initial good putting by a junior to mean he or she has God-given putting talent (Figure 15.5.1). I can't tell you how many adults used to be good putters until they lost it (a little bad practice is all it takes).

Here are some ways to help your kids become good putters forever:

1. Children learn more quickly and more clearly (their brains are less cluttered, information becomes more deeply embedded), so make sure that what you teach them is correct.

2. Don't take away the fun (this goes for all beginners, not just kids).

3. Keep concepts simple. Let them play games in which intuition can teach them good principles. They will love to use feedback devices if you make a game of it.

4. Play games for score, with competition appropriate to their skill levels.

5. Habits learned young die hard. Make sure they learn good practice habits

Figure 15.5.1:
When juniors learn the fundamentals of good putting, they can keep getting better as they age, and that is fun!

right from the start. Keep their putters short rather than too long, and keep changing putters as they grow so the same (presumably correct) putting stroke continues to work.

6. Start teaching kids golf on the green. Let them get comfortable with putting first, then move them progressively back, ending at the driving range. (Unfortunately, most golf instruction is just the opposite. Giving them the satisfaction of seeing the ball go into the hole first is important to both their learning and long-term success.)

It does my heart even better to see older golfers putt well (Figure 15.5.2). If you're no longer a kid and you want to improve your putting, here's some inspiration:

1. Never give up on putting well:
   a. The yips can be cured (old habits die hard, but they can be unlearned and forgotten after 20,000 good strokes).
   b. William Rockwell, who grips his putter with only his toes and leg, finished 157th in the world, beating several Tour pros along the way. If Rocky can do it (and he can), you can too (Figure 15.5.3).
   c. If 95-year-old Ed Alofs can lead the World Putting Championship finals, which included four U.S. Open winners, why can't you at least stop three-putting so often?
   d. Most golfers practice putting in such a way that it is almost entirely worthless (if not harmful). But it's never too late to start a "real" improvement program. This book is your first step to doing so successfully.
   e. Don't be disappointed by manufacturers' claims of better putting from their magic wands (they have to make a living, too). But believe

Figure 15.5.2: Age need not affect your putting. Left to right: Bob Murphy, Bob Charles, George Archer, and Dave Stockton, all over 50, can putt with anyone on the planet.

Figure 15.5.3: Attitude has a lot to do with your ability to learn to putt. Bill Rockwell stood on one foot in the rain, holding his putter between wet toes, as he competed in the 1997 World Putting Championship. Now would you tell me again what problem you have in your putting that you can't solve?

me, the "magic" has to be in your stroke no matter what piece of equipment you use.

2. The Dave Pelz World Putting Championship, which annually identifies the best in the world, is coming. We have developed a scientific way to measure the best putter over a 72-hole competition. When you have a chance to qualify at your home club (by competing in your club putting championship), why not try? You can't win if you don't participate (Figure 15.5.4).

Figure 15.5.4: Len Mattiace (left) and Raphael Alarcon (right) won the first two World Putting Championships (plus $250,000 each) over all the U.S. Open winners, kids, women, seniors, and international stars. Maybe you can win the next WPC (after reading this book and a little practice).

15.6 Get Your Arms Around It

Let me admit right here and now that I don't fully understand everything about putting yet. But I have given you the best information I have as I write this book. Stay tuned for new developments in the coming years, because I know our research will learn much, much more, and develop better tools for learning to aim, make better in-line-square strokes, and read greens (we're already working on devices with 3-D visuals, and they are showing promise). As we continue to work and study—testing golfers, greens, putts, balls, and how they all interact—information is coming in almost daily. Part of our mission is to keep you informed.

Throughout this book, I've tried to alert you when I'm going to say something that I think is especially important. Here's another one: *The better you putt, the more enjoyable the game becomes.* As greens continue to improve, golfers learn to make better putting strokes, learn to read greens better, and learn to concentrate better, and they will make a higher percentage of putts than ever before in the history of the game. So one simple question: Why shouldn't you? The only reason you wouldn't want to putt better is that you don't want to beat your fellow competitors, shoot lower scores, enjoy the game more, and have more fun.

Modern research has proven that the physical motion of putting is not difficult to do; in fact, it is the simplest action in golf. If you can hit the ball at all with a driver, you have more than enough coordination and talent to be a very good putter. But putting is difficult to learn to do. Good putting involves doing many things right, as well as many things "not wrong," and that makes it seem complex. But difficult? No, not really.

You Putt As You Prepare Yourself to Putt

In golf, as in life, you become what you see yourself becoming if you prepare yourself to become that way. For reasons I don't understand, golfers expect golf to be easier than it is. (Maybe they *want* golf to be easier than it is, which I *do* understand.) Golfers think they can buy a better game, or if they take one lesson and learn how to swing a club, the game will become easy.

They expect that after they learn how to hit a shot and hit it once, they should be able to do it perfectly every time for the rest of their careers. I'm sorry, but that's not golf.

Steve Elkington (Figure 15.6.1) is one of the best players I've ever worked with. He knows how to hit all the shots, and that includes putting. But as talented as he is athletically, he still practices his putting stroke, and he still hits all the other shots four to six hours a day, six days a week, *and* he plays 18 holes almost every day.

Do you really think you can do your job—sitting behind a desk or behind the wheel of a car—for most of your life and expect to repeat those motions as well as Elk can? Sorry, but it's not going to happen. I teach my schools, and have written this book, staying loyal to my belief that dealing with the realities of the game is the best way to improve. This means having realistic expectations about your game and your possible improvement. Without question, you can putt as well as Steve Elkington. But you've got to be willing to do what it takes to get there before you do.

Figure 15.6.1: Elk is a great player, but he still works on his putting game, trying to improve (and keep you from catching up).

Once you learn how to putt, you must groove your stroke, work on your feel and touch, and read lots of greens before any of it will become a habit. Great putters build great strokes out of habit. Nobody who is any good at putting thinks his way through his putting strokes.

Attention to Detail

Even putting, which is the simplest swing in the game, has 15 building blocks. Ignore any one of them at your own peril. While it is not difficult to putt, there are many factors vital to putting success, and you have to have a handle on all of them to be consistently successful.

The complexity of putting is one of its greatest aspects. The motion is simple enough that anyone can do it, and a few do it surprisingly well without knowing quite how. But much of putting is very subtle, so much so that it slips past most golfers by masquerading as art, God-given talent, or luck. Figure 15.6.2 shows four U.S. Open champions I have been fortunate enough to work with, all of whom have been referred to as "gifted putters." While each one of them putts great, I know from personal experience how hard they worked to putt that well, and it was no gift. They earned it!

The more you understand, simplify, and habitualize your stroke, the more you can concentrate on the right things at the right time. For example, a "look" (with focus and attention) is better than a glance when you want to see and feel how far away the hole appears to be. A focused look is a vital ingredient to getting your feel and touch for distance.

Figure 15.6.2: Four champions putted wonderfully well to win seven U.S. Opens among them. But great putting was not a gift to them. They were not lucky. Payne Stewart, Lee Janzen, Tom Kite, and Andy North worked hard and deserved to make every putt they made.

But sometimes a glance is better than a look. When you are in your putting ritual trying to create your perfect-rhythm prestroke motions, and don't want to think or engage the brain in anything other than the feel of repeating your preview stroke, a quick glance is better than a focused look. Knowing such differences will advance your putting skills.

Strengthen your mental and management abilities. Organize your practice to work on your weaknesses (while maintaining your strengths), and attend to all 15 building blocks of your putting game. Train your subconscious mind to feel and control your putting while your conscious mind stays busy executing your preview stroke. Build your confidence by forming a clear picture in your mind's eye of what you are going to do, as well as how and when you are going to do it. Once you see and feel how you want to stroke your putt, do it (and do it within eight seconds).

Practice Smart
A few final thoughts. Hard work is never enough. Of course, hard work is essential for good putting, but it is not sufficient. Only smart hard work, on the right things and in the right way, will help you reach your putting goals (Figure 15.6.3).

If you will embrace the concepts of putting that I have presented in this book, getting your arms around all of them, not only will you begin to appreciate the skill involved in putting, but you also will start enjoying the fruits of your labor when you work on improving. Always keep the big picture in focus. See the forest *and* the trees: Play the true break *and* make those noncompensating, pure-in-line-square (pils) strokes.

Figure 15.6.3: Lee Janzen practices hard . . . and smart. There is no other way to be great.

I've probably thought more about putting than most golfers, but I never think about putting when I putt. I have my priorities straight, so I only think about ball tracks, speed, and the size and feel of my stroke. If you understand the game well enough to concentrate on the real issues, the putting game becomes simple.

At the risk of sounding like a commercial, I recommend that you read my *Short Game Bible*, because, believe it or not, how you pitch, chip, and blast from the sand can help your putting. You'll learn that it's more important where you putt from than how well you putt, because when you leave yourself shorter putts, you'll hole a higher percentage of them.

My measurements show that while the Tour pros have been improving their putting skills for years, the same is not true for amateurs. It's now time for the rest of you to start improving, too. You *can* putt better; you *can* score better. The move has begun. Now the choice is yours: Lead, follow, or get out of the way!

You will putt better if you simply:

1. Learn the rules of the putting game.
2. Understand enough about your putting game to learn your weaknesses.
3. Practice smart on the right things, with good feedback.
4. And remember, *nothing* rolls like a well balanced ball started on the right line at the right speed (Figure 15.6.4).

If you've come this far, I know you are serious about wanting to improve your putting game. So put your arms around it, and enjoy!

Good putting to you!

Figure 15.6.4: *Nothing* rolls like a well-balanced ball started on the right line at the right speed!

In honor of my friend . . . Payne

Addresses

Dave Pelz Golf
1310 RR 620 South
Suite B-1
Austin, TX 78734
Phone: (512) 263-7668
Fax: (512) 263-8217
Web site: www.pelzgolf.com

Dave Pelz Scoring Game Schools (3-day school) and
Dave Pelz Scoring Game Tour (1-day clinics)
1310 RR 620 South
Suite B-1
Austin, TX 78734
Phone: Enrollment: (800) 833-7370; Offices: (512) 263-7668
Fax (512) 263-8216
Web site: www.pelzgolf.com

The Dave Pelz World Putting Championship
1310 RR 620 South
Suite A-16
Austin, TX 78734
Phone: (888) 972-7888
Fax: (512) 263-7946
Web site: www.worldputtingchamp.com

Learning Aids

Learning Aids available from Dave Pelz Golf

Dave Pelz Truth Board™	Dave Pelz Putting Track™
Teacher Putting Clip™	True Roller™
Elevated Aimline®	LazrAimer™
Putter Rails™	Teacher Putter Tape™
Elk's Key™	Pathfinder™
Putter Straws™	Phony Hole™
Ball Mask™	Tru-Putt™
Teacher Straws™	Teacher Triangle™

Books available from Dave Pelz Golf
Putt Like the Pros
Dave Pelz's Short Game Bible

Tapes available from Dave Pelz Golf
Developing Great Touch
Amazing Truth about Putting

Synthetic Putting Greens by:
SportCourt Golf
939 South 700 West
Salt Lake City, UT 84104
Phone: (800) 421-8112
Fax: (801) 975-7752
Web Site: www.sportcourtgolf.com

Resort and Teaching Facilities

The Boca Raton Resort & Club
School Location: Boca Raton Country Club
501 E. Camino Real, P.O. Box 5025
Boca Raton, FL 33431-0825
School Enrollment: (800) 833-7370
Resort: 800-327-0101
Web Site: www.bocaresort.com

LA Quinta Resort & Club
School Location: The Ranch at PGA West
49-499 Eisenhower Drive
La Quinta, CA 92253
School Enrollment: (800) 833-7370
Resort: (800) 598-3828
Web Site: www.laquintaresort.com

The Lodge and Spa at Cordillera
School Location: The Club at Cordillera
P.O. Box 1110
Edwards, CO 81632
School Enrollment: (800) 833-7370
Resort: (800) 977-3529
Web Site: www.cordillera-vail.com

Centennial Golf Club
Simpson Rd.
Carmel, NY 10512
Clinic Enrollment: (800) 833-7370
Golf Club: (914) 225-5700
Web Site: www.centennialgolf.com

Pinehurst Resort & Country Club
P.O. Box 4000
Village of Pinehurst, NC 28374
School Enrollment: (800) 833-7370
Resort: (800) 487-4653
Web Site: www.pinehurst.com

The Homestead
Hot Springs, VA 24445
School Enrollment: (800) 833-7370
Resort: (800) 838-1766
Web Site: www.thehomestead.com

Barton Creek Resort and Club
8212 Barton Club Drive
Austin, TX 78735
School Enrollment: (800) 833-7370
Resort: (800) 336-6158
Web Site: www.bartoncreek.com

Photo Credits